Coming
to Terms

Coming
to Terms

A Study in Memory and History

Henry F. May

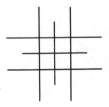

University of California Press
Berkeley   Los Angeles   London

University of California Press
Berkeley and Los Angeles, California
University of California Press, Ltd.
London, England
©1987 by
The Regents of the University of California
Printed in the United States of America
1 2 3 4 5 6 7 8 9 10

Library of Congress Cataloging-in-Publication Data
May, Henry Farnham, 1915–
    Coming to terms.

    Includes index.
    1. May, Henry Farnham, 1915–   2. May, Henry
Farnham, 1915–   —Family. 3. Historians—United
States—Biography. I. Title.
E175.5.M39A3   1987   973.9'092'4   [B]   87-5071
ISBN 0-520-05969-7 (alk. paper)

To Hildy and Ann

Contents

Introduction

This is a book about growing up and coming to terms with parents, self, and society. Everybody goes through this process differently, and probably nobody remembers it quite accurately. For trying to recall and describe it, I have two advantages. First, I have an unusually good collection of family documents, running from the eighteenth century to the present: I and other members of my family have had a good share of the pack-rat instinct. Second, as a historian I have spent my life working with the past. Autobiography is after all a kind of history. This is among other things a book about American culture, of which I am both a professional critic and a part.

I have therefore tried to combine memory and history, mental recall and documentary research. All history that is much worth reading combines an effort for objectivity with an acknowledgment of subjectivity, but here the mixture is a little different.

I have tried to avoid several kinds of anachronism. First, of course, there is the easy kind—the kind that concerns movie directors who have to find the right costumes and decor for 1850 or 1900. I have tried to learn what it was like in Boston in the 1870s or in Denver in the 1890s, and to remember what it was like in Berkeley in the 1920s or at Harvard in the 1930s. I have had to work harder to avoid a more important kind of anachronism: anachronism of thought and feeling. I have tried to imagine how different life seemed before World War I, and to remember the hopes and fears of the Depression years, the age of Roosevelt and Hitler. Above all, I have tried not to impose the judgments of later life on a story of youth. In passages in which I look back from the present, I make it explicit that this is what I am doing.

Both my purposes and my sources are reflected in the organization of this book. Part I is straight memory; it is about my childhood as I can recall it and about my parents as I saw them when I was a child. Part II is straight history: it deals with my ancestors and my parents as I have managed to find out about them, with emphasis on the aspects that I think have affected my own development. There is more about my father and his family than about my mother, not because he was more important to me, but because the record is fuller. In Part III I move back from history to memory, and deal with the story of my own growing up and gradually achieving some degree of independence. Here I hope that the historical investigation carried out in Part II enriches my understanding of what I can remember. In combining these two approaches, my main purpose has been to understand myself by looking at the past. Another object has been to make a small part of the past more real by seeing how it lives in my own temperament and experience.

Dealing with one's own parents at length as I have done in Part II raises a special variant of the general problem of subjectivity and objectivity, the problem of filial piety. I have tried in writing about them to respect my parents as I would any subject and also to understand them in their own times and places. To reflect the shift from memory to history I have varied the names I use for them. When I am dealing with my memory of them I refer to them as "my father" and "my mother." When I am talking about their own youth, I use their first names, Harry and May. (My mother, confusingly, was named May R. May.) In discussing my father's mature career, I call him May, as I would if I were dealing with Jefferson or Wilson.

In one important way this book differs from many recent American autobiographies. Most of the best of these have been written by people coming from immigrant or minority cultures, and their main subject has been the struggle to come to terms with America's dominant Anglo-Saxon and middle-class culture. My own roots are within this dominant culture, though from a section of it slightly marginal, especially where I lived. Perhaps this difference turns out to be less important than it seems; everyone's heritage is both a strength and a burden in a fast-changing, kaleidoscopic country and world.

Part I

Childhood
Remembered

1

A House
in Berkeley

Where I was brought up in Berkeley, the roaring twenties did not roar. It is true that the songs my older brother and sister sang around the piano puzzled and sometimes mildly shocked my parents: "Margie," "Ma, He's Making Eyes at Me," "Insufficient Sweetie." My sister had an all-out struggle with my father over wearing lipstick (she won). My parents stopped the *Chronicle* when it gave front-page treatment to the Fatty Arbuckle scandal, which grew out of a wild party in the St. Francis Hotel and gave rise to lurid accusations of rape and murder. Yet as I think back on the conversations I overheard, the way the house and furniture looked, the way we lived, what I remember is a massive sameness, a deep security troubled by a slight but growing sense of decline.

Funny things might be going on in some mythical place like New York. Crazy-looking modern art was a subject for jokes in *Life,* and the papers had editorials about the strange ways of the younger generation. None of this, however, seemed to affect Berkeley, still less the Claremont district, still less Our House. This house was a comfortable frame-and-stucco building of no particular style or shape. It was built in 1911, on a small curvy street named El Camino Real by some ambitious realtor. It stood in the newish Claremont district, mostly inhabited by well-to-do businessmen and lawyers who commuted to San Francisco on the Key train, which they caught between the grounds of the Claremont Hotel and the Berkeley Tennis Club. Like many houses in the hills, ours had three stories in front and five, including a dirt-floored subbasement, in back. There was a big climbable pepper tree on the lawn in front, wisteria and roses up the south wall, and a small terraced garden in back, in which my father worked incessantly.

In my early childhood there were vacant lots on both sides of our house and many others up and down the street. These were our inexhaustible playgrounds. In fall we slid down the steep slopes of dried grass on wooden sleds with greased runners. In spring the boys pulled tufts of grass with hard chunks of dirt hanging to them for clodfights. Thrown right, the clods would sail a bit on their grass comet tails and land with a satisfying smack. Clodfights were perfectly friendly, carried on from forts, with sanctuaries and agreed rules of war. One vacant lot, on the hill above our street, was excellent for flying kites and also for wildflowers, lupines and California poppies and others, that we picked in huge short-lived bouquets for our mothers. During the late twenties new houses were built on most of the lots, and the more daring boys (I was not one) climbed on the scaffolding when the carpenters stopped work. Gradually the street filled with houses. As I look back at them in my mind I see a conglomeration of styles—Bay Area brown shingle, white-and-green New England colonial, and Spanish with pink walls, wrought-iron grilles, and niches for nonexistent saints.

Before we moved to this house (in 1919 when I was four) we had lived on Ridge Road, just north of the University of California campus, in a house my older sister told me was much nicer (I can summon a few faint impressions of brick terraces and a large flat garden). Still earlier my parents had lived in Denver. Packages came sometimes with Colorado celery or candy from Bauer's. I had the impression that Denver was much richer, grander, and generally better than Berkeley. But the distant past was not really important. Our House, where I lived from 1919 until 1937, when I went away to graduate school, was safe, a little boring, beloved when I was away and thought about it, but for the most part simply taken for granted.

If I were suddenly placed back in this house as it was then, I am sure I could walk from top to bottom in the dark without touching a wall or a piece of furniture. I can still go from room to room looking at the furniture in my mind's eye. What then seemed sacred and inevitable now looks to me comfortable, mildly opulent, in certain cases even beautiful, and remarkably old-fashioned for the Bay Area in the twenties.

Nothing in the house, as far as I can remember, was regional in origin or inspiration except, in my mother's bedroom, a small painting of the Carmel coast and a framed quotation by John Muir in praise of the Sierra. Most of the furniture I grew up with and took for granted was, I now realize, inherited from my father's family and reflected New England taste of the past. No important piece except for the dining-room set had been made later than 1890. Several dated back to the very beginning of the nineteenth century and even earlier. The living room, rather dark with grasscloth walls and a heavy wooden mantel above the fireplace, had most of the best pieces—a Willard banjo clock, a tall secretary of about 1815, mid-Victorian swan-neck chairs covered in dark red plush, a mahogany table with a green Tiffany lamp, tall silver candlesticks with glass lusters. The living room was separated from the dining room and hall by red velvet portières, pulled back by Mungie when dinner was announced. The dining-room furniture had been bought by my father at about the turn of the century, and my mother and sister disliked it. It was massive golden oak, and the chairs had brown leather seats with brass nails. The best china and silver stood on the sideboard and in glass-fronted cabinets. On the dining-room walls were large sepia photographs of Raphael's *School of Athens* and two photographs taken by my father in Mexico: a domed church on a hill, a dusty road with men in sombreros. Over the small serving table was a wood sculpture of a dead bird, hanging by its feet.

Off the dining room was my father's den. In this were brass humidors, Canton-ware tobacco-jars, an ebony horse holding a thermometer, small plaster busts of Shakespeare and Daniel Webster, and a full-length plaster statue of Thackeray wearing a frock coat and tight trousers. On the walls were photographs of Lincoln, Wilson, and the Massachusetts Whig lawyer Rufus Choate; also a cartoon of Theodore Roosevelt haranguing an exhausted-looking woman labeled Europea. Here, as in the living room, most of the wall space was taken up by books. These tended toward standard editions of English or New England novelists and poets and historians, mostly green or red or calf, often with gilt lettering and marbled endpapers.

None of my school friends lived in a house that looked anything like this. The impression, according to some current acquaintances who remember it, was stately, dark, and a bit intimidating. Since nothing ever changed, the look of opulence continued into the thirties, when the family's palmy days had ended and money worries hovered, circling ever closer.

In my childhood there was a lot of entertaining, mostly in the form of dinners for two or three couples. These were always somewhat formal: my father would wear a dinner jacket, my mother a long dress. Once in a while, when there were more people, things got elaborate. A cateress joined

Mungie in the kitchen, adding touches—for instance torturing the butter into butterflies or nests of eggs, instead of the butterballs Mungie regularly made with two paddles.

Of the people who came to the house, I think only a few were real friends—a few Harvard contemporaries of my father and still fewer women who had gradually become close to my shy and private mother. The dinner-party circle also included neighbors, people from the Piano Club or the Town and Gown, "society" friends of my richer and more socially ambitious aunt and uncle, and a few professors. These last, I knew, were much to be respected for their learning, but I often heard them pitied for their poverty. Like us, most of these people had one servant, a few had an additional gardener, or a "couple." A lady who "did all her own work" was regarded as brave and a little eccentric.

From my point of view, dinner parties were all right in my early childhood, when I was allowed to sit on the kitchen stairs in comfort, listening to the grown-ups' conversation from time to time when swinging doors opened for Mungie to carry in food, wondering what good things would be left over to eat. Later, when I had to sit still at the table and be polite, the time passed slowly.

The year was punctuated by the usual American seasonal festivals, celebrated with as much attention to tradition as festivals in Italy or Japan. On most of these—Valentine's Day, Easter, the Fourth of July, Halloween, birthdays—we followed the same rituals as our neighbors. Thanksgiving and Christmas were perhaps a little more formal than in some houses. This was especially true when we went, every other year, to the house of my aunt and uncle, who invited a good many outside guests and played slightly stiff games after dinner (spin the platter, hunt the thimble). For the losers there were mild forfeits. Formally dressed grown-up men had to "bow to the wittiest, kneel to the prettiest, and kiss the one you love best." I think everybody played safe and kissed his own wife, but a good many knelt in front of my aunt, who rather expected this tribute.

I can remember once when the Fourth of July, one of the best holidays, was ruined by my father's sense of what was right. We always saved our money for months to buy fireworks. The ordinary ones—firecrackers, flashcrackers, son-of-a-guns, torpedoes—we set off ourselves and they banged away all day. At night the sparklers, roman candles, pinwheels, flowerpots, and burning houses were used up first, and then, as a climax, my father would set off a few rockets. The time I am thinking of, my brother and sister had gone to a circus without permission. They were ordered to stay in the house, while my father went through the whole ritual with me alone, both of us hating every minute of it.

On Sundays my father always went to the Episcopal church. If my mother had a headache or for some other reason couldn't go, it was understood that one of the children must spontaneously express a desire to go with my father (there could be no coercion in religious matters). Because my father had been shocked by the vehemence of a battle in the vestry of nearby St. Clement's Church, we walked past St. Clement's for two miles to St. Mark's. As a child I could feel a slight thrill when the big gold cross was carried up the aisle in processional, but not much from the rest of the low-church service. The long canticles—"O ye whales and creatures that live in the sea, praise ye the Lord"—seemed excruciatingly boring. When I could, I passed the time by reading in the more mysterious parts of the prayerbook, trying to understand what the Churching of Women was about, shuddering a little at the burial service. When the sermon came I tried to pay attention and sometimes was moved by the homilies of Mr. Hodgkin, obviously a good and kind man, to resolve that I would try to be better. Finally, with the collection one was in the home stretch, and with the last hymn and benediction I started slavering for the roast chicken and vanilla ice cream with chocolate sauce that would be ready when we walked home.

On Sunday night Dad read from the Bible or a book of adapted bible stories. On the whole I enjoyed this, especially the Old Testament stories—Joseph and his brothers, or David and Jonathan. Sometimes the parables of Jesus seemed to be saying something terribly important that I could not quite understand. Later in the evening Mother played the piano and we sang hymns, mostly of the rather too sweet kind written in the nineteenth century for children. This was entirely enjoyable.

From as early as I can remember, I said prayers when Mother came to say good night. First the rhymed one starting "Gentlejesus Meekandmild, Look upon a little child." Then a series of petitions for family, health, goodness, and the whole world. Then, after Mother left, a series added by my own superstitions, for protection against everything I was really afraid of, ending that nothing bad might ever happen to Mother.

Neither precepts nor doctrine were pushed. My parents, I later learned, did not allow us to go to Sunday school like the other children because they thought the teaching was so poor it would turn us against religion. The slow regular influence of observance was left to its own effects, and a little later the intellectual rebellions of dawning adolescence were received tolerantly. Mother was made uncomfortable by overt discussion of matters that to her were sacred beyond discussion. My father, who had always struggled with his own doubts, respected mine. (In the very long run, my parents' hands–off policy was to prove a success. As a young man I tried hard for years to reject religion entirely, but finally in middle age found that I could not.)

I knew that my father really cared about politics and that

while the neighbors were nearly all Republicans, we were Democrats. My father revered Woodrow Wilson, and I remember as a very little boy being taken to somebody's apartment to see him pass by (it must have been on his tour of 1919, when he was struggling for the League of Nations). After a long wait, I saw a parade of black cars. In the last one, long and open, a man was bowing and taking off his high silk hat. This was the first time I had seen such a hat worn—my father had one, but it was on permanent loan to my brother, who pulled things out of it during his magic shows. My father told me I must always remember seeing this great man.

On a typical election day in the twenties, my father, one of the few Democrats in the neighborhood, would walk cheerily to the polls, stopping to tell Mr. Kett, who was mowing his lawn, that he was going out to cancel his vote. In 1928 most of the neighborhood felt more strongly than usual against Al Smith, a Catholic with a New York accent and Tammany Hall associations. A few were a little frosty toward my parents. Later, in the New Deal period, political feelings were to get a lot stronger. In the Claremont district, the few who like my parents remained loyal to "that man in the White House" seemed to their neighbors deluded if not actually treasonable.

I knew that democracy was the best form of government, even though I could not help thinking kings and queens would have been more fun. I gathered too that my parents and their friends did not think the people running things were anywhere nearly as good as the great men of the past.

In theory my New England father, unlike my English mother, was a democrat as well as a Democrat. We were forbidden to say the words *common* or *common people* because these words sounded as though ordinary people were inferior. We were to be polite to all grown-ups. Yet it was evident that only certain kinds of people, who dressed and talked in certain ways, came to the house for dinner. All of these were white, and nearly all Anglo-Saxon Protestants. The only Negro (then the polite word) whom I saw was Tim, the bootblack on the corner by the commuter train, and Tim was genial in the "Yas, sho' boss" manner. Italians were gardeners or vegetable dealers except for Cousin Umberto, who had married a cousin of my father's. Umberto had been a Bersagliere officer, now worked for the Bank of America, and tried ardently to convert my father to Catholicism. (My father agreed to keep a della Robbia plaque of the Virgin in his room for a specified period, then sardonically reported that it hadn't worked.) Sometimes Umberto or his daughter, my cousin Jessie, would remind us—amazing thought—that in Rome *we* would be wops. My mother's singing teacher was Jewish, and when he and his family came to dinner there were reminders first that we mustn't serve pork or bacon or say anything that might hurt their feelings. Chinese were picturesque and intriguing. My Uncle Arthur, given to pronouncements, threw out his chest in a bold burst of liberalism and said that he would just as soon have a Chinese gentleman to dinner as any other gentleman, but I can't remember that he ever did. My Auntie Margo, more socially ambitious than my parents, cultivated some of the San Francisco consular corps. A dignified Chilean, with long sidewhiskers and elaborate manners, was one of the regulars at her home, where we often went. All these were exotic exceptions. Normal people were like us. It never occurred to any of us that there was anything wrong with the incessant flow of jokes about Abie and Ikey, Rastus and Mandy, or even Pat and Mike, though I did not really understand how Irishmen were different.

Sometimes people talked about The War. I have a faint memory of my mother in a Red Cross uniform collecting money—perhaps this was during the flu epidemic of 1919. One of the second-class Christmas decorations was a red-white-and-blue ribbon that had been hung on the tree ever

11

since the armistice. Like the neighbors, we hung out the flag on national holidays, but on Armistice Day my father insisted that it was wrong to hang out only Allied flags because this was a celebration of peace. Either the German flag must be hung out too, even though the Germans had caused the war, or only the American. To children the Great War and all wars seemed part of the past—terrible but romantic. Sometimes we wondered whether anything as exciting would ever happen again.

My parents and their best friends complained a good deal about America's vulgarity and lack of culture. These complaints puzzled me because they seemed to conflict with the patriotism propagated at grammar school. Not only was this the country of Washington and Lincoln, but according to the big green geography it produced more steel and wheat and almost everything else than any other country. Once I burst into a deprecating dinner-table conversation: "But *I* think this is a *great* country." My parents were horrified that I had misunderstood them so badly as to question this. When I pushed the matter further, on one of my walks with my father—times when serious, polite argument was always encouraged—he admitted that he thought the very greatest country in the world was still England, though in some ways America was better and more promising.

Throughout my childhood, one of the most important things to learn and one of the hardest was good manners. One got up when a lady came in, one didn't talk much when grown-up guests were present, and above all one ate neatly and correctly. This last caused me the most trouble since I was absent-minded, and I was constantly being sent from the table for lapses—chewing with my mouth open or holding the knife and fork in the wrong hands. My mother, English and for certain special reasons a bit insecure in her American environment, would talk about the importance of manners as part of the difference between gentlemen and ladies and other people. My father never used terms like these: there were just ways one acted and ways one didn't.

Culture was even more important than manners, and for both my parents it was far more than a badge of class. My father passionately loved literature, and my mother music. The graphic arts were comparatively unimportant. There were oil paintings in gilt frames on the walls, some of them supposed to be "good," most of them blackened by decades of fireplace or furnace smoke, none of them ever looked at.

If a well-informed social historian suddenly found himself in our living room in 1925, he would, I think, expect to walk out into a Boston suburb. Instead, all around lay Berkeley and California. Berkeley in those days was a quiet, rather staid university town of about twenty-five thousand, attractive to well-to-do commuters. I hardly ever saw the flat part of town, where there were small factories and a population of Italians, Finns, and a small number of highly respectable blacks, some of them railway porters or cooks. The three parts that I knew as a child were Claremont, the campus, and North Berkeley.

Claremont was full of houses much like ours—some much bigger and handsomer. I knew the names of everybody within ten or fifteen houses on each side and was known in the local stores. One reached the campus by walking about two miles, crossing on the way the grounds of the California School for the Blind and Deaf, where there was an exciting life-size statue of two Indians fighting a grizzly bear who had bitten halfway through the arms of one of them. Nearer the campus one passed fraternities, where tall young men in sweaters and cords lounged on the porches, watching for girls to go by. The campus itself was huge, mostly made up of white stone buildings and green lawns, surmounted by the tall campanile that bonged the hours. To the west were the broad dusty fields where the ROTC marched. From most of the campus one could see either San Francisco Bay or the swelling oak-dotted hills.

I knew that North Berkeley and the few blocks south of the campus were supposed to be more interesting than Claremont, mainly because they were close to the University. A few of the family's university friends suggested even to a child some very special quality. The Misses Hilgard, for instance, were daughters of a famous agricultural scientist and lived on Bancroft Way. Miss Louise was tall, musical, a little scatterbrained perhaps, and devoted to my mother and my aunt, whom she called the Pink (of Perfection). Miss Alice was handsome, slightly severe looking with her brushed-back iron-gray hair and her pince-nez, erudite and dryly humorous. The Hilgards' pleasant frame house was surrounded by an impeccably tended garden. One story has it that Professor Gayley of the English department came up to the front door carrying, in mock horror, one leaf that he had found in the sandy path. The Hilgards, like many others, employed college boys to take care of the garden, probably paying them very little but supervising their manners. (One of the boys, Miss Alice reported once in a horrified whisper, had to be told not to *expectorate*.) When each boy graduated, he received a gold watch. Next door to the Hilgards was a particularly rowdy fraternity with which the Hilgards were in a state of intermittent war. Shrill female screams, carefully faked, sometimes rang out from the upper floors in the middle of the night, freezing the blood of the ladies next door. Yet at the appropriate times the fraternity house asked the Hilgards in for tea with parents, and the tone in which the ladies told about the scandalous goings-on was as much amused as really horrified. Much later, when I had learned about such things, I found out that the Hilgards, unlike most family friends, were political liberals, members of the ACLU and friends of Oswald Garrison Villard, the editor of *The Nation*.

On the campus Sanskrit and Greek plays were presented in the Greek Theater, and each spring I was taken to the Parthenia, a dance drama in which young women in beautiful gauzy costumes ran trippingly across the grass under the auspices of the physical education department. In fall, when a new class appeared, the streets near the campus blossomed with horrible posters, threatening death and worse to freshmen who wore jeans or cords or didn't wear dinks on their heads. When the Memorial Stadium was being built (in 1922), I was often taken to watch the steam shovels scooping out the mighty crater. Of course I was for Cal as soon as I heard about intercollegiate football.

Behind the town lay the Berkeley hills, to me as a child and later as an adolescent the most beautiful and inviting wilderness in the world. One could walk up the dirt road behind the Claremont Hotel and branch off onto trails. Eventually one would get to lonely hillsides, brown in summer, green in winter, flowery in spring, as I thought all the world should be. Finally one came to dense and fragrant pine woods—to me part of immemorial nature, though they had actually been planted twenty years before by the water company. In openings one could see the campus, the town, and beyond them the Bay and the white towers of the City.

One could see the City also from our front window. The Bay spread below us and on the other side, after the sun went down into the Bay, lighthouses winked from the two sides of the Golden Gate and Alcatraz in the middle, and San Francisco glittered in more and more splendor. To get to San

Francisco one took the Key train for half an hour and then waited on the pier for the ferry, looking at the barnacles and starfish on the pilings. When the boat warped carefully in, people streamed aboard. Some met their regular bridge group for the half-hour's trip, others went to the galley for excellent corned beef hash and apple pie à la mode. For a child, the best of all was to stand on the stern with a bag of bread fragments, tossing them to the gulls who circled in endless formation, usually catching the crust in effortless flight, a few feet from the water. For the last few minutes people crowded onto the bow, watching the Ferry Building come closer and closer until the boat ground alongside and people rushed out into the noise of shouting paperboys and streetcar conductors: " 'Xaminer, Chronicle, Call. Get your San Francisco papeh! All the way up Market, City of Paris Shopping District!"

In the city people walked faster, looked brisker, and were far more various. In Chinatown one very occasionally saw a queue, in North Beach the signs were in Italian and there were wonderful pastry smells. In Union Square everybody was always dressed up—men wore suits and hats and women black dresses and hats. Naturally! This was the City!

As a child the rest of my California included Mount Tamalpais with its funicular winding endlessly up through the bay and madrone, and Carmel, still a village smelling everywhere of pines, dusty roads, and the ocean. When we had a car we went for long drives through Contra Costa County, often between rows of walnut or fruit trees. Several times we drove for two interminable days all the way to La Jolla, next door to Mexico, where my father's sister lived in a small pink auto-court surrounded by bee-buzzing lantana. One summer after my brother learned to drive, we made it all the way to Tahoe, first putting the car on a riverboat to Sacramento and then struggling up the steep and winding Strawberry Grade, lined with cars waiting with their hoods up for the engines to cool down. There we stayed for a wonderful month in a cottage at Glenbrook, on the Nevada side. My father and brother fished, while I played with friendly kids who didn't know my dubious place in the home-playground pecking order. When someone caught a lake trout it was served for dinner with ceremony. Every Saturday night a three-piece band ground out "Moonlight and Roses" while the slightly older kids solemnly circled.

The East existed only in school geography books or very occasional and baffling group reminiscence. Snow was an exciting legend, except once when a freak sprinkling of white caused the schools to close. Winter meant greenness. In summer, of course, the hills smelled of dry grass in the afternoon sun before the white fog rolled in through the Golden Gate. An old house was one built in 1900. That my parents' furniture, books, and loyalties went back even farther than this and were associated with other parts of the country was something I sensed dimly and only later came gradually to understand.

Yet almost from the first I was made to understand that a few things about our life were odd. My father was much older than other fathers and knew nothing whatever about football, baseball, or cars. Other children did not have to be quite so polite. No house in the immediate neighborhood looked like ours inside. None of my friends read many of the books that I picked up in the living-room bookcases and read sitting in the pepper tree—Stevenson, Scott, Kipling. In some way we were different—maybe better as my mother insisted. But I remember asking God to make me more like the other boys.

From quite early, I remember hearing my parents arguing in worried tones about money. There would be serious sessions in my father's den, from which Mother would emerge wiping her eyes. Once or twice there were solemn family councils, in which we all were told we must cut down. My head full of stories, I sometimes wondered for a few minutes whether there would be enough to eat.

There always was, and in early years Our House was a secure citadel most of the time. The really important people in my life were my parents, Mungie the maid, and my older brother and sister. From my earliest memories, my mother represented one set of feelings and my father another. The battle between the two has gone on in me all through life and is the main subject of this book. For this reason, and also because I think my significant elders were interesting people and representatives of social types long gone, I want to do my best to describe them. I will present them first as I remember them and then as I have learned to understand them by studying their papers, their origins, and their vanished worlds.

2

The Family

I remember my father as an old man: handsome, vigorous, often genial; yet also often grim, sometimes fierce and frightening, and always—I slowly realized as I got older—more than a little sad. I knew that I had to love him and felt guilty because I usually did not. A believer in self-discipline above all, he seldom allowed himself to demonstrate the affection he felt. Once, when I had been sent to bed before dinner for some infraction of rules, he came up to see me with his face twisted as if in pain. "Good night, my dear little boy," he said, and kissed me on the cheek. I was astounded and also embarrassed. Dad just did not behave like that.

My father was fifty-five when I was born, and by no means a young fifty-five. Even in photographs taken shortly after I was born, the man holding the baby is bald and thin, and his face is lined. I remember him as usually dressed in a dark-gray suit, often with a striped shirt and a deep-red tie. When I planted a ritual kiss on his cheek before going to bed I felt bristles and smelled tobacco.

Though usually uncomfortable in his presence, I was proud of my father. I didn't have much idea what it meant to be a lawyer, but it sounded all right. I liked to draw and could always have as many sheets as I wanted of white paper with a small printed heading: Special Assistant to the Attorney General of the United States. I boasted to my friends that my father was older than their fathers. Most of them could answer that their fathers were richer. When they came to the house I could see that he impressed them, and I worried lest they might do something he disapproved of. The main thing everybody knew about my father was that he was painstakingly honest and expected others to be the same. You could not imagine his condoning even the most harmless half-truth.

My father believed deeply in hard work and achievement, yet during my childhood it was obvious that he did not have enough to do. I can barely remember the days when he used to leave by Pullman for Washington, D.C. Later, when he took me for one of our festive outings in San Francisco, we would drop into his law office at the Nevada Bank Building, say hello to the secretary, and look for mail. Later still, he gave up that office and moved his law books home. What used to be the spare room upstairs was fixed up as an office, with *his* father's ancient gold-and-black wooden sign over the door, several ancestral justice-of-the-peace commissions in black frames on the wall, and a massive square desk of polished wood. No client, as far as I know, ever came.

At one time he wrote a series of lectures on law and history, to be given at the University Extension. They were duly announced but hardly anybody came and they were abandoned. More and more, as I was growing toward my teens, I realized that there was a family conspiracy to keep Dad occupied—playing beat-your-neighbor or rummy, reading aloud, or going for incessant short walks through the neighboring streets and up into the hills.

Often, when I went with him for a walk the tension lightened and we were able to enjoy each other. I loved books and so did he, especially, I now realize, the books he had read in the eighties when he was a young man. He loved to read aloud *The Idylls of the King,* his voice shaking when he came to Guin-

evere's tragic fall from virtue: "Liest thou here so low . . . ."
Fielding he considered coarse, but echoing his favorite Thackeray said he believed *Tom Jones* was the most complete picture of a whole man ever made. When I was a child and he and Mother read Thackeray aloud, over and over, I was free to listen, but he told me that I would understand Thackeray better when I was older. He had read some of my favorites, Scott, Stevenson, and Kipling. He loved history, especially the works of Parkman and Voltaire, whom he read in French though he could not pronounce a word of that language.

As we walked up and down the hilly streets and the trails in back of them, there was a lot to talk about and a lot to learn. And in certain formalized ways we acted as equals on these occasions, wrestling for his cane when I was little, arguing about history, politics, or religion as I got older. In these arguments he was always just and never invoked authority. When I told him, walking home from church, that I did not believe in God, he said he hoped that some day I would be able to. When I said much later that my teachers thought the United States had been led into the war by British propaganda, my father, a devout Wilsonian, said I must have misunderstood them. Once I asked him what he would ask for if he could have one wish—a million dollars, a new house? "Peace of mind," he answered.

Dad was against prohibition, and drink was never regarded in our family as evil. Once in a while he would talk about old days in Denver when he had been having a good time at the University Club and could not remember which floor he lived on. With a chuckle, he said he had gone back to the ground floor and started over. There were a few prewar bottles in a small compartment under a seat in his den, and at Christmas Mother would try to persuade him to let her use some real brandy on the plum pudding. Once in a while he made Welsh rarebit for supper, always regretting that he had to use near beer. Since he believed strongly in keeping the law even when he opposed it, there was never any bootleg liquor in the house. But at some time in the late twenties he found out that it was legal to have naturally fermented wine. The Italian Swiss colony delivered some kegs to our basement. From time to time, their cars carefully parked a few doors down the street, men from the company would come to look at, or tamper with it—I think my father rather carefully refrained from knowing. In the last few years before Repeal we had bottles of dry sauterne for parties.

Sex was another matter. Discussion of it was unthinkable. I could read almost anything in the family library but had to get my titillation from pretty sparse sources. Books about French history discussed kings' mistresses, but my parents would not make clear just what one was. Shakespeare was the juiciest writer available, and he could hardly be prohibited. *The Rape of Lucrece* and *Venus and Adonis* had plenty of stimulation for a vigorous though uninformed imagination:

> Now is she in the very lists of love,
> Her champion mounted for the hot encounter.

Movies were carefully chosen, and when my father took us to a wrong one by mistake we would file solemnly out whenever he was shocked. (Actually, in the twenties, before the Hays Office tightened up, it wasn't easy to find the right film for a boys' birthday party—even *Old Ironsides* had a nude girl in a slave market that we all knew about and were waiting for.)

Yet even here there were odd exceptions. Later when we went to Paris, Dad took my seventeen-year-old brother, though not me, to all the classic nude shows, the Folies-Bergère and the Casino de Paris. Paris was different and always had been, and that was what one did there. Once, after I had acquired a fairly full underground knowledge, my father and I were walking in the hills. A man and woman, a bit disheveled, emerged from the chaparral and said, grinning, that they had been picking flowers. To my surprise and some embarrassment, my father guffawed.

Of course his authority was absolute and very seldom put in question. I remember his spanking me only once or twice. He didn't do it well. When I finally, after years of saving, was allowed to have a dog, Dad insisted that the dog be disciplined too. At night Lindy (named like many dogs after the Lone Eagle) was put in a pen in the yard because it was supposed to be good for him. When he whimpered, Dad would go down and beat him with a slipper instead of letting him into the basement. He was fond of the dog and clearly hated to do this.

Dad had a sense of occasion, and there were times when he could suspend some of the rules he rigorously enforced on himself and the rest of us. He enjoyed most parties. I can picture him carving a roast at the head of his table, smiling over the good food and well-set table, bantering with his guests. After dinner there was often bridge, and Dad was known to be a good player. On such occasions I could glimpse a very different person from the tense, unhappy figure I saw most of the time—here suddenly was a man who loved company and was not at all shy. Once I went with him to a church fathers and sons' dinner. He was slated to make a speech, and I was worried lest he sound too formal and old-fashioned. To my surprise he was just right—brief, deprecating, and with a perfectly acceptable funny anecdote.

Most of the rules were off on one kind of occasion he clearly liked—a special outing on which he took just one of his three children. When it was my turn, he and I would start after breakfast, taking the train and boat to San Francisco and then the streetcar uptown. We would usually have lunch at

23

Solari's, a typical old-fashioned San Francisco restaurant—dark wood, mirrors, ferns, and behind a large portrait of the late Mr. Solari an arrangement of palms and American flags. I could order anything I wanted—a favorite was tagliarini followed by baked alaska. Usually Mrs. Solari, plump and pleasant, would stop and talk. She remembered Dad from the times when he had lunch regularly at Solari's. Once she promised me that when I was in college I could bring a group of my friends on the house. (Unfortunately, by the time I was in college the Depression was on hand and Solari's had gone broke and closed.) After lunch, my father and I would take the streetcar again, to the Cliff House to look at the seals, or to Golden Gate Park to see the buffalo, the aquarium, or the museum. Usually these occasions came off well, though by the time we were on the Key train coming home conversation between the two of us sometimes flagged, and I was glad if he bought and read a newspaper.

From the early thirties on, the good times became fewer, the grimness and sadness more pervasive. Part of this, I well knew, was worry about money. Once my father, who usually dressed well, bought a badly made cheap suit that made him look foolish. For a while the house was for sale, and I was deeply troubled to see a For Sale sign on the lawn near the pepper tree. It didn't sell, and eventually the sign was taken down. We resigned from the country club and the tennis club. We got rid of the car, which had never been very important in our lives. In the thirties our standard of living was an odd one—a house full of elaborate furniture in a good neighborhood, an old maid who could not be fired, and no car. Only the level of the family meals was never cut—I don't think my mother really knew that there were any alternatives to the round of steaks and roasts. And behind everything, damping every family occasion, lurked the question, What would happen when the money was all gone? We were living, I later learned, on what remained of my father's investments. Even before the crash of '29, some of them were turning out badly.

Other worries than money fell on my father in his late sixties. At a time when one should turn the worrying over to another generation, he had to deal with my mother's desperate illness, unprovided for by insurance. By about 1932, when I was in high school, this and other worries became too much for him and he started to become more and more obviously forgetful and absent-minded. By the mid-thirties his mind wandered and the words straggled. Instead of being frightening, he was pitiable. By the time I graduated from college, in 1937, he was fast losing ground and in 1939 he died.

This combination of memories—the strong but somewhat frightening father of my childhood and the sad, failing old man of my adolescence—was so painful that it was a long time before I could set about trying to understand my father. When the time for this came I had been a professional historian for many years, and the best road for me started way back in the middle of the eighteenth century in Attleborough, Massachusetts. Gradually I learned to see more clearly how strange Berkeley, California, in the 1920s must have been to a man from Boston who had graduated from Harvard in 1881. Slowly I came to understand better and appreciate more both the vigorous, genial man I had occasionally glimpsed and the tense, unhappy man I had usually known. Both, I have come to admit, are partly recapitulated in my own character. I often wonder whether if it had not been for the extreme age difference and its consequences, my essentially uneasy relation with my father might have eased and warmed as I grew up.

Though my father made the family decisions and set the rules, my mother presided, subject to his occasional veto, over our daily lives. She provided the family with two important things that my father, for all his virtues, could not: a light touch and expressed affection.

25

My mother was twenty-six years younger than her husband. I remember her in the late twenties—her early forties—as beautiful, with her specially white, soft English complexion and wavy dark hair. For all three of her children she had an inexhaustible store of love and warmth, and a considerable flow of high spirits. She was something of a mimic and could "do" the cockneys she remembered from her childhood in London suburbs. Music was her passion, and the year she had spent studying singing in Paris was the high point of her life. She loved Impressionist pictures, remembered the excitement of hearing the dramatic singer Yvette Guilbert, and often strummed on the piano a melody from *La Bohème*. Her piano playing was not particularly good, though she could manage accompaniments for family singing. As a singer, though, she had real talent and training. For parties she sometimes sang the trivial ladylike songs that the company loved, but for herself, and increasingly, she worked hard on Schubert, Schumann, and Mozart (the only good music I really know well are the lieder I remember her singing by the hour).

To her children, she seemed to radiate happiness, coming from deep inside. She seemed to like being with each of us, understood our differences, and never played favorites. Her sense of humor was robust when she was not worried about proprieties. I can remember her and her sister, Auntie Margo, in helpless tears at a Laurel and Hardy movie. Yet I can also remember a good many mornings when she stayed in bed with a "sick headache"—a migraine that could paralyze her for a day or two.

Not very long ago I met a woman who had occasionally worked in the house as a "college girl," which meant that she worked for low pay, sometimes including meals, and was not to be treated as a servant. To my utter surprise, she said that she had disliked Mother and remembered her as formidable and severe. She was certainly formal in most relations—I can hear her on the telephone saying, "Yes, Mrs. Smith. Really, Mrs. Smith? Oh no, Mrs. Smith," even to a close friend. Parties, especially big ones, were a challenge and an enterprise, to be worked on for days in advance. She loved her spectacularly handsome and much admired sister, Marguerite, but was also a little jealous of her. Part of her own charm was a girlish quality, fresh and pretty and lacking self-confidence. The formal manners, I now understand, were a necessary protection outside the family, and especially in dealing with the wives of my father's friends, some of whom were quite old enough to be her mother. While my father was somewhat sad and stern at home but gregarious and easy abroad, my mother was all love and happiness at home and full of timidity abroad. Yet later, in several terrible ordeals, she was to find somewhere the courage to overcome this timidity and to emerge from her trials a strong, wise, and free woman. Perhaps the strength was always there, under many layers of convention. Studying her history, harder to get at than my father's, I have learned to understand some of her fears—the underlying courage remains mysterious. I suspect that it may have something to do with an unquestioned, unarticulated religion.

My sister Elizabeth and my brother John were respectively eight and six years older than I was. My sister was fond of me and spent a lot of time playing with me, reading to me, and teaching me (she taught me to read before I went to kindergarten and later undertook French). My brother usually seemed little interested, beyond an occasional avuncular piece of advice or present (his excellent Meccano set, which I never took to). I thought of him as handsome, successful, and popular—all the things that I was not. This, I learned much later when we became very good friends, was not at all the way he saw himself.

Each of the three of us had a special relation with each

parent. Mother understood our different tastes and ways and seemed to enjoy the differentness. Each of us dealt differently with our father. Early, Elizabeth was clearly his favorite. She feared him less, loved him more, and sometimes spoke or wrote to him in a light and bantering manner. Partly, I think, this was because she had known him as a younger and especially as a happier man. Yet my brother, only two years younger, feared Dad as much as I did. Unlike me, however, he chose the path of evasion rather than that of obedience and resentment (defiance did not occur to either of us). John stayed away from the house a lot and kept his own counsel. When he was sixteen and we got a car, it turned out he had long known how to drive and this was accepted. I would have asked permission to learn, been refused it, and sulked.

As the youngest, I was petted and protected too much, and I continually complained of being treated like a baby. Sometimes, usually wrongly, I felt excluded by the other four. They played bridge together, and sometimes talked about things I didn't understand. Once or twice, when I had behaved badly, I overheard them discussing what to do about it. This seemed to me deeply unfair; despite being older, John and Elizabeth belonged in the category of kids, not grownups. As younger brothers will, I grew up subject to sudden, unreasonable resentments and a very mixed attitude toward authority.

The family circle included three other important relatives. Not far away on Tunnel Road, in a house much grander than ours, surrounded by a garden much bigger, lived the Rickards—Uncle Arthur and Auntie Margo, my mother's sister. Uncle Arthur looked a little like H. G. Wells, with a pink face, rather projecting eyes, and a gray mustache. He had the air, which I was later to get to know among some kinds of academics, of wanting everybody to know right away that he was a man of distinction. (Later I learned, to my surprise, that he more or less *was*.) An Englishman, he lost no opportunity to deplore American vulgarity in particular and modern decadence in general. A typical pronouncement was that Bernard Shaw was a monkey thumbing his nose at all that was good and decent. In genial moods, Uncle Arthur would tell over and over about half a dozen anecdotes, most of them reflecting favorably on himself. One was about an audience with the queen of Spain, whom he had asked how to pronounce *Los Angeles*. "Lose Anggheles," she had apparently answered, with a guttural growl. Uncle Arthur, bowing, had gravely replied, "I will tell my people." When we Mays heard this one coming it was all we could do to look at Uncle instead of at each other. Auntie Margo, however, looked straight at him, her eyes bright with interest. This, she knew, was her job, and she did it magnificently.

Few people really liked Uncle Arthur, and I was aware that my parents were not uncritical. In his case, I could go to the very edge of the strict rule that children never criticized grown-ups. By the time I reached adolescence, however, I learned that if one was *very* cautious and respectful it was possible to have interesting conversations with Uncle Arthur. He had been a prominent mining engineer, had spent time in Russia, Alaska, and several parts of Africa. He had written half a dozen books about his travels, an autobiography, and a history of mining. When he learned that I too liked to write, he presented me with his little manual on *Technical Writing*— itself an excellent piece of writing, brief, clear, and useful.

Unlike her husband, Auntie Margo was immensely loved and admired in Berkeley. She had been an Edwardian beauty and was still flamboyantly handsome, with huge gray eyes, penciled eyebrows, and (in evening dress) massive white arms. She had, even more than my mother, the gifts of a mimic and was also a skilled raconteur. She sang light songs with great charm and talked cleverly, usually about nothing whatever. She was warmhearted and always loyal to her difficult husband. She dressed fashionably and when our fortunes declined sent barely used clothing to my mother. For Mother this was not easy. She knew, moreover, that all over town people constantly sang Marguerite's praises, adding, "Of course, May's really very nice too."* From a child's point of view Auntie Margo was a fairly satisfactory aunt. Every now and then she would ask me to spend a day at her house, playing in the garden with the child of the Japanese gardener. There would be plenty of candy and plenty of demonstrative affection. If, however, Auntie promised to take me to Chinatown next week, I learned not to count on it.

For all the glitter, there was real sadness in Auntie's life. I never saw my first cousin Tommy, the Rickards' first child. Tommy spent his time upstairs with a nurse. From what I heard, a handsome child and then a handsome young man, he never advanced beyond the mental age of six and died in his twenties. The Rickards' other son, John, was a little older than my brother and sister; rather silent, of intellectual tendencies, and melancholy. In his late teens he began his revolt against his difficult parents and lonely upbringing by announcing, all of a sudden, that he was about to marry a young nurse who had come to the house to take care of his mother in a minor illness. She may have been almost the first girl he had met.

The other important relative, as different as possible from the Rickards, was my father's sister Harriet, always known as Tante, pronounced the German way in two syllables. Tante was short and fat, with a smiling brown face and piled white hair. She exuded self-confidence and good nature. I learned the essentials of her story rather early.

---

*My mother's first name, as well as her married surname, was May. Needless to say, this confused many people during her lifetime.

After working in her youth as a court reporter, she had received a legacy giving her, for life, a small but adequate income and all her medical expenses. From then on her main activities had been travel and taking care of her excellent health. She had been all over Europe many times and then had gone on to North Africa. In her little house in La Jolla there were postcard albums with pictures of prewar Vienna and Berlin and Rome, and photographs of Tante on a camel in Tunisia. Tante was particularly fond of camels. Everywhere you looked in her small living room were wooden camels, ceramic camels, and whole camel trains in cross stitch.

Tante had an uncomplicated but shrewd mind and a generous heart. Her Christmas box was a work of art. There were five or six presents for each of us, bought at sales all through the year. Usually there were a few things saved from her travels—for instance a Florentine leather wallet. Every Christmas Tante's box was opened first.

I enjoyed her visits to Berkeley, but my parents didn't entirely. She would arrive to delighted greetings and very soon retire to the spare room for a few days in bed. The doctor would come and give her some pills or an enema. Her room would be a cheerful mess of pieces of paper, bits of cloth, medicine bottles, and odds and ends. She insisted that this was her kind of order, and that she could lay her hands on anything instantly, but the apparent chaos bothered my neat mother. I learned that for some reason, Tante did not entirely approve of my mother. Once, in fact, I overheard her saying to herself under her breath, "That woman is a fool," and I knew whom she meant. Such moments of irritation passed quickly, but between Tante and my father ran a current of more serious tension. They were of opposite temperaments and I think her visits put a strain on his disciplined courtesy.

Several times I went to stay with her for a month in La Jolla. In general I had a good time, watching the porpoises from her window, swimming every day at the cove, and in the evening listening with her to the radio. She loved both Amos 'n' Andy and Cecil and Sally. One of the few drawbacks was that Tante, strong-minded and determined to do her duty as the grown-up in charge of a child, continually grilled me about my bowel movements and dosed me with laxatives at the slightest hint of nonperformance.

A little later I learned that Tante felt very strongly about the old May furniture in our house. In her strong opinion—all her opinions were strong—my mother would have no right to any of the family pieces after my father's death. Not that she would take anything away; she did not want it for herself. But it was up to her, as a true May, to say what went to whom eventually, and she enjoyed planning the division and telling us about it.

This completes the circle of significant elders except for one. The remaining person was so important to me and her exact position so hard to explain that she needs a chapter to herself.

3

Almost Family

About Mungie, our maid, no documents exist, but my memories are vivid. She did not change essentially, so I will tell her story now from when I first remember her up to the time of her death.

Once when I was reading Tolstoy, I realize that I *did* understand some of what he said about serfdom. He hated the institution and worked for its abolition. Yet he knew that serfdom, paradoxical like all human institutions, could foster love, gentleness, and spiritual beauty.

Mungie was a member of one of the smaller servant classes of America, the women whose marriages had not worked out. She was not an Irish or Polish girl fresh off the boat. She was the daughter of a German farmer from Illinois and remembered a few phrases of dialect German. She was the same physical type as those stringy women—with their blue frizzy hair and their slacks and high heels, their cross voices and unhappy faces—whom one sees all over the Southwest, where they have come from Iowa or Illinois and found Nothing. Mungie was of an earlier midwestern generation: her hair was thin and straight, her knees and feet knobby, her clothing simple (on her days off, pink hats with flowers), and her face full of goodness and wisdom.

Her real name was Mary Grossman Thompson. We never

heard much of anything about Mr. Thompson. The story was the Victorian classic melodrama. He took to drink, beat her, and sold the furniture. At some point she had a miscarriage. Finally, about 1910, Mr. Thompson disappeared and Mungie had to go to work. After a couple of short jobs she came to us, about 1914, and never left.

So Mungie was a servant, and there was a lot wrong with that. She ought to have had a house and family of her own, and instead was "just like a member of the family" with us. As a matter of course, she lived in a small dampish room in the basement. It had its own bath and was not uncomfortable, but it was hard to heat. She suffered much of the time from rheumatism, and more and more from arthritis, and she worked all the time. To me, when I woke up on the sleeping porch—then thought hygienic (pretty cold in Bay Area fogs)—the most reassuring sound in the world was to hear Mungie banging around in the kitchen very early in the morning, slamming the screen door, rattling the garbage-can lid on the back porch, and humming tunelessly but cheerfully to herself. She cooked our three meals, almost always well and for parties excellently, cleaned the house constantly, and filled in her time mending, darning, and ironing. When she first came to us, in the family's palmy days, there had been other servants, and she had once been just a cook. But waitresses and laundresses came and went rapidly; Mungie could never get along with other women working in the house and preferred to work harder and run her own show. Her tactics of boycott and subtle interference were resourceful. This was especially the case with women who were hired to take care of the three children, and especially of me, the youngest. They would institute regimes of strict discipline according to the fads of the day, which Mungie would ignore, and the more we were forbidden to sit in Mungie's kitchen, the more she would lay out alluring cookies. Sooner or later the competition left.

34

When the family's already declining fortunes were made worse by the general crash, Mungie's wages were cut from whatever they had once been, probably nothing spectacular, to twenty-five dollars a month. As my parents saw it, there was nothing else to do. We couldn't afford a maid, couldn't get rid of the fairly big house. Mungie, by now more knobby-kneed than ever and by no means beautiful, was unemployable elsewhere. And anyway, it was unthinkable to her or to us that she could leave. That is what I mean by saying she was something like a serf: she was tied to the house and worked almost without pay. We were tied to her also; getting rid of Mungie was one of the few economies never even considered.

A serf, not a slave: she had her rights. Her room contained the mementos of her shattered respectability. A picture of her in turn-of-the-century pompadour and shirtwaist looked like nobody I had ever seen, except in the expression of the eyes. On the wall was an engraving of Siegfried rescuing Brunhilde, about whose meaning she had long stopped speculating, and a brightly colored painting of some pansies done by Mungie herself. In my more belligerent moods I would loudly insist that it was just as good as any other picture, but without much conviction. On her day off she liked to take me for long streetcar rides. I can still smell the combination of hot wicker, stale cigars, chewing gum, and sweat that pervaded the streetcars as they clanked up the Berkeley hills for miles and miles, stopped at the end of the line, and clanked back down again. On Sunday she went to the First Baptist Church, and she contributed to it a tithe of whatever she earned. Being an American and not a Russian peasant, she voted. After politely asking my father what he thought, she almost always voted the other way. The only time she felt strongly, however, was in 1928, when her minister told her that Al Smith was a boozer. With the same good reasons that made many women of her generation prohibitionists, she hated and feared booze. When we got wine in the house, and then when prohibition ended and cocktails were an occasional indulgence, she would serve them correctly. But she herself would never even touch the excellent wine jelly that she made for parties.

Like Tolstoy's serfs, whose horizon did not extend far beyond their villages, Mungie knew very little indeed of the world she lived in. She knew we had fought the kaiser but not why. When the family went to Europe for a year, leaving her to work for our fortunate tenants, she heard my accounts with interest, but her questions made it clear that she thought it no more reasonable one should go to England via New York than the other way round. She knew how to make and serve company dinners and dinners for all kinds of festive occasions, like birthdays and homecomings. She cooked with pride and accepted praise with pleasure, flattering the special tastes of each member of the family. Beyond this, she knew that Jesus had saved us, that all people had their good and bad sides, and that life was hard and had to be endured.

Her relations with the family were close, but special. Her birthday was celebrated more or less like the others, and after she served the Christmas dinner she would come in the living room for the present giving. But she had no statutory share in family power and thus, like servants in all cultures, had to defend herself by sabotage and persistence.

Her relations with my father were those of mutual respect without much intimacy. She thought him a fine man and a smart man. In the twenties she invested her savings on his advice, and when she lost them did not blame him since, as she explained, he lost much more. My father, who was a stickler for his own special brand of democracy, frequently insisted that she was probably the most completely good person he knew. He would discipline us for teasing her, which of course we did all the time. As long as we still had a car we took her to church on Sundays, going on to our own church and picking her up at hers afterward. My father would make a great point of jumping out of the car, opening the door for her, and handing her in and out.

With my mother, where the association was closer and the collaboration constant, the relationship was a very complex combination of affection and warfare. My mother, being English, never quite gave up her badly mistaken belief that it was possible and desirable to make Mungie over into a proper English servant. Mungie retaliated by exaggerating, mincingly, the correct manners my mother tried to teach her, sometimes going so far as to call my sister "Miss E-liz-a-beth" in a derisive tone. One battle she won, gradually but decisively. My mother thought it wrong for Mungie to speak while she was waiting at table. This was hopeless. When somebody said something funny, Mungie choked with laughter; when somebody said something wrong, Mungie corrected him. My mother fortunately did not have the heart to be consistent about this. When Mungie was really irritated with my mother, she would tiptoe about the house, telling me in a stage whisper to be quiet, "because your mother's terrible nervous today." Yet the two women spent many happy hours sitting at the kitchen table discussing plans for the day. And when my mother was dying, Mungie was the last person she called in to say good-bye.

Mungie was fond of all of us three children. I had a special place as the youngest, who had been a new baby when she first came. Obviously enough, I took the place, to some extent, of the baby she should have borne. Whether or not it is good for a child to have somebody's absolutely unconditional and uncritical devotion I do not know, but I had it. Mungie was undemonstrative. She complained constantly about having to open the screen door every fifteen minutes for my dog, who more or less lived under her stove, and still more when, as often, he was joined by one of my friends' dogs. Yet she put out food for them all the time, just as she had wonderful cookies and glasses of orange juice always ready for all children. We played tricks on her sometimes and ignored her a lot of the time.

When I went to school I heard a lot about democracy, and it occurred to me that there was something wrong about the cold little room and the twenty-four-hour days with only one day or afternoon off a week. "She's better than you are," I would shout at everybody—everybody, that is, except my father. (He would have agreed, but nobody ever shouted at him.) The rest of the family found my egalitarian belligerence amusing, and of course I never refused any of Mungie's services for a minute.

Long years later, when my parents died and the family broke up, Mungie continued as long as she could to work for my sister, hobbling about a much smaller house, cooking, and pressing clothes. Eventually this became impossible and she was moved to the King's Daughters Home in Oakland. There she made few if any friends, but when we went to see her she always said she was fine, that everybody was nice to her, that we all had a nice movie last night. Though by that time, bony and crippled, she was not obviously attractive, my little daughters fortunately took to her, and she spent a lot of time embroidering pillowcases for them with straggly rickrack. Occasionally she spoke of old age, illness, and death. There was, she said, a little light inside of her that kept going in spite of everything. As long as it didn't go out, she was all right.

I wish the story could end on that note, but it can't. One day, after I had been busy or out of town or just neglectful, I heard that she was dead. When I got to the Home, I learned that in her last hours she had been fearful and lonely. The little light, which had burned clearly all her life, had gone out just a few hours too soon. It is one of the regrets of my life that I was not there.

My brother and I arranged the funeral—when the funeral director learned she had been at the Home, his interest ebbed and the prices came down—and it took place from my sister's house. We had gotten in touch with Mungie's relatives, though of course we assumed, as the "families" of serfs and servants always assume, that she had really belonged to us. What a mistake! In the first place, Mungie was a free woman in her own heart and belonged to nobody (unless to Jesus). In the second place, she belonged to her family, who turned up and soon made this quite clear.

My sister invited them to her house before and after the funeral. They were different both from us and from Mungie: southwestern in accent, as she had not been, and modern in clothes and ideas, as she had been still less. We tried to get along, the two groups eyeing each other warily. So this is Mungie's real family—this must be the daughter of the sister she always went to visit in Los Gatos, but just who is the old man with the weather-beaten face? So these are the folks Aunt Mary worked for all these years. Dutifully, we all trooped to the funeral parlor, and saw poor Mungie, all glossy with wax and rouge—a sight that gave me nightmares for a long time. We sat more or less together listening to the perfunctory and sentimental words of a preacher who knew nothing about Mungie.

Then we went to my sister's house for supper. With some hesitation I asked the stringy old man whether I couldn't give everybody something to drink. Well, now, he said, I don't guess a little drop would hurt us, and he poured himself a generous whiskey. With the second glass his face cracked: "What if Aunt Mary could see us now!" he said. We all roared; tears came to our eyes, and for just a moment we were all her family, and therefore each other's.

4

The Smell
of Europe

Despite a few clashes of temperament, despite underlying and growing money worries, our family gave friends and visitors an impression of deep security and mutual affection, and this was not by any means a wrong impression. It was my mother, who gave the family almost all her time and strength and understanding, who held things together. As the money shrank and my father grew shakier, this was to become a heroic assignment.

Much was good about my early upbringing; what was wrong with it is obvious: the age and remoteness of my father. If a father's function is, in part, to teach a son the skills he needs to get along in life and to serve as a model, I hardly had a father. My father represented authority and discipline at a distance, and the result was that I grew up disliking both but feeling guiltily that they were necessary. His expressed principle was that being grown up meant forcing oneself to do things one disliked doing. I long thought, most reluctantly, that he was probably right. Now I think that this view needs a great deal of dilution. It may be necessary to do unpleasant things, but the virtue never resides in the unpleasantness. Fortunately, my mother represented, without saying so, a quite different principle: there is no virtue in anything done without love.

For whatever reasons, in a conflict of family values or in my own makeup, I grew up with too many fears and too much guilt. The fears were of many kinds. I was so afraid of high places that I could hardly climb a tree or even the steps of a slide. I was afraid also of supernatural forces and went in for complex propitiatory formulas. I had nightmares. The worst of these would start as I seemed to be walking, in the twilight, past a small park at the foot of our street. I would know that witches were going to jump out at me, and sure enough they did. At this I screamed as loud as I could, waking myself up and disturbing neighbors several houses away.

Mine must have been almost the last American generation in which children grew up absolutely ignorant about sex. This did not prevent me from having fantasies, which I considered bizarre, disgusting, and unique to me. At one point when I was about ten, I got my first inkling of comparative anatomy. A somewhat older boy had a club that met in a tent. There were girls as well as boys, and to be initiated each person had to take off all his clothes and be examined. This seemed to me the height of depravity, and I was terribly alarmed when my mother found out about the practice. Of course she expressed shocked disapproval, but was not nearly as horrified as I had expected, and the matter was very shortly dropped.

Some of my difficulties were matters purely of temperament, but in addition there was the problem of our differentness from other people. When I first went down the hill to John Muir School, a block away, I found that I had too fancy a vocabulary and also, apparently, a touch of an English accent from my mother. That was bad enough; worse was the fact that I didn't know the bare beginnings of the rules of football or baseball. I had a very hard time for many years learning to throw or catch a ball. I was good at most of my studies except woodworking shop, which boys had once a week while the girls had cooking. Perhaps part of my trouble came from the fact that there was no tool in our house but a hammer. I am afraid that this was linked with a deplorable and snobbish feeling that handwork was not our business. Wood shop was called "manual training," and I assumed that it had something to do with being manly. At least boys were supposed to love it, as they were required to detest music classes. I pretended to rejoice with the others when Thursday, manual-training day, came around, but in reality I dreaded it and did my best to work up a sore throat so I could stay home.

I was perceived at school, not altogether wrongly, as odd. Sometimes I was waylaid on the way home from school—not witches but actual boys darted out from behind bushes, scaring me, spilling my books, and pushing me around until they tired of it. My increasing resort from this and all other troubles was to escape into books. I would get Mungie to give me a big glass of orange juice and would sit for hours in a branch of the pepper tree with a volume of Scott or Stevenson. In my fantasies, of course, I was always brave and universally admired.

By the fifth and sixth grades things had improved a bit. I had discovered one sport at which I was competent, soccer, and would even play in serious after-school games between the high fifth and low sixth. I was lucky enough to have one really good teacher. Miss Stone, who taught fifth grade, was an angular, rather homely midwestern woman who told us not to talk the way she did. "You shouldn't say 'ask,' the way I do, you should say ahsk, the way Miss Martin does. You listen to her; I just can't make that noise." Miss Stone had traveled all over the United States and could tell us what New England or Chicago or the southwestern deserts really looked like. She had a sense of humor, the right mixture of skepticism and affection toward children, and she always knew what was going on in her class.

Even in the worst times there were important compensations. I always had a few close friends, who accepted my oddness and forgot about it. Fears, nightmares, hangups—all could disappear in a moment of shared enjoyment.

#

In 1926, the year I graduated from grammar school, the process of learning to get along was interrupted by an astounding piece of family news. We were going to Europe, and for a whole year! Europe to a bookish American kid was a magic word, and Europe became the sole subject my father and I talked about in our incessant walks in the hills. What countries should we go to, what would we see, what would it be like? Anywhere was possible except Germany—my father's feelings about the war were too strong for that. What it eventually boiled down to were long stays in England and France, with a brief trip through Belgium.

Under the circumstances to go at all was a brave decision. Many of our friends had made brief European trips, but to take three children out of school, rent the house, and live abroad for a whole year was something different. Doubtless it seemed a good time—I was just out of grammar school, my brother just out of high school, my sister (who did not much want to go) finishing her second year at the University. To my mother it meant a chance to see her beloved half-sister and formidable stepmother, to return to England, where she had grown up, and to Paris, where she had spent a wonderful year studying music. For my father it meant revisiting Paris and

43

London, the great centers of the traditional culture he loved. It also meant spending a lot of money when there was none coming in, and his worries about this were sometimes to cloud the adventure. Yet I think none of the five of us ever regretted the decision. For me, this year abroad was the single most formative experience of my childhood. In an effort to explain why, I want to recall it in some detail.

To move a family of five from the West Coast to Europe in those days meant a big job of getting train tickets, reserving steamer passages, packing trunks for the hold and suitcases for the cabin. Finally we all got aboard the Southern Pacific train at the Berkeley station in a mood of shared excitement and mild hilarity. My father, greeted by porters he knew and sniffing the familiar train smells associated with better times, was at his happiest. Family discipline was relaxed. Sent to my upper berth at my usual bedtime, I could get away with sticking my head out and talking to the grown-ups late at night. It was summer and very hot. We had the choice of closing the windows and sweating or opening them and breathing cinders—not all the locomotives had switched from coal to oil. Dining-car meals were heavy: heavy food was served on heavy linen held down by heavy silver. The black stewards were deferential and also jocular. After meals I sat on the observation platform at the rear of the car, listening to strange grown-ups talking while the men smoked their cigars, and the Nevada sagebrush, the tiny mountain towns, or the flat emptiness rushed past.

We stopped for a week at Denver. I had always understood that this city was something like Paradise, and found that this impression was quite true. My parents, who had had their happiest times there and left only ten years before, were entertained night and day. We stayed in a big frame house with a family of their closest friends, whose daughter, a few years older than I was, had the job of keeping me happy while the others went to grown-up parties. She taught me to play chess, I had ice cream sodas whenever I wanted, and we went to the movies most nights. Finally, to my regret, we got back on the train for Chicago and Montreal. I had been told that this trip would be a great experience and had resolved to keep a diary. In Chicago I duly and pompously recorded my awe at the huge crowds rushing about, and with great originality compared them to ants. This was the first and last entry in the diary—life was much too interesting for conventional literary sentiments.

On our nine-day voyage from Montreal up the St. Lawrence, past the battlements of Quebec and across to Southampton, our lives were regulated by the odd, utterly conventional routines of Atlantic travel, unchanged from the nineteenth century all the way to the 1950s, when the liners finally surrendered to the airlines. We went cabin class, which was not first-class splendor, but nearer to that than to third-class austerity. The grown-ups sat in the deck chairs in the morning, wrapped in rugs. Young people like my brother and sister played deck games and danced every evening. For the children there was a free new world to explore. To my surprise I found myself for the first time an accepted leader, elected president of the secret club that met on the boat deck, in demand for games of hide-and-seek among the lifeboats and behind the stacks. Nobody knew that I was used to being considered odd. I had never had such a good time.

One morning we started seeing seagulls—tiny ones, not like those of San Francisco Bay. Land appeared in the distance. People packed up and gathered in groups in the dining salon waiting for the customs men. When we went ashore my mother cried at the first blue-helmeted policeman, the first red pillarbox with the royal GR. We were met by a hired car, big enough for us and our suitcases—the trunks came later. From Southampton to Bournemouth we drove

45

through a bright-green landscape. My mother pointed out thatched cottages. Finally we turned into a gravel drive and were met by two people, new to me but clearly important, whom I was to call Granny and Auntie Nina. I had to make a great effort not to laugh at their way of speaking, which sounded to me exactly like comic parodies of extreme English accents.

While the grown-ups made conversation, no doubt a little stiffly at first, Granny gave me an orange and told me to go and play in the garden. The orange, regarded by her as a great and unusual treat, was larger and more tasteless than the oranges I took for granted at home. In the garden California poppies grew with other flowers among the rockeries instead of in vacant lots, and I learned that here they were called *Eschscholzia*. Everything, it was clear, was going to be different—perhaps better.

The house was named Tresillian, after a Cornish village. It was on Westminster Road East, in Bournemouth West, near the Branksome Towers Hotel. Westminster Road was lined by trees and bordered by hedges. All the houses were fairly large, most were of brick, most had large gardens, each had several servants. Most, I think, were lived in by elderly people whose families visited them in summer. All had names, often with the feudal pretensions of Branksome Hall or Westminster Grange. The large house next door was modestly called Westminster Cottage. It was presided over by ancient Mrs. Topping, whose granddaughter Daphne became my daily playmate. The house was full of trophies of far-flung hunting expeditions. Pythons coiled around the standing lamps, tigers glared glassily from under the piano, fierce heads loomed from the walls of house and coach house. Mrs. Topping did not like automobiles and was driven around town in a horse-drawn vehicle, in which to my delight I sometimes had a ride. I was impressed by my hostess's ability serenely to ignore the horse's natural functions taking place a few feet in front of her nose—the loud farts, the emergences and plops, the sudden cascades of urine.

From Tresillian we could walk down the beach through Branksome Chine, full of pines and rhododendrons. There were rows of bathing huts. We often had tea in Granny's hut. I had learned that *tea* meant a regular meal, with sandwiches and cakes or scones. This was the somewhat select Westbourne beach. If I walked a mile or so along the sands I could come to Bournemouth beach with its amusement pier. Here there was a theater where pierrots sang slightly off-color songs and, much more intriguing, a Punch-and-Judy show. I soon became very familiar with this weirdly archaic and satisfyingly violent drama—Punch beating Judy, both tossing Baby back and forth, the Crocodile biting people in the head, Punch dead and being tossed up and down in his coffin. On the beach near Bournemouth pier unemployed veterans made careful sand statues of Britannia or the British lion, and people gave them pennies. Even a child was aware of unemployed veterans in England then.

Tresillian itself was brick with white trim and bay windows. On the ground floor were two principal rooms. The drawing room contained the piano, the best furniture, and cases full of the best china and books. It was used only for guests or music. The far more comfortable living room, with a couch and ordinary furniture, opened into the garden, which, though not large, had its shrubberies, its kitchen garden, and room to set up clock-golf on the lawn. Up the steep stairs were three floors of bedrooms, getting smaller as one went up to where the maids lived and visiting children stayed. Reading matter in the house—something I quickly investigated—included a few strange and baffling children's books dating back to Granny's childhood in mid-Victorian times. If I got desperate there were the bound volumes of

Punch in the drawing room. Cartoons in the earliest volumes had women in crinolines and men with spreading whiskers; the current issues depicted comic charwomen, bizarre American tourists, and young people in blazers and flannel bags or big hats and short skirts, referred to in the captions as the Bright Young Things.

Granny herself was kind but formidable; Auntie Nina affectionate and companionable. She had stories about being a nurse in the war, and I later heard that she had lost a fiancé in France. I became and remained very fond of her. It is clear to me now that both were absolutely determined to make a success out of the challenging visit from an unknown American family. I suspect that Granny wanted to make up for some less than happy episodes of my mother's youth. Everybody tried hard and in general things went well. My mother, in the difficult mediating position, clearly found herself more American than she had realized. She told me, only a little later, that she was irritated when Mater or Nina would suggest that dear Harry might like a whiskey-and-soda or a nice glass of port, without its occurring to them to offer dear May anything. My aunt Nina has told me recently that there were some episodes when my mother was upset enough to withdraw to her bedroom with a headache. My father seemed to find no difficulty in calling a woman about his age "Mater." My sister, fresh from a California sorority, was startled to find that she was expected to efface herself and wait on the men. I had very few troubles except to pretend that I always liked the food. The suet puddings were all right, but gooseberry fool was a challenge—supposed to be a great treat but to me sour and soupy.

The two maids, usually referred to together as "Rose 'n Ella," were pink-cheeked and very young. I was astounded that they called me "Master Henry," sometimes even "sir," but of course we became friendly. When I asked Ella if she had ever been to London, where we were about to go, she was astonished that I would think this possible. She had never been even as far as Southampton. Sometimes on an afternoon Rose 'n Ella would take me to Poole, probably by tram. What they liked best to do there was to look at the Woolworth's; I preferred watching the peacocks in the town park.

Granny and Auntie Nina were well acquainted in Westbourne, and there were constant parties—tennis and charades for the young people, teas and musicales for my parents. When my mother sang, she was at first surprised that people went right on talking and clinking teacups. The great occasions for me were the frequent picnics. Auntie Nina drove the Morris-Oxford, named Angelina. We went to towns in the New Forest, to Studland, best of all to Corfe Castle, a towering feudal ruin in the Purbeck hills. Its gaunt shattered towers looked down on a storybook village. The village inn was called the Bankes Arms, and I learned that in the Civil War Lady Bankes had herself led the defense of the castle against the Parliamentary forces. For longer trips, with packed lunch and careful planning, we went as far as thirty or forty miles to the cathedrals of Salisbury and Winchester, where the stone knights slept, their feet on their hunting dogs, their swords at their sides, in the dim light.

Once, in central Bournemouth, there was a fair with tents and games and a pageant. The pageant had two subjects—British history and the Empire. Druids in sheets draped one way were followed by Romans with sheets draped another way, and the historical part ended with soldiers from the Great War. In the Empire procession, people wore Indian or Zulu or Maori costumes long preserved in trunks in their attics. The band played "Land of Hope and Glory":

Wider still and wider, shall thy bounds be set.
God, who made thee mighty, make thee mightier yet.

I sang as loudly as anybody, but yet was not without a few American qualms. It all seemed to conflict a little with what I had learned in school about the triumph of democracy.

Tory ideas were of course taken for granted in my grandmother's whole circle. The goodness and charm of the royal family, the sadness and heroism of the war, were not things to joke about. Somehow, though they had been allies, one could never really trust the French. The leaders of the Labour party were uncouth and dreadful people. Once on a picnic we came to rest in a field under some oak trees, and were approached by a man in corduroy breeches who I learned was a bailiff. (This was exciting; there were bailiffs in Robin Hood.) He asked us to leave since this was Lady Something's land. While we were packing up, the owner herself appeared and started to lecture to us about private property. My grandmother immediately answered that she entirely agreed and was a landowner herself. (She owned a couple of small plots of land in Cornwall and had tenants who occasionally sent her pheasants.) The lady's manner immediately changed and she said we could stay if we wanted, but Granny, standing on her dignity, insisted on withdrawing. I was surprised about all this and ventured to ask Granny about it, and was told how important it was to respect landowners. Remembering grammar school world history, I said that sounded to me almost like the feudal system. "Indeed it is," answered Granny, "and a very good system too." I was both shocked and intrigued.

After a few weeks in Bournemouth (we were to return for longer visits there) we all took the train for London. The first thing I noticed was the grime—touch anything and your finger came away black. Underground stations with intriguing names—Knightsbridge, Earl's Court, Marble Arch—turned out to be unexciting. Of course there were a few surefire attractions. The best was the Zoo, always exciting from the animal smells and sounds as one approached it to the tropical feeling of the reptile house. I read Harrison Ainsworth's *The Tower of London,* a romantic summary of Tudor history for children, and here was the great grim Tower itself, with its messages scratched on dungeon walls.

It was The Season, still a time for traditional splendors. I loved to watch the guards, in their busbies and red coats, marching briskly up the Mall with the band playing the current hit song "Valencia" in military time. We saw the Royal Tournament at Olympia, which included a simulated attack on an Arab or Afghan fort. We saw the royal family and Field Marshals Allenby and Haig reviewing the household troops at the ceremony of Trooping the Colour. On the streets, men took off their hats passing the Cenotaph, or when a royal car went past with the two little princesses, Elizabeth and Margaret Rose. After church on Sunday people still paraded in Hyde Park, the men in gray toppers and ascot ties. At least once I saw big black cars with coronets on the door. I met a boy my own age who was in a public school and wore—unbelievably—a black bowler. "Only the louts wear caps," he proclaimed, looking at mine. It was, after all, the London of the last gasp of empire and aristocracy—the London of Evelyn Waugh—also, shortly, the London of the General Strike. From a much later perspective, I find this the least attractive period of English history. Aristocracy and empire survived, wounded by the war, defensive and nervous, unclear about function and future.

Finally we left England, by a rough passage to Ostend. My brother, looking green himself, had to help a very sick lady to her cabin; the deck became slippery with vomit. Of our trip through Belgium I have only a few scattered impressions. One morning my brother and I woke up in a room on the top floor of a hotel overlooking the central square of Bruges. Down below a market had blossomed with tents and stalls. When we went down we found women in white caps, men wearing wooden shoes. I can remember the smell of the canals, the swans, my father's bald head covered with mosquito bites. At Ghent the castle of the counts of Flanders was the best castle so far. Surviving medieval details included stone toilets, with holes in their seats giving conveniently on the courtyard below. Of Brussels—a city I was later to live in for a year—I can remember little that impressed me except, of course, the statue of the little boy urinating, somehow in Europe not shocking but amusing and acceptable, even to my parents.

Paris, on the other hand, gripped my eleven-year-old imagination powerfully and the grip has never weakened. It was, of course, an imagination fed by books. I had recently read *The Three Musketeers*. In the low-ceilinged ill-lit salon of the Hôtel des Saints-Pères I reread *A Tale of Two Cities*. In Paris, it was easy enough to believe in the cruel tortures, the grim Bastille, the crashing guillotine.

For a while my brother and I took French lessons at the Ecole Berlitz near the Opera. There one was supposed to learn just by talking "like a child." Occasionally, however, a teacher, first looking cautiously down the hall, would whisper an English equivalent or even a handy grammatical rule. I learned more talking to hotel employees and store clerks.

Pictures imprinted themselves on my mind for good. Walking across the Seine at the nearest bridge, I saw the gray river flowing between its tree-lined embankments and, very close, the towers of Notre Dame and the Conciergerie. Then, walking through the Louvre, I could see on the right the symmetrical grandeur of the arches, the formal gardens, the obelisk. Best of all was the Left Bank, where we lived. Without knowing why, I liked the narrow dark streets, the gilt horses' heads marking the horsemeat butchers, the swinging capes of the policemen who strolled through the streets at dusk. A little farther away from our hotel there were big black doors and cobbled courtyards, and beyond them the Invalides, with its museum full of knights in armor. Often we went to stroll in the Luxembourg Gardens, where French children played with hoops in formal ways I did not understand, and the brooding giant looked at his reflection in the Medici fountain.

In the hotel there were times of boredom, whiled away talking to the two ladies behind the desk, reading, drawing pictures. I liked the food—the main course was usually veal, the dessert sometimes elaborate chocolate pastries called *religieuses* (black with white whipped cream and therefore looking like a nun) or vanilla ice cream swimming in rum. I was allowed a little wine. Our meals were usually served by a very kind old man called Monsieur Jean. He had an odd knob on the back of his bald head that I could hardly keep from staring at. When I went out with my mother, we often stopped for chocolate and napoleons or babas at a pâtisserie.

Winter came on and it became, for a California boy, very cold. I can feel the wind blowing down the river as I walked with my father on the quays. At corners men sold roasted chestnuts—I didn't much like the taste but this, like everything, seemed to me to be exactly as it should be. I discovered a shop in the Rue Bonaparte in whose windows were beautiful lead soldiers—the best of them carefully and accurately painted Napoleonic regiments—grenadiers, Polish light horse, cuirassiers. I was sure that these were far too expensive for us, but was to find some beside my bed Christmas morning. In the holiday season the department stores had superb animated window displays: I remember the jazz band whose members winked and smiled as they played, and a street panorama featuring a crowd of American tourists whose heads turned in unison up and down, from side to side, as their guide pointed.

I learned, with slight apprehension, that my parents were thinking of sending me to an American boarding school at Grenoble. Before this happened, however, I got what seemed to be a super-cold, with a raging sore throat and terrible wheezes. It became more and more difficult to get my breath, and I was delirious with a high fever (I seemed to be in a box I couldn't get out of). Finally diphtheria was diagnosed. I acutely remember bouncing over the cobbles in a taxi on the way to the American Hospital at Neuilly, and arriving to find that they had expected a much smaller child and had prepared a crib. Sitting in a wheelchair struggling for breath, I knew that I was very sick. I can't say whether or not the possibility of dying quite crossed my mind—probably, since my mother was right there, it did not. The crisis passed, and then I got almost sicker than before with a reaction to the horse serum that was then used to treat the disease—I broke out in spots and again developed a high fever. My mother, who seldom left me during the crisis, developed shingles and spent a few days in the hospital herself. I stayed there five weeks, and after the first days enjoyed it enormously. There were no other children, and I was made much of. There were family visits every day, usually with presents. At first, while I was in a private room, I talked a lot with the nurses. These were mostly Russians, some of them beautiful, one of them—I learned from the others—a princess. One had splendid stories about escaping from the Bolsheviks in a freight train across Siberia, another taught me Russian phrases.

After about two weeks I was moved to the men's ward. There I got along excellently with the men in the other beds, and learned quite a lot. One man had been a soldier in the war, and had married a Frenchwoman and stayed. One was black, and it should be recorded that in 1926 his presence in the ward somewhat upset my mother and sister. A young man I liked used to read aloud from Milt Gross's *Nize Baby* ("itt opp all the Proon-joos," etc.). Once I stopped him and said, "Shh, here comes Mr. Glickman." "What of it?" asked my friend. "Didn't you know, he's Jewish," I answered. He gave me a long incredulous look. "What in hell do you think I am?" he asked. I was deeply embarrassed but had learned something. I was by no means completely happy when time came to leave the ward and go back to the Hôtel des Saints-Pères.

Soon after this episode, undoubtedly far more terrifying to my parents than to me, we all left Paris to look for some sunshine in Menton, on the Italian border. There was no more talk of school—probably the time for enrollment had passed. I am not sure how seriously my parents had thought about it—they never seemed to feel very strongly about schools.

Menton was not a fashionable Riviera town like Nice, Cannes, or Monte Carlo, all of which we briefly visited. I have learned that it catered to middle-class English tourists. We encountered tweedy types walking on Cap Martin. There was a shingle beach with an old stone pier from which one looked across the bay to the Old Town, rising from the water with brightly colored walls and red tiles to the church tower flanked by cypresses. The best times were family walks, sometimes joined by other American families from the hotel, on easy zigzag trails through the terraced olive groves with views of the dark blue sea. We walked to the Chapel of the Annonciade, to Roquebrune with its Saracen castle, and to small villages—St. Agnès, Gorbio, Castellar, and others—ancient piles of tumbled white stone and red tiles, inhabited mainly by black-shawled old ladies who spoke only Italian. The Hôtel Turin, where we were staying, furnished sandwiches of strong Swiss cheese on strong dark bread.

After a month in Menton, we went back to Paris, stopping in Provence. In Avignon we saw the huge papal palace, the ruined bridge, the medieval towers across the river in Villeneuve. In Arles and Nîmes we saw Roman amphitheaters and arenas, temples and tombs and aqueducts, all baked orange by the sun.

When we got back to Paris it was still cold, and my parents decided that I should spend the spring in Bournemouth. I did not really want to leave Paris. My father took me across the Channel. We had a fairly good time on the journey. He delivered me in Bournemouth and went back to Paris. Once again Granny and Auntie Nina made an immense effort—a twelve-year-old American boy was still to them an unknown species. Again there were picnics, by now in country full of primroses and cowslips. Somebody had lent my hostesses a Yorkshire terrier—it was the first time I had had a dog almost my own. Neighborhood boys and girls were invited to tea several times a week, and their parents invited me—once to an incredibly elaborate children's party with professional clowns and a conjurer. In pictures taken that spring I look entirely like an English boy—white shirt, gray shorts, a belt buckle like a snake.

Like an English boy at school, I missed my mother in this first separation. I wrote her daily letters, which she kept. These seem to me now a little young for my age, a little too much designed to be what she would most want to hear, full of pat descriptions and inept drawings. On the other hand, one surviving letter from my mother in Paris seems to me now a perfect letter to a child—affectionate but not patronizing, telling me about plays she saw, full of eager anticipation of the good times we would have in England when she came.

Finally the family gathered again in London, and I was horrified to find that my mother had bobbed her hair and didn't look at all as I remembered her. This shock soon abated, however, and as far as I remember our remaining weeks in England were pleasant. When the day came to leave, Granny and Auntie Nina went with us to Southampton, this time by train. I could see that both Auntie Nina and my mother were having a hard time holding back the tears. In those days it was a long trip from England to California—who could tell when they would see each other again?

Again I had a fine time with the other children on the ship—one boy's parents asked me to visit them in Maine, which I knew we couldn't afford. When we reached Boston it was dreadfully hot. The huge hotel seemed to all of us repellent after the cozy Saints-Pères, the food almost inedible. Faneuil Hall and Old North Church were only mildly interesting after Europe, and when my father wanted to take us to see Harvard one especially hot morning we all rebelled and simply lay around fanning ourselves. After another long train trip we found ourselves actually at home, with Mungie and my aunt and uncle to welcome us. The house looked unbelievably the same.

#

I have described this European year in some detail because it was my first great remembered experience. The long-range effects on my development were important, though it is not easy to understand them and very hard to balance the good and bad. Of course my childish attachment to traditional and genteel culture was greatly strengthened. I had heard—and doubtless owlishly repeated—too much conventional chatter about what was and was not picturesque. Deeper than this lay the beginnings of a feeling for the past, a sense of its continuous presence and endless fascination. Love of the past for its own sake is a dangerous and addictive drug, but I doubt if anybody studies history without a touch of it. My senses had been cultivated and made acute. Wet smells could bring back the garden at Tresillian, cold winds recalled the pale-gray embankments of the Seine, spring rains the fruit trees blooming in cracks in the medieval towers of Villeneuve, across the Rhône from Avignon. Foundations had been laid for national prejudices. England I loved and hated—I felt that it was partly mine and partly very strange. France, on the other hand, was all of a piece, aloof and elegant. These feelings have become more complicated but they are still there. As to my own country, my feelings about that were challenged and deeply stimulated. Working them out was to take much of my life.

Against these undoubted riches there was a lot to balance. I had spent a year not only in Europe but also almost entirely in the company of grown-ups. This was not by my wish—I had longed for company my own age and missed my friends at home. The few times that I had encountered contemporaries stood out, even amid all the other excitements. I spent one afternoon in Paris playing soccer up and down the corridors of an apartment with some French boys—children of the acquaintance of an acquaintance. Afterward we went to see Harold Lloyd in *The Freshman,* and I had had the prestige of an interpreter, explaining about college stadiums and rooting sections. Once on the beach at Menton a boy from the Old Town had turned up and we had had a fine time building castles. The teas at Bournemouth had been a little less satisfactory because more supervised, while the gang on both the boats had been splendid.

The family was different after the year in Europe. My sister, to whom I had so far been close, was left behind, to study music in Paris for another year. My brother was almost grown up. In Europe, to impress his friends at home, he had had pictures taken smoking a Dunhill pipe, standing just outside an actual bar. Now he was going away to Stanford. In Europe the alternations in my father's moods had become more extreme. Sometimes he was almost exuberant, at other times he was consumed and paralyzed by worry, mainly over money. It was on the trip, where the family spent long hours close together, that I learned that while I could not defy his orders, I could sulk and scowl and get away with it.

I was going back to start junior high, a rough passage for most shy and bookish kids, and doubtless I would have had a hard time in school even if we hadn't gone away. But certainly adjustment to normal American life and the beginnings of adolescence was made far more difficult by this strange and exciting year, during which I had been almost completely withdrawn from the important process of learning to get along with my equals in my own time and place.

In Europe the family had been too close and isolated a world. From the time of our return other worlds were gradually to become more important. Yet all challenges had to be handled with the resources I had got from my upbringing and my two very different parents. Therefore, in order to understand and explain myself better, in the next part of this book I turn to quite a different enterprise. I will be shifting keys in my mental computer from the mode of memory to the mode of history. As a historian, I am going to try to look at both my parents (I know much more about my father) in their own settings, at the experience of life before I knew them, at the families that formed them as my family formed me, and at the cultures that formed the two families.

Part II

Roots as Found

5

Attleborough
and After

Long after the deaths of both my parents, after I had been a professional historian for many years, I was helped toward a deeper understanding of my father and his background by an odd coincidence, a dramatic coming together of professional interest and family history. The coincidence grew out of a historical project I particularly enjoyed, my assignment by Harvard University Press to edit Harriet Beecher Stowe's novel *Oldtown Folks*. This book is in part a conventional Victorian romance, but the other part is the most penetrating and imaginative account ever written of New England Calvinism and the society it formed and reflected. Harriet Beecher had been bruised and damaged by this fearful and logical set of doctrines in her youth, and she looked back on it with a wonderfully complicated mixture of hate, respect, and even affection. A paragraph will give the flavor of her ambivalence:

On some natures theology operates as a subtle poison; and the New England theology in particular, with its intense clearness, its sharp-cut crystalline edges and needles of thought, has had in a peculiar degree the power of lacerating the nerves of the soul, and producing strange states of morbid horror and repulsion. The great unanswerable questions which must perplex every thinking soul that awakes to consciousness in this life are there posed with the severest and most appalling distinctness. These awful questions underlie all religions,—they belong as much to Deism as to the strictest orthodoxy,—in fact, they are a part of human perception and consciousness, since it cannot be denied that Nature in her teaching is a more tremendous and inexorable Calvinist than the Cambridge Platform or any other platform that was ever invented.

Part of the reason I enjoyed working on *Oldtown Folks* was that I shared Stowe's mixed feelings about New England Calvinism. Perry Miller, the great historian of American Puritanism, had been one of my graduate school teachers. Miller, himself a product of the iconoclastic twenties, had rescued the Puritans from people who had thought them mere bluenosed Fundamentalists. An atheist himself and something of a romantic tough guy—a learned Hemingway—Miller had admired the Puritans for their sheer courage. They alone, he believed, had dared to look man's fate straight in the face. Since the God of the Puritans willed everything that happened, he must have known before the beginning of time the fate of each individual he had made. All were inadequate and sinful; yet by divine edict some were saved and some were lost. The implications of this fearful conclusion had been worked out with great subtlety.

Miller wrote a brilliant and controversial biography of Jonathan Edwards, the great theorist of New England Calvinism, making him over into a modern existential philosopher. Taken straight, Edwards's own writings fascinated, attracted, and repelled me as they have many readers during the last two hundred years. There are aspects of Edwards that are not difficult to love. His imagination and aesthetic sensibility raise him far above other eighteenth-century American theologians. His oddly aristocratic disdain for all practical or prudential morality, his unselfish love of vastness and beauty for themselves can be deeply attractive to people who, like Perry Miller, are fed up with the morality and aesthetics of Middletown or Zenith, Ohio. Yet it is impossible to separate these attractive traits from Edwards's iron system of determinism. Those who are prevented by God's own inscrutable decrees from being able to love him are necessarily objects of his hate. Edwards's descriptions of their sufferings, both endless and intolerable, draw on his great poetic talents for the ability to convey feelings of terror and despair.

Edwards grips many people who read him, whether they like him or not. His New England successors, who worked out his doctrines with plenty of intelligence but far less depth of feeling, are a more special taste. Yet they too have their admirers. These stern "farmer-theologians" had all been ardent supporters of the American Revolution, denouncing the waverers and the lukewarm in Old Testament language. After the Revolution they fought fiercely against every sentimental or liberal departure from consistent Calvinism, and just as fiercely against the political heresies of Thomas Jefferson and of all who seemed to them to fall under the influence of infidel and Jacobin France. Once radical, now consciously reactionary, these preachers spoke for the values of the Puritan past. Some of them had a following well into the nineteenth century, especially in rural New England, hardly at all in the urbane and enlightened city of Boston.

In editing *Oldtown Folks,* I had identified one of Stowe's most powerfully drawn characters, "Dr. Moses Stern," as one Nathanael Emmons of Franklin, Massachusetts, perhaps the most painstaking, uncompromising, and for some the most powerful of Edwards's disciples. Emmons himself had appalled Harriet Beecher in her youth by preaching one of his typical funeral sermons over her sister's fiancé, a virtuous and brilliant young man who had been drowned at sea.

Looking straight at the young man's family and fiancée,

Emmons had demonstrated, sorrowfully and gently but inexorably, that it was impossible to know whether this excellent youth was saved or lost. Whatever his merits, he could not be saved without a special experience of divine grace exerted in his favor, and we had no way of determining whether he had received this or not. This sermon, understandably, did a lot to drive both Harriet Beecher and her sister away from their ancestral Calvinism.

Yet Stowe's novel gets most of its power from the fact that she respects and admires Dr. Stern, his icebound system, and the bleak society for which he spoke. In her correspondence she often refers to the surviving archaic rural Calvinists of her own youth as "my people," contrasting them favorably with the smooth, cheerful, up-to-date Bostonian Unitarians represented by polite authors like the senior Oliver Wendell Holmes. What I suddenly realized through a series of coincidences was that these small-town Calvinists were, in factual and not merely in sentimental terms, my people too.

My first intimation of this connection came in Widener Library at Harvard, when I was reading Emmons's sermons in connection with my Stowe project. I found one funeral sermon that had been preached over the wife of the Reverend John Wilder of Attleborough. I knew that my grandfather had come from Attleborough and was named John Wilder May. A very little detective work showed that Nathanael Emmons, Stowe's Dr. Stern himself, had preached over my grandfather's grandmother. But the connection proved to be much closer than that, and to understand it I had to look hard at my own ancestry—a subject that in itself had never interested me much.

Thinking back to childhood, I realized that, on the one hand, my father had never talked much about his family. On the other hand, there had been suggestions that he cared about his origins. In his study hung the justice-of-the-peace commissions of his father, grandfather, and great-grandfather, the last, in the name of Elisha May, signed with the flamboyant autograph of John Hancock and dated "in the fifth year of the Independence of the United States." In a bookshelf in his "den" was a May genealogy, carefully compiled by several Mays, including my grandfather, in 1878. The record began with John May, a sea captain who after several voyages settled in Roxbury, Massachusetts, in 1640. The editors of the genealogy, wistfully hoping to discover aristocratic connections, tried hard to connect the Roxbury pioneer with a distinguished, even occasionally knightly family of Mays in Mayfield, Sussex. This effort came to nothing and my father spoke of it with sardonic humor. It was not that he had no family pride, but rather, I think, that he did not like what was real and solid to be mixed with foolish vanity.

In our attic at home was a large box marked Old May Papers. Once or twice I was shown some of the older documents. I found them mildly interesting, since I was a bookish and romantic kid who liked anything that was really old. Once in the 1950s I took out this box and went through the early family papers with a Berkeley colleague who was a distinguished colonial historian. Many of them were of some historical interest. There were revolutionary civil and military commissions, a correspondence about the supply of beef for General Gates's revolutionary army, eighteenth-century church documents and land transfers, tavern bills and a receipt for the tax on a coach, records of the court of a village justice of the peace, and a few revealing personal letters. All the early documents, of course, were written in the fine durable ink, on the good heavy paper, and in the clear elegant handwriting of the eighteenth century.*

---

*My father gave one document away, to a friend who believed in prohibition. This was a letter making sure that for an eighteenth-century ordination there would be plenty of rum for the quality and cider, well-worked, for the rest.

What my colleague and I had not looked at closely was the collection of sermons in the box. Neither of us then was primarily interested in American religious history, a field that later came to attract me intensely. More recently, I got out the papers again and looked through them carefully, concentrating especially on the sixteen sermons, preached from 1773 to 1844. All but one of these were printed—in early New England well-known preachers often published their sermons, especially those preached on public occasions. Down to the next-to-last, preached in 1836, all were Calvinistic. Three were by Nathanael Emmons himself, and others were by identifiable followers of Edwards. Four were Whiggish election sermons—a term that needs a little explanation. Once a year in early New England, a prominent preacher was invited to preach before the general court, ceremonially gathered in the presence (before 1776) of the royal governor. In these sermons, the New England Israel is always ritually urged to remember its special destiny and repent its misdoings. From 1763 on, the preachers almost invariably urged the people, while the governor gritted his teeth, to resist injustice and oppression. One of the sermons in the family collection is an election sermon by Nathanael Emmons. Another is a particularly famous and fiery wartime polemic of Nathaniel Whitaker, preached in 1777, calling down the "curse of Meroz" on all who were lukewarm in the holy cause of the Revolution—those, for instance, who had qualms about confiscating Tory goods. I was not at all surprised to find several later political sermons that were vigorously Federalist, one lamenting the death of the divinely appointed leader George Washington and another, of 1798, denouncing the infidel and menacing rulers of Revolutionary France.

Even more interesting to me were the seven funeral sermons preached over members of the May and Wilder families, two by Emmons and all but one in the special ultra-Calvinist mode of the Emmons school. All cultures, we are told by anthropologists, develop ways of dealing with death. The recent American way tries to minimize grief or explain it away. That of early Attleborough was the very opposite—grief was dwelt on and rubbed in, but yet associated with an inevitable divine plan. In one sermon, that over Mrs. Wilder, Emmons himself was at his very gentlest, almost daring to believe that God had decided to save "that amiable and excellent Child of God, whose remains now lie before us." The most moving were two successive sermons preached by Elisha Fisk of nearby Wrentham over the three children and then over the wife of Dr. Calvin Martin (son-in-law of Elisha May). These four had all perished, as often happened, in the same illness. Fisk warned the widower and remaining children against two dangers—first, insensibility, which rejects any of the grief or pain inflicted by the Lord; second, dejection, which can be self-indulgent and may even lead to rebellion against the divine will.

Such calls for fortitude and realism represent for me the admirable side of Calvinism; its less attractive side was also apparent in some of the family papers. Almost the only personal letter of Elisha May, the first member of the family to achieve provincial eminence, is a harsh denunciation of somebody who has slandered him. In the most vindictive Calvinist manner, making full use of Old Testament language, Elisha May forgives his enemy and leaves him to his own remorse and God's inexorable judgment. As late as 1830 Mrs. Eliza Wilder May, my great-grandmother, makes a personal covenant with Jehovah, in which she, the worst of sinners, surrenders her destiny to his disposal in the hope of his grace and protection. This document, almost in the style of seventeenth-century Calvinism with the addition of some nineteenth-century sentimental rhetoric, was written when Jackson was president and Emerson was preparing to announce, a few years later, the divinity of all men.

I was a good deal struck by the coincidence that I had worked hard and long trying to understand the thoughts and feelings of people exactly like these whose writings had been in a box in my upstairs closet. Obviously one of my Calvinist ancestors would have seen the clear finger of God, and a nineteenth-century geneticist the no less inexorable power of inherited mental traits. Having my own habits and prejudices, I tend rather to invoke the influence of cultural history and especially of fashions in raising children.

The short road between ultra-Calvinist provincial Attleborough and my father's upbringing in a Boston suburb can be quickly mapped with the aid of a little family history. The original John May who arrived in America in about 1635, though unfortunately not connected with the knightly Mays of Mayfield, Sussex, was at least a freeman and church member of Massachusetts Bay Colony. One of his sons, also John, stayed in Roxbury and became the progenitor of a rising family. The Mays of Boston and Roxbury achieved respectability and sometimes even distinction in a typical Boston manner. One was colonel of the Boston regiment in the Revolution; another was one of the "bold rebels" who dumped the British tea into Boston Harbor. A little later another was churchwarden of King's Chapel and a philanthropist on a modest scale. Several were prosperous merchants; at least two were well-known abolitionists and reformers. One married Bronson Alcott and achieved an unenviable immortality as Marmee in the novels of her daughter Louisa. Since they did not move their money from commerce to manufacturing, the Mays never came close to sharing the wealth and power of the Cabots and Lowells—the new group that ran Boston by the middle of the century and were only rarely abolitionists or reformers. The Boston Mays continued to live and think in the manner of the older elite—upright, complacent, equally devoted to progressive reform and to the best literature.

Until they decided to study and publish their genealogy in 1878 the Boston Mays had no idea that they were connected with the provincial Calvinist Mays of Attleborough—the introduction to the genealogy specifically makes this clear. The Attleborough Mays were descended like the others from the first and second John Mays. The latter, whose oldest surviving son stayed home and sowed excellent seed, had only modest means and seven children. When he grew old and blind he gave some thought to providing for his two youngest sons. He expressed the hope that each of these would learn a trade, and left each a plot of land, to become his at the age of twenty-one. One of these tracts was on the Massachusetts–Rhode Island border, in what later became the town of Attleborough. This region of southeastern Massachusetts had once been part of the "Old Colony" of Plymouth, and even after Massachusetts Bay took it over in 1671 was known for its cranky independence. Its inhabitants looked to Providence, Rhode Island, as their commercial and intellectual capital and were never much influenced by Boston. From very early, the region produced Baptists, Separatists, and other thorns in the flesh of the Bay Colony's religious establishment. The preachings of the Great Awakening had fallen on fertile ground. The town of Attleborough in particular was radically Calvinist in religion and radically Whig in politics. Its citizens were among the first to answer to the circular letter from the Boston Committee of Correspondence by denouncing all connection with Britain in rhetoric drawn from the Old Testament. The region's historian, J. H. M. Bumstead, says that in this area land was bought and sold a lot, and new men often came to replace the traditional elite. One of these new men was Elisha May.

Elisha is the first May whose papers I have in any quantity. Most of them are concerned with land acquisition, and this clearly paid off in status. Elisha May became successively selectman, coroner, justice of the peace, member of the committee of correspondence, major and then colonel in the local militia, member of the governor's council, moderator of the town meeting, and presidential elector. Whereas his father in formal documents was either "yeoman" or "husbandman," Elisha was now "gentleman" or "esquire." He became, that is, the local magnate. For several generations before this first success, the rural Calvinist Attleborough Mays had lost all connection with their polite and prosperous Unitarian cousins in Boston.

In Boston some families kept their prestige for many generations, but in provincial Massachusetts society was more mobile. People like Colonel Elisha May were not necessarily able to pass on their hard-won status to all their children. Only one of the colonel's sons was graduated from the nearby College of Rhode Island (later Brown University). The rest had their ups and downs, usually as farmers. Only the sixth son, my great-grandfather Lemuel, managed to climb back up the social scale. His papers are full of the buying and selling of land, shares of cotton factories, and estates of insolvent debtors. It is this son, not any of his older brothers, who became almost as prominent locally as Colonel Elisha, holding almost all the same positions in local government.

All this time, while Boston and Harvard were going Unitarian, the Attleborough Mays clung fast to the old faith. Colonel Elisha and his family sat under the uncompromising

Calvinist John Wilder, and Wilder's daughter Eliza married Elisha's son Lemuel. Church records show that both Lemuel and his wife, my great-grandparents, were admitted to the First Church "upon full profession" of its Calvinist faith, and it was Eliza Wilder May who made the covenant giving herself wholly to God.

Within the next generation, that of my grandfather, the family's social and geographical location shifted, and the religious pattern began to shift with it. John Wilder May, Lemuel's second son and my grandfather, named after the Attleborough minister, achieved some success after a very hard struggle. His father was able to send him to Phillips Academy, Andover, and then the University of Vermont (family tradition says because it was cheaper than nearer colleges). After graduation he tried farming for a year or two and then kept school two or three seasons in Attleborough (this was the usual desperate last resort of nineteenth-century college graduates with no particular profession). Then he moved to Roxbury, apparently without knowing that it was full of comparatively well-to-do relatives, and studied in the office of a local lawyer. He was admitted to the bar in 1859, never built up much of a practice, but after some struggles became selectman and then member of the General Court. In 1869 he was elected district attorney of Suffolk County. In 1878 he was appointed chief justice of the Boston Municipal Court and held this position until his death in 1883.

John Wilder May did not talk much about religion, but he attended a Congregational, not a Unitarian, church near his house in Dorchester. Its minister, E. N. Packard, remembered by my father as an unconvincing preacher, in one of his few published writings deplored not only Unitarianism but also "the liberalists within our own ranks" and blamed this internal treason on "the old unvarying enmity of the soul of man to his God." Judge May himself, however, seems to have turned away to some degree from the harsh old theology, while keeping in his personality the deep marks of both his inherited Calvinism and his hard upward struggle.

In 1850 he married his cousin Elizabeth Thurston Farnham. Her grandfather, one of the sons of Elisha May, had left Attleborough for Winthrop, Maine, in 1790. There, according to the genealogy, he achieved local prominence through his natural abilities, despite a limited education. His granddaughter married Henry B. Farnham, who became sheriff of Bangor. Their daughter Elizabeth apparently was given her middle name after a local clergyman, David Thurston, who is remembered in Winthrop history as a strict Calvinist, a reformer, and an abolitionist. As far as I can tell, the Mays and Farnhams of Winthrop and Bangor were exactly the same kind of people as the Mays of Attleborough—Calvinist, hardworking, and intermittently successful: farmers, lawyers, occasionally legislators or judges.

Despite this somewhat forbidding background, Judge May's wife and cousin had a gentler temperament than her husband. A girlhood diary of 1849–50 gives a picture of a gentle, emotional, sentimental adolescent who falls in and out of friendship with girls and is flattered and excited by the attention of boys. The weather is usually terrible, illnesses frequent, and churchgoing incessant (sometimes three times a Sunday). Yet there is also the lyceum, where she once heard Horace Greeley—"*I like him,* but he is not a very *pretty bird*"— occasionally the circus, and once a thrilling trip to Boston by boat and train. In Boston Elizabeth not only visited the statehouse and the churches and roamed pensively in Mount Auburn Cemetery, but went up eighty feet in the "Fandango" in the Public Garden and saw Edwin Booth act at the Boston Museum.

Judge May's personality is revealed and his religious tendency suggested by a letter to his small son Harry, my father, written when Harry was seven years old. John Wilder May describes a visit, with two of the still younger children, to the Bangor office of Grandfather Farnham, the sheriff. This is followed by a look at "the poor people in the lockup":

These people, you know, are bad people. They lie and swear and steal and get drunk and do other naughty and wicked things and so Grandpa has to take them and put them in prison to make them behave better. There is one little girl in there not much older than you. She has been taking things that did not belong to her, that is, she has been stealing. She seems very unhappy as all bad boys and girls must always do. I hope you will remember that to be good and kind and obliging to others is the way to be happy, and to be bad and unkind is to be unhappy.

This is one of a number of surviving letters written by the judge to his little boy, usually when Harry was staying with his Maine cousins. The letters are always concerned for Harry's welfare and manners. They are affectionate in their way and report on the farm animals, on the Dorchester place, and on the doings of the other children. They never fail to take some opportunity to inculcate a moral lesson:

It will always make your dear papa and mama happy to hear that you are good, obliging, generous, polite and kind to others, because this is the way to make yourself loved, and to make friends. Boys who do not care for others and do not wish to do them kindnesses and favors, are generally not much cared for by other people.

In his efforts to make Harry a good boy, the judge never refers to God, the Bible, or any specifically Christian doctrine. Children must be good so that people will like them and be helpful to them when they are grown up. In a way familiar enough to students of Max Weber, the judge's inherited religion, still practiced on Sunday, seems mostly to have turned into bourgeois morality.

It is in the nineteenth century, not earlier, that certain kinds of New England reformers and moralists believed it to be their duty to bring to bear every possible coercive influence in order to change the character of criminals, paupers, drunks, orphans, and, still more of course, their own children. These were people who clung to the rigid discipline inculcated by the ancient faith without its fundamentally egalitarian belief in the sinfulness of all men. Real Calvinists, after all, know that they have to be virtuous without indulging any hope of reward. They know too that it is impossible to make bad little boys and girls good, even by locking them up.

When Judge May died in 1883, at the age of sixty-four, the Boston press published a number of long obituaries, resolutions by bench and bar, and statements by people who had known the judge. These lay special stress on Judge May's integrity, never questioned even by those he had sentenced. As district attorney, we are told, "he used none of the arts of the demagogue to win popular applause and perpetuate his hold on the place"; indeed, one memorialist suggests that he had "almost too much" integrity for such an office, and that it was remarkable that he was reelected. Next to his integrity, the obituaries stress the judge's learning; he was the author of two standard books, one on criminal law and one on insurance.

May's indictments when he was district attorney usually resulted in convictions and his judgments on the bench were seldom overturned. His eulogists concede but usually approve his severity. Some of them insist that underneath it lay a particularly kind heart. One says that the judge hated especially to send to prison young boys, accused by their rich employers of first-time petty thefts. I do not find it hard to believe either in the severity or the underlying kindness.

Though the tone of these obituaries is not that of Attleborough funeral sermons, it is still New England, and some of the writers consider it their duty to point out the faults as well as the virtues of the deceased. A number refer to the judge's brusqueness of manner, which sometimes left the wrong impression. And several suggest a basic unhappiness in the life they are praising. Just when May reached the bench, his wife died, and one obituary suggests that he never got over this blow. To supplement his "honorable poverty"—and perhaps to escape his sadness—he worked far too hard, editing legal works in addition to his major writings. Overwork and lack of vacations, one eulogist implies, contributed to his death at sixty-four. His pictures show a leonine head with long white hair, a high forehead, piercing blue eyes, and a grim slit of a mouth. Yet it would be a mistake to make Judge May into a caricature. An uneasy and often difficult father, he was occasionally capable, as we will see, of showing both understanding and affection to his son. Letters show that his close friends loved him, and there is evidence that his provincial stiffness at times lapsed into geniality.

As district attorney and judge, May had finally become a successful Bostonian, and he was recognized as a relative by his Boston and Roxbury cousins. He was invited to help with the May genealogy, contributing the part on the Bristol County branch that finally convinced the Boston Mays of the truth of the connection. There are records of occasional social relations between the judge and his Boston relatives.

Yet the gap must have remained a real one. The Boston Mays were Unitarians who often sent their sons to Harvard, were a part of the wide current of reform and uplift, and remained continuously well-to-do for several generations. John W. May's immediate Attleborough forebears, including his mother and father, were holdout Calvinists. No Attleborough May had been to Harvard and only a few to any college. Those who had become lawyers and merchants had done so by very hard work, and not a few had lost out in the struggle. Most had remained close to the farm. The brusqueness and severity that his admirers recognized in the judge were no accident.

My father, Harry May, was brought up in relative security and complete respectability, but far removed from the world of fashion and wealth. He went to Roxbury Latin School and then Harvard and acquired many of the habits and tastes there prevailing. Yet it takes no antiquarian flights of fancy to see under the Bostonian polish the uneasiness, sadness, and rigidity, the constant self-questioning, the iron integrity that go back for their origins to the Attleborough of John Wilder, friend and protégé of Nathanael Emmons.

6

A Puritan
at Harvard

The center of Harry May's childhood world was his august, demanding, formidable father, who constantly urged Harry to improve himself. His mother in her letters is far more tender and very occasionally verges on the playful. The house in Dorchester, spacious and almost in the country, must have been a good place to grow up. In photographs it is tall, thin, and utterly unpretentious. Its one high gable is lost in elm branches; a barn and connecting passages are added on at the rear. Letters refer to a cow, and the judge hired a couple of men at times to help with the haying and other chores.

Harry was the oldest surviving child (a sister had died in infancy). A sister, a brother, and then another sister appeared at regular two-year intervals. Very early, and all his life, Harry felt the special responsibility of the oldest. When he was thirteen his father wrote him from New Brunswick a letter implying that he had been in charge of the other children: "We hope to find all well, and to have the best of reports about your efforts to make Hattie and Johnny and Lily, and all the rest happy."

Whenever Harry could, he loved to go visiting relatives in Maine. There were lots of lively cousins and above all, in

Bangor, Aunt Laura and Uncle Sidney, a childless couple who were deeply and uncritically devoted to him. In one letter his aunt writes, "Uncle Sidney calls you his boy and we talk about you a great deal and hope you will come and visit us this summer again." Harry's parents remind him that he mustn't outstay his welcome, and his mother declares, playfully but not without a hint of jealousy, "You need not think I have forgotten you, or concluded to let you *live* with auntie, for I couldn't possibly spare you." Occasionally one of the children spends a week or two with cousins in Attleborough or even Buffalo.

Harry grew up on the edge of a great city with slums and fashionable quarters, but his world was mostly one of green landscapes, white wooden houses, and rocky coasts, linked together by fast, familiar trains. This was the 1860s, yet nothing survives in writing that links Harry May's childhood with the horrors and glories of those years. But I remember his telling me that he remembered seeing an uncle brought home wounded from the war, and that the only time he remembered his father crying was at the death of Lincoln.

A few family friends, with whom the parents dined soberly at frequent intervals, were part of Harry's world. None was as close as the Storey family. Charles M. Storey had been John Wilder May's law partner in Roxbury and was an affectionate, devoted friend. His son Moorfield, later a well-known Boston reformer, had worked in John Wilder May's office when May was district attorney. In 1867 Moorfield Storey became private secretary to Senator Charles Sumner, and thenceforth was a part of the very top circle of Boston reforming society, as Judge May's family was not. Yet the Storeys kept in close touch with the Mays, and Moorfield remained a friend and correspondent of my father all his life. The comparison is instructive: Moorfield Storey, unlike Harry May, was a committed reformer, passionately devoted to such causes as Philippine independence and black civil rights. According to an admiring biographer, he never doubted any of his opinions, whereas Harry doubted all of his. I am tempted to ascribe this temperamental difference in part to Storey's standard, optimistic Unitarian religion, the faith of upper-class Boston, as against Harry's post-Calvinist tendency to inward searches and doubts. In part Storey's confidence surely reflects the complete social and financial security of his family. "I never thought," Storey is quoted as saying, "whether the family was rich." The Mays thought about this a lot, and knew that they were not.

In due time Harry went to Roxbury Latin School, which had been founded in 1645 for the purpose of preparing some local boys for Harvard (one of the original Roxbury Mays had been among the founders). In the seventies, when Harry went there, Roxbury Latin was still mainly concerned about getting boys into Harvard, recently grown demanding in its admission policies. It succeeded with about twenty-five boys a year, far fewer than its rival Boston Latin. In 1877 Judge May writes in high good humor telling Harry that he has been admitted to Harvard without conditions, and that Mr. Collar, the headmaster and a family friend, has praised his last year's performance. A couple of the neighbor boys have been conditioned in Greek. The judge urges Harry to work hard and keep up his good start—advice that the boy was not to take.

We know little about Harry's first year in Cambridge, and nothing directly about a terrible blow that fell on him in the middle of his sophomore year. In 1878 Elizabeth Farnham May took ill and died, leaving her husband sadder and grimmer, and the children in his sole charge. Thinking how I would have felt if my mother had died, as she came close to doing, when I was that age, I can understand how the loss must have affected my father. Shortly after this major disaster, Harry started keeping a diary. For the rest of his college years and for a few years after graduation, he recorded not only the outer events of his life but also his inner feelings. The diary makes a remarkable portrait of a certain kind of young man in the changing Harvard and Boston of the early eighties. To me, reading it is an invaluable experience. I knew my father only as an old man. Now I discover him in his youth, passionate, full of hopes, fears, self-doubts, and potentialities.

Harvard in the late 1870s and early 1880s was at once the best, the most modern, and the most fashionable of American colleges. Charles William Eliot, who carried through but did not begin most of the modernizing, had started his long presidency in 1869. Since before the middle of the century, Harvard had been changing from a sleepy, pious, provincial school with prescribed classical curriculum and memorized recitations to a modern university with some elective courses, some lectures instead of recitations, and professors selected both for learning and gentility, not for piety. From a college designed primarily to make country boys into ministers, it had become the preserve of the new top financial class of Boston and its suburbs, designed primarily to make sure that their sons were well-educated gentlemen. The famous and exclusive clubs reigned over Harvard social life, and at the top that life was part of fashionable Boston. Both academic and social standards were raised. Tuition had recently risen, to $150, housing cost more, and students were expected to dress better. According to one careful examination, both the rising standards and the increasing expenses were part of an almost conscious effort on the part of the Boston rich, who provided ever larger endowments and dominated the governing boards, to keep Harvard for their own kind and cut down the number of country boys and ministers' sons.

One kind of Harvard atmosphere is suggested by the Harvard novels of the period, which deplore misfits and grinds and treat with admiration the rich, easy-going, high-spirited, and athletic young men who drink a good deal, barely manage to keep from getting involved with Boston actresses, and are only occasionally bothered by academic requirements or college rules. The *Harvard Lampoon* of the period has cartoons making fun of Irish goodies and muckers, Jews, Catholics, and the nouveaux riches (Mr. and Ms. Isaac Shoddy). Languid young men wearing wing collars, loud checked suits, and very long overcoats are caricatured more gently. In its prose, cartoons, and general tone the *Lampoon* is clearly straining for the assured snobbery of *Punch*.

Harry May occupied an uneasy middle rank in the stiffening Harvard hierarchy. He was not foreign-born and had gone to an acceptable if not really prestigious school. Neither Theodore Roosevelt '80 nor his friend Owen Wister is mentioned in the diaries, and it would be most surprising if they were. Being one of the swells was out of the question for Harry—both money and inclination were lacking. The ways of those he called "the money men" made him uncomfortable. His father often found it hard to find cash for the young man's ordinary expenses. Harry lived in college but went home to Dorchester, on the horse-cars or on foot, for weekends.

More important than Harry's social status was his complex and divided temperament, which both helped and hindered his college career. One side of him was very gregarious. Often seven or eight men turned up in his room of an evening. Most nights he played cards—at first poker and later whist, at which he became expert. He liked going for walks with friends and singing on summer evenings under the elms of the Yard. He sometimes disliked paying calls, though these usually went well enough once the ice was broken. In winter he enjoyed sleighing parties on the Brighton road or coasting down Park Street. In summer he went with friends on carefully planned camping trips in Maine or New Hampshire. He went as often as he could to the theaters in Boston, seeing at first everything from farce to opera bouffe, delighting in the new comic operas by Gilbert and Sullivan, but turning more and more to Shakespeare's plays, in which all the great English and American stars appeared. At first uninterested in opera, he learned to love it by going with other Harvard men to "supe," which meant to serve as an extra in a crowd scene and get in free.

Occasionally Harry smoked a cigarette, noting the fact in his diary. Despite some pressure from Dorchester church circles, he stoutly refused to take a temperance pledge, deciding that he did not think cider, beer, or ale harmful. Wine was more suspect, being associated with the high-living set, and hard liquor never mentioned except for a welcome swallow of brandy on a rainy camping trip. Clearly, Harry tried to be one of the boys, and was—up to a point. Once, in his sophomore year, he even got caught "ragging a sign" (stealing a store sign for display in his room, a very common undergraduate offense).

As throughout his life, his friendships ran deep. He was involved in the lives of his intimates, worrying about their examinations, engagements, and family troubles. Often he and a friend would spend long evening hours discussing marriage, the future, or religion. Several of his college friends remained close throughout his life.

As with most of his college generation, clubs were important. Harry was not among the 30 percent of his sophomore class selected for the Institute of 1770, whose members were eligible for the Hasty Pudding, the prestigious waiting and final clubs, and for fashionable Boston society. (The names of the sophomores who *were* selected were published in the Boston papers, in exact order of social rank.) In his freshman year Harry became a member of the Everett Athenaeum, a group that read each other's papers and discussed topics of historical and current political interest. He took the Athenaeum very seriously, objecting when a "ring" tried to seize control of it.

The Athenaeum's lighter moments were not easy for Harry. Twice he did his best with comic readings and was not happy with the result. When he played a country doctor's apprentice in an Athenaeum farce, things went better and he kept the program. The Athenaeum supper at the end of sophomore year was the best evening he had had so far in college. Nobody took wine, but the party ended with singing in the Yard beneath the summer elms.

In his junior year club life presented Harry with a moral dilemma. He was invited to join Pi Eta, sometimes known as "the pie eaters," a club for those who had not made the Institute. Several of his friends belonged, but Harry knew the club had a dubious reputation, social and possibly moral. After many doubts, he accepted, but immediately regretted his decision, concluding that the club "would be likely to bring me down rather than I to bring it up." His regret became real chagrin when he heard intimations that had he not joined Pi Eta, he might have been elected to the Signet, the top intellectual society and one that was not altogether lacking in social standing. One of the Signet Society's rules forbade members to belong to Pi Eta or the Pudding. After many agonies Harry offered to resign secretly from Pi Eta so that the club would not be damaged. His resignation was accepted with some generosity and without the secrecy, though the remarks of a few Pi Eta men hurt Harry. Finally the Signet did invite him to join. After making quite sure that the one member said to oppose him had been notified in time to object, Harry accepted.

The Signet immediately became the center of his college life and remained so during his last two years. His diaries report in detail his opinion of the papers presented, and he presented his share, working on them far harder than on any college assignments. The club usually met for papers, followed by an excellent spread and often a late walk. On April 1 of his senior year Harry joined the others after the meeting in "leap-frog, high-kicking, jumping, etc.": "We kept it up till 1 o'clock. We threw away all dignity and enjoyed ourselves, all of us I guess. At any rate, I didn't have any time to think of the blues."

Harry took the Signet very seriously, working hard on committees and worrying about the caliber of the new members. The society brought him important friendships and intellectual excitement. It also raised his social standing, and there is evidence that he was quite conscious of this. He continued occasionally to go to Athenaeum meetings, but advised one friend not to join that society "unless he was sure that the others in the ten [chosen] were the right sort of fellows, because I think there is a small chance of the societie's [sic] rising to a position again where it will do a fellow any good."

Though he still disliked the swells, Harry was also uncomfortable around people who were noisy or coarse mannered, in or out of college. One fellow student was "a little too 'California' to be agreeable as a companion." He was surprised to encounter a very agreeable Yale man and wished all Yale men were as pleasant. He was pleased, one summer, to find one of the friends of his Maine relatives a part of "the best society of Portland."

Harry was an intelligent and thoughtful young man, and most of his close friends were at or near the top of the class. George Lyman Kittredge, one year behind him at Roxbury Latin and Harvard, was barely outside his most intimate circle, and Harry may have been one of the first to observe (from Signet papers) that Kittredge was an outstanding scholar. Yet his own diary and the college records show that Harry never rose above mediocrity in his studies.* His

---

*In his freshman year his rank was 132 out of 229. The class shrank to 197 the following year and Harry placed 107. In his junior year he went up to 95; his nearly disastrous senior year set him back to 145 out of 196.

method of study was, as he well knew, a poor one—in his words periods of "loafing" alternated with short, intense days and nights of "grinding." He never makes excuses, but is even more severe with himself than are his teachers. A typical diary entry says: "Wrote a forensic on the Ideal gentleman which is worse than any theme or forensic I have written and that is saying a good deal." He kept a few of his longer papers, including one on Disraeli that he submitted for a Bowdoin Prize (he didn't expect to win one, and was right). These papers are better constructed and written than any but a few written by undergraduates now, but they are wooden and unexciting.

Yet Harry May studied under a number of the Harvard stars of the day and enjoyed some of them. He heard Simon Newcomb lecture on political economy, Benjamin Pierce on physics. He took pride in never missing one of Charles Eliot Norton's polished lectures on art and enjoyed hearing Francis James Child, of Child's *Ballads,* read Shakespeare aloud. Young Dr. William James baffled him—he wasn't sure whether James was vague or mixed up on philosophy or whether he himself had no head for that subject (his favorite was history). Once he mentions reading his examination aloud to Dr. James: "he didn't like it nor I either." When James gave a lecture on "the hygiene of the genital organs," Harry wrote that he was glad such a lecture could be given.

If one looks for a reason for Harry's poor academic performance the immediate answers are easy: poor study habits, too much time spent playing cards. The question remains, Why should a young man with literary tastes, intellectual friends, and some ambition to succeed waste so much time, even as he fully realized the consequences? The answer surely lies somewhere in his complex inner conflicts.

Harry's real education at Harvard came from the Signet,

conversations with friends, and reading. Harvard formed his taste: most, though not quite all, of the books I remember in his library were books he first read in college. His great favorites were Thackeray and Tennyson. Somewhat more surprisingly he enjoyed Swinburne. About "Henry James, Jr.," whose stories were currently appearing in the better magazines, he had mixed feelings. "An International Episode" seemed to him too clever. He was attracted by Edwin Arnold's *The Light of Asia* and had some affection for the manly Christianity of Thomas Hughes. When he heard Hughes talk in Boston he found him just like Tom Brown at fifty. Some French literature seemed "malignant." Of the New Englanders, Francis Parkman was a great favorite, while James Russell Lowell is mentioned only occasionally. Emerson, Thoreau, and Hawthorne, none of them much in vogue at Harvard, hardly appear in his early reading.

In politics Harry May was a liberal Republican, barely beginning to look at the Democratic party as a possible alternative. He detested Ulysses S. Grant and, like many New England reforming Republicans, he strongly disapproved of dubious Republican politicians like Roscoe Conkling and James G. Blaine. It never occurred to him, in college or later, that morality could be for a moment separated from politics. A trip to New York and Washington in the spring of 1880 did a good deal to broaden his knowledge of his country, but his reactions were still those of a young New Englander. The opulence of New York impressed him but he ended in some disgust: "I don't want to live in a city where the doormats have to be fastened with padlock and chain." In Washington he was charmed with Mount Vernon, impressed by the government buildings, but severely shocked by the depravity of the Arlington Theater, a low resort on Pennsylvania Avenue. The Supreme Court awed him, but the Congress distinctly did not. The House looked like a crowd one might find at a popular lecture. Few hesitated to spit on the carpet; many smoked, walked about, or conversed until the speaker had to shout at them. The Senate was much more quiet and dignified. To Harry's surprise, the Senate Democrats did not present a worse appearance than the Republicans and the "Confederate Brigadiers" were "not at all horrible in appearance." In Norfolk, Virginia, a Negro school interested him more than anything he had seen on the trip, and left his general opinion of Negroes "decidedly better" than before his trip. Later in the year, perhaps thinking over his exposure to the South, he asked himself a question which, while it certainly shows no extraordinary enlightenment on racial matters, does demonstrate that he was trying to think about them: "It must be admitted that the Negroes are inferior morally as well as mentally but isn't this entirely the result of circumstances and won't they develop as well as we in time with the same advantages."

So far we seem to have the portrait of a fairly standard late-nineteenth-century collegian, a young man with a bookish bent, fairly standard political and literary tastes, and gregarious habits. But another current runs through the diaries—a current of rigidity, censoriousness, deep self-doubt, religious intensity, and concern about the meaning of life and death. I am tempted to call this the Attleborough effect: clearly it is partly attributable to Harry's upbringing, partly to his relation with his father and siblings, partly to a series of severe shocks starting with the death of his mother. In the young man, even more clearly than in the old man I remember, one can see gusto and warm affection fighting a hard battle, not always successful, with melancholy and tension.

The diaries are full of self-criticism. Harry wishes he were better organized and more confident, knows he is sometimes unkind or tactless to his friends, and deplores his lack of social grace. Sometimes even his successes embarrass him. In his junior year he is invited to be an usher at Class Day but reflects that "the honor is slight, may be given from a mistaken idea, and probably won't sit well on me though I think it will be a good thing to try myself in such a position and no one will be hurt if I fail." When he tries on a new spring suit, he finds it lighter in color than he had expected "and more stylish than I have a right to wear or wish to," but decides that to wear it, now that he has it, will be only a very small evil. When a close friend praises him, he is uncomfortable: "It has a bad effect on me to have people say so much good about me and to me. I need to be sat on oftener for my own good."

Not surprisingly, much of Harry's uneasiness was centered about his relations with girls, which were always a bit tentative and never entirely successful. In his junior year Harry's roommate Jack, a more cheerful and worldly lad, tried hard to persuade him that in order to meet girls he should learn to dance. Harry was invited, through Jack, to join the Phoenix, a mixed social club, and agreed to try it: "I don't expect to get great enjoyment from it but think a certain amount of the society of ladies is a thing I need." Sometimes Harry enjoyed the club and he liked a number of the young ladies, but the dancing was a painful failure. Lessons and hard work didn't help. Complaining to his diary that he would rather be whipped than go to a dancing lesson, Harry kept grimly at it:

I did miserably and not only had a wretched time myself but my partner must have suffered torments.

I can dance only one way and that not very well.

I don't know how to conduct myself on such occasions and suppose I ought to learn how but it seems pretty nearly a waste of time.

Finally he gave up, but still went to the club and still enjoyed some of the girls—those who were not either "fresh" or "silly." Though he enjoyed sleighing, he says once that it is mainly good for those "who enjoy an excuse for making the girls snug." In the next sentence he regrets that so many fellows have special girls that all the good company on such sleighing parties is taken early. Harry envied those like Jack who had easy social relations with girls: "I think it is an excellent thing for Jack and would be for me or almost anybody." As for getting engaged, that seemed to him good for some men and not for others: "However that may be I am unattached and shall be only the loser by staying so."

Harry strove hard for purity and integrity, and in doing so was often betrayed—as he well knew—into censoriousness. In his freshman year, going dutifully to college baseball games (he never liked sports), he was disturbed when he learned that Harvard had made use of a man who had entered law school "on purpose to play." Yale might do this, but he wished Harvard wouldn't. He was understandably and deeply shocked when he learned that some southern fathers gave their sons money to pay prostitutes.

His severely moral principles sometimes got in the way of his love for the theater. Unconsciously echoing the dominant Common Sense criticism of the previous generation, he found a blood-and-thunder melodrama seen in Washington even more harmful to the public mind than the "merely low, vile exhibition" he had seen at the Arlington in Washington. This sort of play taught otherwise decent people "to expect love to be carried to frenzy and grief to madness or suicide in real life." He was—and almost knew he was—a bit in love with Adelaide Neilson, an English actress praised by a contemporary critic for "her rich, dark-eyed beauty, her grace, her pensive charm, her integrity, her golden voice." Enchanted, Harry went to Miss Neilson's every performance. When he learned that she was said to have a bad character, he was disturbed. He continued to see her act, however, and when he read of her death in August 1880 he concluded that her acting had done more good than her character harm.

Sarah Bernhardt was another matter. It was good, Harry thought, to see a great actress, but Bernhardt was a woman of notoriously bad principles. He was glad to learn in the paper that the best New York society had declined to receive her. When he saw her in *Camille* he found the play "Frenchy." The acting was fine but the final impression unpleasant: "I couldn't help thinking of the likeness of the actress to the character."

Harry's most severe inner troubles centered around his Dorchester home, and especially his relation with his father. Of course he missed his mother, especially on the anniversaries of her death: "Every time I go home it seems worse to me. I couldn't enjoy it to see Nellie [a relative] there and think how different it is from what it used to be." A succession of housekeepers either proved inadequate or left too soon.

Harry and his father each made a brave effort to understand the other. Sometimes the judge, pressed for money, had to delay sending his son's allowance, but whenever possible he was generous. At his first class dinner, in February 1879, Harry was the only man with a short coat and it was his father who, when he heard this, insisted that Harry buy a swallowtail. Probably with a good deal of pride in his Harvard son, the judge congratulated Harry first on Pi Eta and then on the Signet and agreed to provide the extra money. Often Harry brought friends home for weekends and the judge tried hard to unbend. Once, to Harry's great surprise, his father joined Harry, his friend Will Lane, and his sister Hattie at whist: "The first time I ever saw father play cards, he played better than any of us."

Once the Signet met at the Dorchester house. "Father took all the pains he could to have the meeting at home a success and thought about more little things than I have known him to before for a long time." The father and son sometimes enjoyed talking politics and often agreed. Harry admired his father's reading aloud (Webster's reply to Hayne) and wished he could do as well. Once Harry, discussing family problems with his father, realized that "he has deeper reasons for some things he does than I look for."

And yet the two could not really get along. "Blue about home matters" is a constant refrain in the diary. Sometimes there were crises. In September 1881, he wrote: "Father and I had a long talk about my senior year and he expressed disappointment in me and the fear that I shall never accomplish anything. I am sorry that he feels so for I don't." In June 1881, when Harry was getting near graduation, relations hit bottom: "Got a note from father which makes me feel sorry that I didn't exercise more self-control last night when I left home. I felt grieved at what seemed to me harshness and came away without saying good-bye. I ought not to have done so."

The censorious side of Harry's character came out strongly in his relations with his siblings, whom he often calls "the children." He especially disapproved of Hattie, two years younger, whom he found obstreperous and ill-behaved. Harry thought his father far too indulgent to her and constantly urged him to crack down. Less often, he took the same position toward his brother: "Jonny needs lots of reining in and don't get it." Lily, his second sister, was sickly and Harry worried a lot about her. Quite obviously, Harry sometimes projected his own shortcomings onto his brother and sisters. He wished that they would like father more. Just after his own failure at dancing, he carried on a persistent campaign to persuade his father to keep Hattie and Johnny from going to neighborhood dances that he considered (socially?) "promiscuous."

Harry was always happy to get back to Cambridge, and still more when he could spend time in summer with his Maine relatives. In his freshman year, however, Grandfather Farnham, whom Harry had admired, died. Even before this he had learned that his favorite, his cheerful and loving Aunt

Laura, was very sick. In June his father told him that Aunt Laura, only thirty-six at the time, was likely to die any moment. A few days later, learning that the blow had indeed fallen, Harry and his father took the boat for Portland. There they learned that Laura's death had been one of "horrible suffering" (we do not know from what disease) and that she had been "wholly changed" before the end. This dreadful shock clearly helped bring into Harry's consciousness his deep and uncomfortable religious doubts:

Uncle Sidney bears it in the spirit I think a true Christian ought to be able to. He talks freely about her and I only saw him break down even slightly two or three times. Some memories of things that can never happen again were too much for him. But this is not inconsistent with the really Christian view of death: that all is for the best on the whole and that the Christian dead is better off after death than before. Grief in such a case is only for one's self and the others who are left behind. Uncle Sidney is a splendid man and is of a family of good people. I wish I could believe fully in the Christian view of death.

Harry worried a lot about what he did and didn't believe. This sort of religious intensity was hardly the rule at Harvard in his day. When his father asked him about scoffing at Harvard, the collegian answered, perhaps a bit loftily, that there was far less of this than outsiders believed. This was probably true, but indifference was not uncommon. The largest group of Harvard men was, of course, the Unitarian, the next Episcopalian, and the third Congregationalist. But in Harry's class a postgraduation survey found twenty-five undecided about religion, fifteen agnostic, and a total of twenty-three others belonging to a series of vague classifications including "nonsectarian," "rationalist," "deist," "theist," and "uncertain."

Harry struggled hard with religion, both as ultimate concern and as guide to life. In this he was out of tune with most, but not all his Harvard contemporaries. He was also unlike his father, who nominally accepted Congregational orthodoxy but turned it into a strict version of middle-class morality. Harry was far more like his Attleborough ancestors, who had longed to attain certainty and found it hard. He was also, however, a young man living in a center of religious liberalism and tossed by the breezes of Victorian doubt.

On weekends at home, Harry usually attended both church and Sunday school (meaning after-church religious study for adults) at the family Congregational church in Dorchester. He liked Mr. Packard, the minister, but shrewdly rejected his standard formulas. When Mr. Packard explained, for instance, "that we ought to have faith enough in Christ to take his word for it that what he asked was all right and give up the little scruples we had against it," Harry added, "he seemed to me to beg the question." Even from his beloved Uncle Sidney, Harry could not accept an orthodox view in the Edwardsian tradition: "Uncle Sidney believes that the only motive that can influence a man besides direct or indirect selfishness is love of God. I believe love of man is a motive that inspires the good done by some good men."

In the Sunday school, Harry sturdily resisted the spiritual assaults of Miss Carruth, one of the teachers, who wanted desperately to convert him to evangelical views and practices and was, if I read the evidence correctly, more than a bit in love with him. She constantly badgered him, with no success, about the temperance pledge: "Miss Carruth said she didn't see how any young man who had any self-respect could refuse to sign it. I refused as did some of the others." On another occasion Harry defended evolution against the Sunday school majority "though my knowledge of the subject is too slight to allow me to argue much about it." Miss Carruth continued to push him hard about his lack of clear religious commitment.

After S. S. I had a talk on religion with Miss Carruth. We spent half an hour but no impression was made.

A letter from Miss Carruth shows that she thinks I am weak and lack true manliness. Perhaps so. I have tried to defend my position, if I may call it so, by argument and have completely failed. I can't define my state of mind at all but think I am not doing wrong.

He was willing to send Miss Carruth his picture and to correspond, but showed some embarrassment and irritation when she went too far. One letter from her "was the kind of a letter that makes one feel complimented but puts one in a curious position. I know how I feel towards her and think it would be best to tell her frankly all she cares to know about my beliefs &c." Characteristically, he felt guilty after rebuffing her missionary endeavors: "She is much more liberal than I have given her credit for being and I am afraid I have done her an injustice."

Harry was far more comfortable talking about religion with his close friends, preferably late at night, in a Harvard room or at home in Dorchester on a weekend. Usually, the results for him were distressingly inconclusive:

This evening I have been having a good talk with Billy Noyes on religion, a man's duties &c. I don't know very well what I think about religious matters.

David and I have been discussing religious philosophy or rather he has been giving me his views on the matter for I have none that properly belong to me.

His roommate Jack, who tried to get him to learn to dance, also constantly urged him to become a committed Christian.

Harry, who probably envied Jack's less inward and more decisive temperament, felt that these talks did him good. Like dancing, church membership would probably be good for Jack, he thought, but he doubted that he himself would find it much help.

On a camping trip, one of Harry's companions took "a purely infidel ground" and showed "an intolerance and bad temper that surprised me." In January 1881 still another friend wrote urging him to "become a Christian." "I like the spirit of the letter but shall have to answer him in the old way." Another of his close friends told Harry that he ought to become a minister "but he doesn't understand me." (I wonder.)

All his life a religious seeker, in college Harry sampled Boston churches from Unitarian to Catholic. The college church, decorous and noncommittal, attracted him only when he admired a particular preacher. When Professor John Fiske, an ultra-liberal evolutionary optimist, preached, Harry was bored. He early stopped going to college prayers. Like many contemporary New Englanders rebelling against the harsh doctrines of their fathers, he became attracted to the uncensorious traditionalism of the Episcopal church. At first the service seemed formal and repetitive, but he grew fond of it. He developed an intense admiration for Phillips Brooks, the eloquent and charismatic rector of Trinity Church.

The sect that attracted Harry far the most, however, was Swedenborgianism. The teachings of the eighteenth-century Swedish count, scientist, and mystic had enjoyed a modest growth in New England since the beginning of the century. In Philadelphia, where the sect had its American beginnings, Swedenborg's writings had the status of revelation, but New England converts did not feel it necessary to take literally Swedenborg's accounts of direct divine commission or talks with angels. In his "Historic Notes of Life and Letters in New England," Emerson points to "the slow but extraordinary influence of Swedenborg; a man of prodigious mind, though as I think tainted with a certain suspicion of insanity, and therefore generally disowned, but exerting a singular power over an important intellectual class." This class included in Europe, Coleridge, Coventry Patmore, the Brownings, and Carlyle; in America, besides Emerson and others of his Transcendentalist persuasion, the elder Henry James, who accepted Swedenborg in his own special way and was saved by him from a severe mental crisis.

Swedenborgianism in New England was, like the more Christian type of Transcendentalism, a way to accept Christianity that avoided both dogmatic rigidity and rationalist picking and choosing. The whole Bible was true if it was understood spiritually. All nature, to Swedenborg as to Emerson, was filled with spiritual meaning. As to Edwards, to the New England followers of Swedenborg the constant exercise of God's creative spirit was necessary to maintain all existence. Essentially joyful, Swedenborgianism taught like Whitman that death itself, being part of nature and spirit, was without terror.

It is not hard to understand how this doctrine might attract a young New Englander who had experienced too many important deaths too early. Probably the most important reason for Harry's involvement, however, was the influence of the two closest friends of his last two college years. Both of these remained close throughout their lives, and their surviving letters to Harry are full of affection. One was Will Lane, second in the class, and the other, still more important, was Will Worcester.

For three generations, the Worcesters had been the leaders of Swedenborgianism in Massachusetts. John Worcester, Will's father, was minister at Newtonville and a prolific author. Will himself, apparently a particularly brilliant and charming young man, was to become a distinguished minister, writer, and theological school dean. It is clear that in and after college the whole Worcester family was for Harry a group of superior beings, to be looked up to and loved. Will and his brother Charles were his close friends, Mr. Worcester a revered elder, and Margaret Worcester, for a brief period, more important than any girl so far. Harry visited the Worcesters in Newtonville as often as he could, and many of his summer trips started from their house in Intervale, in the White Mountains. This house, still lived in by Will's daughter, is a typically New England summer place, full of ells and porches and steep stairs, with a sweeping view of the White Mountains.

Will himself seemed to Harry an ideal model, to be admired and imitated but never conceivably equaled. Will was not too straitlaced to play cards at the Signet but was already deeply committed to his beliefs. Once Harry admitted to his diary that he slightly wished Will was more one of the fellows. If he were, he immediately added, he would perhaps lack the great charm he had. Harry rejoiced, somewhat timidly, in his growing intimacy with Will in his senior year and asked for loans of Swedenborg's books. Reading these and discussing the doctrines with the two Wills and others, he hovered on the verge of commitment to the New Church.

Despite all his own efforts and Will's influence, Harry approached graduation still both uncommitted and unhappy about it. He describes his feeling with impressive self-knowledge: "I signed myself Congregationalist in the blank to be filled for the class records but I am not a Congregationalist. I wish I was something more definite than I am in my religious nature which I don't think is at all deficient in itself. That is I have the kind of a nature that is not satisfied without religious faith." Though he tried hard and sometimes thought he had found what he needed, he was never to find a faith free of doubt and tension. It is in this mixture of uncompromising honesty with religious longing only partly fulfilled that Harry May seems to me to show his Calvinist inheritance. And his religious conflicts both resulted from and influenced his mixed nature, affectionate and vigorous but also often gloomy and self-doubting.

Despite his inner troubles and his worsening academic performance, Harry enjoyed the climactic ceremonies of his senior year. Harvard Commencement had been a major New England festival for two hundred years, and Class Day, dating only from the 1820s, was by now almost as important. Seniors were requested to appear for both in "dress suits, white cravats, and silk hats" and Harry was duly measured in Boston for his first really formal costume. It was customary to invite friends and relatives for spreads in one's room, and the judge, though feeling very pinched for money at this point, told his son to do what he thought right about Class Day and "not to be mean or extravagant." Harry spent several days writing invitations.

Apparently it was worth it. Harry's account of Class Day is perhaps the most exuberant entry in the whole diary: "Class day—the most perfect one I can imagine. The weather was just right, the yard was in its best condition, the literary parts were good, the spreads were good, the people were happy." His room was full of flowers sent by relatives. His Roxbury Latin headmaster contributed "a handsome basket of flowers with 1881 in the centre," prudently saved from the school graduation the day before. According to the Boston *Advertiser* the yard was bright with the ladies' pink and blue dresses and the German band played vigorously. The class orator, one Curtis Guild, warned the audience against both greedy monopolies and "communism, the spawn of despotism." What America needed most, he said, was "men in politics who can emerge from the husk of selfish interest, who can sink the idea of political capital and devote themselves heart and soul to the good of the nation."

Commencement Day was clouded by Harry's rueful observation that 109 men graduated with honors of some kind, and only 75 with a plain degree like his. Still, the formal exercises were less uninteresting than he had expected them to be, and only a few fellows drank too much punch. Will Worcester spent the afternoon with Harry, and a number of other men came to say good-bye. The next day he packed his things to go home and wrote in his diary a conventional but deeply sincere comment on his college years: "Shall I ever have four such happy years again? I hope so but I can't complain if I do not." And Harry went home to Dorchester and his father.

#

The next year and a half were among the unhappiest of his life, and at times the diary gives an impression of something like a breakdown. As always, external events were only a part of the story, but there was little really cheerful about Harry's outward circumstances in this period. He did not make a postgraduation trip to Europe, as he had expected to do and as many of his friends did, including the admired Will Worcester. He had chosen law for a profession but did not start Harvard Law School with his college classmates. Instead, his father got him a job in the law office of Frederick O. Prince, the mayor of Boston. This amounted at first to doing errands for Prince and his sons, none of whom Harry much respected. Part of his work was collecting rents in poor districts. For the first time Harry became acquainted with the tenements and even the jail, and gained a new sympathy for the poor. Meantime, he ground through Kent's *Commentaries,* Blackstone, and other standard legal texts, preparing to take the bar examination. Money was very short; in October 1881 he was forced to ask a friend for a loan; that January he could not afford to replace a lost overcoat.

Unhappy and discontented, Harry did some growing up. His reading tastes widened and deepened. In addition to old favorites like Thackeray and Tennyson, he read Milton, the *Rubaiyat,* De Quincey, Macaulay, a little Chaucer, and a lot of Shakespeare. Always somewhat compulsive, he included Latin authors in his reading program and took notes, for "discipline" on his history reading. His theatergoing was mostly Shakespeare, and he learned to enjoy the Boston Symphony as well as the opera.

In his unhappiness, Harry's Harvard friends were more important than ever and sometimes, especially at Signet dinners in Boston restaurants, things seemed almost like "the old days." His small club that included young women usually failed to please him now, and he regretted keeping on with it. It seemed strange when Harvard opened in September and he was no longer a part of it. In June he attended Class Day and was delighted with George Kittredge's triumph as orator, but thought the class of '82 in general very inferior. He was bored once more at commencement. Reading over his journal for the same time the year before, he decided that he certainly had *not* had as happy a year as any of the four in college, but that this was entirely his own fault.

His religious views, activities, and language became, for a brief period, much more conventional. He struggled hard to feel a personal relation to God and to be able, sincerely and unselfconsciously, to pray. He continued to read Swedenborg a lot and was almost, but not quite, able to accept the whole teaching of the New Church. He hoped that Will, whom he sorely missed, would straighten him out when he got back from Europe. He did not like now to go to the Worcesters' church in Newtonville because it seemed, with Will away, too much like an intrusion on a family circle. He became zealous in the Congregational church in Dorchester, attending regularly and even talking willingly with Miss Carruth. He became deeply involved in church committees, organizing concerts and entertainments and joining a discussion group called "the mission circle." None of this strenuous effort seems to have helped.

Much of the time, and eventually to a dangerous degree, Harry disapproved of himself. When his full college report arrived in August 1881, he was dismayed to find it even worse than he had thought. This gave rise to a long confession in his diary. He had done what he wanted and then found reasons. He had acquired a reputation for laziness and deserved it. It was necessary, he decided, that he learn to plod away at unpleasant tasks—right now, at his legal studies. At other times he condemned himself for conceit. Sometimes he thought he was making progress in correcting these faults, but at times his depression was paralyzing. On January 23, 1882, he was unable to write to Will. On the twenty-eighth, "I shut myself up foolishly in my room this evening—there isn't any [reason?] but—I ought not to have done it." On March 31 he started to a Signet dinner but felt too blue and turned back.

Several deaths again played some part in Harry's depression. The assassination and lingering death of President Garfield moved him deeply. The sudden death of one of his most promising classmates stirred feelings of unfairness that he knew were un-Christian. When his Uncle Horace died in February 1882 he had to try to sustain his aunt and cousin, both near collapse.

The center of Harry's depression lay as usual in the Dorchester house, where he now lived all the time. He continually badgered Hattie, urging her to read seriously, study

French, and in general improve herself. Then he decided that he had wronged her and made her pray with him that they become a better brother and sister. (This clearly didn't work; the two were to quarrel intermittently all their lives.) Once he even scolded poor sick Lily until she got into "a terrible state." He worried about John's performance in Dorchester High School and thought his brother ought to get into a business. (Whether for lack of money or lack of ability on John's part, Harvard was never considered for him.)

Worst of all, he failed most of the time, despite the most strenuous efforts, to get along with his father. Once he blamed his father's sharpness with him on failing health, but most of the time thought all the trouble arose from his own gloomy and hostile behavior: "I am ashamed of myself. I have been thinking that I was a Christian and then all the time allowing myself to be knowingly responsible in part for the fact that this home is not a happy one. The way I have acted is indefensible and contemptible." Once he forced himself to beg his father's pardon for his behavior of several months. His father answered that he saw no reason for Harry to be unhappy, that if a few little things had gone badly it was a father's duty to forgive, and that he felt abundantly satisfied with his son. For the moment this made Harry feel much better, but in the long run his father's generosity probably only increased his own self-condemnation. Indulging in his most conventionally Christian language, Harry decided he was an "ungrateful wretch" to be "so unchristian here at home when God is so kind and forgiving in his treatment of me; and continually, so to speak, making advances to me which I reject." At this point, more than any in his diary, he seems to me to be trying to force himself into the beliefs and even the language of his Calvinist ancestors.

Throughout 1881 Harry complained that his father was working too hard and refused to take care of himself. The next year things got rapidly worse, and by September 1882 it became necessary for Harry to take over management of the money and the house. On December 27 the doctor told him his father's condition was hopeless. With this entry the diary was abandoned for a month. John Wilder May died on January 11, 1883. Of course Harry was in charge of the funeral, which was conducted in the Dorchester house by Mr. Packard and a colleague. Some of the letters of condolence that Harry received, including those from the Storeys and that from Senator Edmund Hoar, former attorney general of the United States, were full of admiration and also affection for Judge May. These, and the newspaper praise, must have made the young man blame himself even more for his lack of filial devotion.

One sign of the importance of this crisis in Harry's life is a complete change in the nature of his diary. When he takes it up again, after his father's death, it becomes a dry record of events, sometimes informative but almost never expressing any feelings. It continues like this through the years. Thus most of what I have learned of my father's inner character comes from his own record of 1879 to 1882. Many of the traits of the aging man I remember a half-century later are sharper and clearer in the young man, but there are few basic changes. Both the gregariousness and gusto and the inner doubts and depressions were evident in youth and age. Never quite vanquished, the gloomy tendency was far less prominent in my father's middle years of professional success and growing personal happiness, the years between 1890 and my own earliest memories of him in the 1920s. The diary shows the young man's faults even more clearly than his virtues. Its frankness and honesty make it, to me, an admirable and fascinating document. And young Harry's brave struggles with himself fill me with sympathy. It could hardly be otherwise, since I recognize in my father's self-portrait much of myself.

Harry May's last Boston years can be treated very briefly. After his father's death his diary expresses no emotion whatever except an occasional irritation or, more rarely, an attack of the "blues," briefly mentioned like one of his colds or stomach upsets. The Dorchester house was sold. Harry and his sisters moved into rooms in Boston, and Hattie, always practical and resourceful, learned shorthand and got a job. Conscious of his position as the new head of the family, Harry stopped criticizing Hattie (at least in his diary), worried constantly about Lily's health, and concerned himself with John's rather unsuccessful efforts to support himself as a mill superintendent.

In 1884 Harry passed the bar examination and immediately began to try a few cases. In 1887 he formed a partnership with William Choate, a Harvard classmate and friend who, according to Harry's diary, had been so lazy in college that he had almost failed to graduate. The prospects of the partnership are described in a poem preserved in his papers, possibly written by his new partner:

MAY & CHOATE
Three Pictures

I. April, 1887
The smell of varnish fills the air,
And brightly shines the slippery floor,
And polished is each ugly chair,
And fresh the paint upon the door.
With trust that mocks at Time and Fate,
With faith that holds all fear remote,
With spirit high, and hope elate,
Begins the firm of May & Choate.

II. July, 1887
The senior partner grimly looks
About the dull and cheerless scene;

106

His eye surveys the dusty books,
The pens unused, the dockets clean.
The junior slakes a ceaseless thirst,
He little recks the warning note
That tells the tempest soon to burst
Upon the firm of May & Choate.

> *III. October, 1887*
> At last arrives the hour of dread,
> A raving throng the entry fills,
> They wildly curse the wretches fled,
> And madly wave their unpaid bills.
> Within, the Sheriff's keeper sits,
> Black is his eye and torn his coat;
> So ends with constables and writs
> The short-lived firm of May & Choate.

The firm's actual history was not quite this dismal, but it is clear that business was slow. Harry had plenty of time for Harvard reunions and Signet dinners, which became fewer, for his reading program and mountain trips, and above all for a very busy social life, much of it shared with Hattie. There is no indication that Harry much enjoyed the round of church sociables, lantern slides of travel, bowling parties, ice-cream freezings, berry pickings, and progressive euchres. Once or twice, revealingly I think, he notes in his diary, as something extraordinary, an evening spent alone.

The real center of his life in this period was once more the Worcester family. More and more of his time was spent in their house, walking with Will and his brother and sometimes his sister, and talking religion with "Mr. Worcester." Finally Harry was able, however temporarily, to overcome his doubts and join the Worcesters' church as a Swedenborgian communicant. He quickly became a very active one, teaching in the local Sunday school, trying to read Lamb's tales and English ballads with a boys' club in the North End, going to local and state church conventions, and helping to found a new Sweden-borgian church in Dorchester. Yet there are still signs that Harry had difficulty in accepting the mystical part of Sweden-borg's teaching: "*Friday, November 9th, 1888:* I went to S. S. teacher's meeting at Mrs. Montgomery's. Mr. Rich led us and talked entirely about the Spiritual sense of the lesson in a way unintelligible to me."

Forty years later, when my mother wanted to tease my father a little, she would utter the word "Margaret," and he would look at once a little guilty and a little pleased with himself. Margaret Worcester, Will's sister, was a high-spirited, intelligent, and striking-looking young woman. Her favorite niece, Mrs. Margaret Worcester Briggs, who still lives in the New Hampshire summer place where Harry and Will started many of their mountain trips and is still an active Sweden-borgian, has told me a story current in her family. According to this tradition Harry proposed marriage to Margaret at some time in these years. She refused, then changed her mind, and asked her father if he thought she might reopen the matter. Mr. Worcester answered that a lady could not do such a thing. Whether this family story is true or not, Margaret never mar-ried. Will did, and when his wife died young, Margaret de-voted her life to bringing up her nieces and nephews. One cannot tell much about this delicate matter from Harry's diary. From 1886 to 1888 there are several mentions of walks and rides with Margaret. On November 11, 1888, Harry "walked to Newtonville to call on Miss Worcester"—not on her broth-ers or father. From then until he left Boston Harry saw much less of the Worcesters. In December 1889 he mentions burning some letters.

Suddenly an opportunity opened for Harry to get away from May & Choate, local church affairs, his dull amuse-ments, his siblings—and perhaps Margaret. At the end of

1889 Harry learned that Senator Edward Oliver Wolcott of Colorado was in town, looking for a young lawyer to join his Denver office. Wolcott was the son of a Massachusetts Congregational minister and a graduate of Yale and Harvard Law School. He had made himself a career in Colorado politics as a straight conservative Republican with the necessary regional aberration of supporting free silver. He was a devoted counsel and later director of the fast-expanding and venturesome Denver, Rio Grande and Western Railroad. The account in the *Dictionary of American Biography* hardly makes him sound like Harry May's favorite type of man:

Wolcott was a large man, always very carefully dressed. His manner towards strangers and enemies was often arrogant, towards friends often free. He was a "high liver," lavish in the expenditure of money, thoughtless in giving. His marriage . . . ended in divorce in 1900. He died [in 1905] in Monte Carlo while in search of health and diversion.

Nevertheless, the young Bostonian was to learn to like and respect the Colorado senator.

They seem to have hit it off well from the start. The day after their first interview Wolcott offered young Mr. May the job, and the next day Harry accepted. He was to leave for Denver February 1 at a good starting salary of $2,400 with increases in the second and third years and after that a free choice to leave the firm or stay. With a few pangs, Harry set about saying his good-byes and winding up his business affairs. A group of his more convivial Harvard friends—not including his closest friends who were serious Swedenborgians—gave him a farewell dinner at the Union Club. The poems written for this occasion once more demonstrate both the wit of his friends and their affection for him. The best of these—again conceivably written by William Choate—also shows how *very* far Denver, Colorado, was

from Boston, Massachusetts, in 1890. The poet rejects lying
reports about churches and schools in the wilderness; he has
read "Bret Harte & Co."

I see the crooked straggling streets
   The shanty-like saloon
Where dwell the bummer and the beat
   At midnight as at noon
The gambler gains his sinful bread
   The drunken cowboy sings
While dangling limply overhead
   The captured horsethief swings.

The court-room echoes sounds of strife
   With oaths the air is blue
The red-nosed judge pulls out a knife
   The red-nosed clerk has two.
Who strives to seize each others' throats
   Each others' features mar?
Who but the Websters and the Choates
   That lead the Denver bar.

To his revolver each resorts
   The shots ring loud and clear
That is the kind of court reports
   That make impression here.
What blood-stained ruffian leaps with glee
   Amidst the hottest fray?
I seem to know him—can it be?
   Yes—it is Harry May.

Enough—it is a sorry part
   To end all with a jest—
The honest loyal manly heart
   We give it to the West.
We've known its worth—its purpose true
   Its trust to Heaven's decrees

Since those old days when life was new
    Beneath the Cambridge trees.

The College cares, the College joys
    Come back to us again
The ties that held us close as boys
    They hold us close as men.
We need no words our thought to tell
    Our hearts speak out and say
"The love of those that love you well
Goes with you Harry May."

The dinner broke up at eleven o'clock, and Harry reports that "I probably indulged myself more than I ought to have." On Saturday, January 25, Harry left home at the usual time, finished drafting a brief, went to another dinner given by his friends at the Tavern Club at one o'clock, caught the train at the Columbus Avenue Station, had an oyster stew at Springfield and went to bed on the rattling Pullman headed West. After stopping at Buffalo and Chicago for visiting and sightseeing, he reached Denver on the thirtieth, just as the rising sun hit the snowy mountains. There he was to spend the best and longest period of his life, twenty-seven years.

7

High Days
in the Rockies

In Denver things went well from the beginning. May got off the train, went to the Windsor Hotel, changed his clothes, and immediately reported at the office of Wolcott and Vaile, his new employers, where he was cordially welcomed. After some searching, and some exhaustion from the thin air, he found a boarding house. By February 1 he was at work, studying a matter of railroad law, and that evening he played whist at the Lotos Club. The next day, Sunday, he went to a service at the cathedral and took a tram ride to nearby Berkeley Lake for a view of the mountains. Despite the fact that the altitude made him gasp for breath, despite the strangeness and some pangs of homesickness, the main elements of young May's Denver life were already in place.

He was just the type of young man Denver needed. The Queen City of the Plains in 1890 was trying hard to get over all vestiges of its recent rough past. It had grown twentyfold since the railroad reached it in 1870 and was now a city of nearly 107,000, the biggest between St. Louis and San Francisco. It was the mining capital of the nation, the railroad center of the West, a brand-new metropolis of the mountains with smelters, refineries, banks, a mint, a mining exchange, and—until the disastrous panic of 1893—a boom psychology.

On Capitol Hill the mining and cattle barons lived in elaborate new mansions—Romanesque, classical, colonial, or plain eclectic—set in wide green lawns. From these they could drive in the handsomest of carriages to the massive stone Denver Club, the center of the city's power. Visitors were housed in the elegant Windsor Hotel, about to be eclipsed by the Brown Palace, which promised to be the most lavish establishment west of Chicago. For pleasure one could dine at Tortoni's, take a streetcar to the brand-new Elitch's Gardens (complete with summer theater and zoo) or see top East Coast stars at the Tabor Grand Opera House or the newer Broadway Theater.

In the exclusive parts of the city, a carefully conventional social life was carried on. Eastern and European visitors were many, some of them on the way to San Francisco, the Yosemite, and Santa Barbara as a sort of American Grand Tour, others fighting tubercular tendencies and planning long visits to Colorado Springs or other luxurious resorts, some hoping for a glimpse of the Wild West and finding themselves at once impressed and disappointed at Denver's civility. Some reported with astonishment, in the best part of town, one could think oneself in Boston or Philadelphia if one had the right introductions, except that the welcome was warmer and the climate much better. For the thrilling fact was that all these amenities existed in the midst of rugged wilderness. Just west of the city were magnificent Alpine peaks—one could see them from the Capitol. Eastward from the city's edge, the empty plains stretched for hundreds of miles. The climate was stimulating—sunny, crisp, and cold in winter; hot but not humid in summer. Some boosters were suggesting that Denver should become the summer capital of the United States.

And yet Harry May's Boston friend, exaggerating in his farewell poem all the clichés of Western roughness and vio-

113

lence, was not all wrong about Denver—at most he was a couple of decades late. Denver old-timers remembered nearby Indian raids and retaliatory massacres. Vigilantism and lynch law lasted in Denver into the 1870s, and there had been an anti-Chinese riot as recently as 1880. Labor relations in the mines were characterized by violence on both sides. The panic of '93 was to bring a Populist governor, Morrison R. ("Bloody Bridles") Waite, whose mildly pro-labor program of reforms caused talk of anarchy and communism in the Denver clubs.

Downtown, the city had just started paving its streets and in summer dust storms from the plains swept between the new big buildings. Railroad bums lived in shanties by the river, fights were common in the city's hundreds of saloons, murders not infrequent. In parts of the city gambling was wide open, and a freely available directory listed the many whorehouses, some of them elaborate. A *Harper's* article of 1893 briefly mentioned the abundant prostitutes but was confident that "the ladies and children never see them, so well separated are the decent and vicious quarters," and at least prostitution and gambling closed down Sundays.

Even more than most American states and cities, Colorado and Denver were owned and run in these boom years by a vigorous, self-confident, and greedy oligarchy. The mines, railroads, and smelters were often owned in the East and even in Europe. Absentee and local magnates normally controlled, through the dominant Republican party, the governor, legislature, courts, and city government. In good times the ruling circles answered all criticisms by pointing to the city's growth and prosperity. Brief setbacks could be blamed at once on eastern interests and local agitators.

Harry May, always a bit marginal at Harvard and Boston, in Denver soon found himself a part of the best society—accepted by the real ruling circle, though he never became rich enough to claim a share of its power. His rigorous personal integrity, good manners, and literary polish were admired—Denver needed these qualities. Yet he was not a prig or a snob. Fastidious about his own conduct and that of his intimates, he was never unable to get along in the often rough and coarse world—of course an exclusively masculine world—of business and power. Purity and refinement, qualities respected by May wherever he found them, were especially the characteristics of women.

I shall treat my father's long Denver period briefly. For one thing, times of busy activity and rising prosperity have a certain sameness about them in all biographies. For another, the evidence is full in some ways and very meager in others. As had been the case since his severe crisis of 1882, his diaries reveal little of his feelings. They discuss his work only briefly. For the most part they are a detailed chronicle of his social life. They give a full picture of one way of life of well-to-do Denver, and between the lines some suggestions of the man's maturing character and personality.

Through the nineties, May was a rising railroad lawyer. His employers, Senator Wolcott and Joel F. Vaile, were close to the centers of Denver power. Wolcott and Vaile represented the Denver & Rio Grande railroad and also the Chicago, Burlington & Quincy. Senator Wolcott's brother Henry was the president of the telephone company and also of the first board of directors of the Denver Club. There are one or two indications in the diaries that May sometimes felt a bit uncomfortable socially in the Wolcott circle—he never was at ease with "politicians"—but on the whole he got along very well indeed with his employers. Occasionally he went to dinner at the Wolcotts' or to parties at their country place. Once in a while he invited Miss Wolcott to the opera. Apparently he particularly liked Mrs. Vaile, taking her wildflowers he picked and once in a while doing an errand for her downtown. Knowing the man, we can assume that all this was for him a part of correct and friendly behavior, and not a conscious effort to curry favor. I must admit that I am a little surprised to find him, in March 1892, writing to thank Mr. Wolcott for some gas company stock he had given him—a fact he records with no apparent qualms. Of course he took for granted travel on railroad passes—the bête noire of later Progressive reformers—and he sent his sister a pass when she was coming West for a visit.

May was always grateful to Senator Wolcott for his help at the beginning of his career. Yet there is evidence in the diary that he was not altogether happy with his work for the railroad. This is hardly surprising. Most of the first cases he tried before the Colorado Supreme Court dealt with accident claims. An injured employee, passenger, or neighbor of the railroad—or sometimes, poignantly, his widow—would get five thousand dollars' compensation in the lower courts. Nearly always the Supreme Court would reverse the judgment and find for the railroad. Even if this sort of employment did not trouble May's humane conscience—and one must remember the power of nineteenth-century laissez-faire doctrine among lawyers—it cannot have been stimulating. On May 8, 1899, he records with obvious satisfaction that it was "finally decided that I leave Wolcott and Vaile and the RR Co." By this time he had enough local reputation to set up an independent legal office, and a different stage of his Denver life was beginning.

During the early part of the young New Englander's life in Denver, there is much evidence of homesickness. He read the Boston newspapers, and when he was in need of inspiration the sermons of the two Worcesters. He wrote very frequently to his sisters, Harvard friends, and eastern relatives, occasionally to Margaret Worcester and even Miss Carruth. In 1891 he made his first visit home, seeing his college friends, his Maine relatives, and the Worcesters. In February 1893 he unemotionally records getting news of the death of his brother John, to whom he had never been close. Of course he went East and took charge of the funeral, stopping to visit Lily in her New York state sanatorium. An eastern visit, mostly for pleasure and friendship, became almost a yearly routine, but more and more clearly the center of his life and friendships was Denver.

In his Denver social life, as in college, May combined a capacity for serious friendship—perhaps his most attractive quality—with a clearly compulsive gregariousness. Within months of his arrival he had habitual associates, some of whom gradually became intimate friends. In his early years in Denver, as at Harvard, he occasionally spent a long evening talking poetry or religion with an intimate. Occasionally he read Thackeray aloud to a really congenial male friend or friend's wife. But more and more of his energy was consumed by an incessant round of calls, dinners, and cards. Bridge and whist, night after night, sometimes until very late, seem to have been almost an addiction. By the mid-nineties, May sometimes had engagements for breakfast, lunch, and dinner the same day. In addition there were cable-car rides, sometimes by moonlight. In 1897 the bicycle craze reached Denver and May took "wheel" lessons, bought a wheel, and started going for long rides in the country, often with large groups of men and women. As in Boston, he went frequently to the theater or opera. Sometimes he was able to see or hear great Shakespearean or operatic stars—Julia Marlow, Modjeska, Emma Juch, Melba—but more often Denver offered lighter fare: *Said Pasha, Castles in the Air, A White Lie, The Heir at Law, Hoyt's Trip to Chinatown.* After the theater it was possible to go to Tortoni's for an oyster supper and some California wine.

As a bachelor, May was attentive to the wives of his friends, taking them flowers or inviting them to the theater. Sometimes he escorted unattached young women and for a while saw a lot of Miss Kountze, the daughter of a rich businessman. Whenever there was a party with dancing, however, he withdrew as fast as possible.

As in Cambridge and Boston, May noted in his diaries the rare evenings he stayed home, and not with pleasure. There is clear evidence that his incessant socializing was partly a defense against the "blues" that still welled up out of somewhere deep in his inner world.

February 26, 1891: I have felt very blue and mean all day—or rather sullen.

December 12, 1893: Bliss went with me to the Orpheum to break up the blues and later we played cards at the club.

Fairly frequent in the first half of the decade, these moods seem to have disappeared by the late nineties—or perhaps there was just no time to record them.

In addition to his professional work and the social round, May put a great deal of time and effort into clubs. In November 1890, when he had just arrived, he joined some other eastern college graduates to form a University Club, which took rank just below the Denver Club. He was also a member of the Denver Athletic Club, where he occasionally went for exercise. In 1891 he helped organize the Colorado Bar Association, in which he was later to play a major role. In the mid-nineties he became part of the Discussion Club, a small group of young men and women who presented papers on conventional subjects very much in the Boston pattern. In April 1894 May presented a paper on "Poetry," always a favorite subject, after an elegant dinner at the Brown Palace. In March 1895 he discussed, disapprovingly of course, "Old Fogeyism." In the same series his roommate, and later brother-in-law, T. A. Rickard discussed "The Duty Educated People owe the State," and one of the young women spoke to the topic "In Doing Good we are Allies of the Divine." He of course joined the Harvard Club, of which he found himself president in 1896. In 1898, however, he found the annual Harvard dinner "stupid and exasperating" and in 1899 did not attend. What sort of thing put him off can be guessed at. Rickard, in his memoirs, discusses with distaste the invariable custom of telling smutty stories in speeches at the dinners of Denver clubs. Thoroughly a club man, despite his straitlaced side, May was by this time in demand for toasts and responses at formal dinners: "To the New Englander in the West," "To Yale," even "To the United States."

In 1893, after living in a series of rooms and "chambers," May took a house and imported the inherited family furniture from the East (a photograph shows most of the pieces I remember in California). He invited his sisters to visit him, and they came for a year, Hattie taking a full part in his social life and Lily coming along when health permitted. Apparently this experiment was less than a success and after a year the sisters went back to the East. Harry continued housekeeping with three other young men, one of them T. A. Rickard. Of course, the young men employed a housekeeper, and sometimes invited guests to breakfast, cards and Welsh rarebit, or even dinner.

All this sounds as entirely innocent and as conventional as it was busy. But young May, an active participant in Colorado life, knew about Denver's wide-open downtown and about the raucous goings-on in the mining camps. He was clearly not without curiosity about such matters. In Leadville on business in February 1891 he records that "in the evening the brakeman of our train showed us a little of the night side of Leadville." And on one June evening in Denver in 1892, according to the diary: "three of us went down to Market St. intending to go through some of the dives with a detective but as we didn't succeed in meeting him we gave up the scheme." One wonders how the young Puritan handled the bawdy drunken conversation that pervaded the Denver clubs late at night. Probably his only sins were inner ones, but once in a while they bothered him. In June 1890 he records that he has lost his feeling of self-respect "and I deserve to." Feeling "mean and blue" about this, he read a sermon of Will Worcester's before going to bed.

Railroad business took May all over the state, to Colorado Springs with its splendid Antlers Hotel, to Pueblo, Leadville, Georgetown, Salida, Trinidad, and Gunnison. Sometimes he went farther, to Chicago, St. Louis, Cheyenne, Yuma, or Sante Fe. Occasionally he went for mountain trips deep into the magnificent wilderness. In the fall of 1892, for instance, he went on a two-week hunting trip with one friend and a guide. They crossed the Continental Divide, often going cross-country over terrain so steep that May thought the horses couldn't make it. They lived mainly on grouse and fish, sighted elk, and at least once the guide killed and cooked a deer. May wrote in his diary that the thick venison steak with onions was "as good as anything I ever ate." Yet I remember he once told me that feelings of remorse made it almost impossible to shoot a deer himself. The style of this sort of expedition is conveyed by photographs of May and others like him. In the midst of granite and junipers, the young men from the city pose in a careful group, dressed in tweed caps, white shirts with neckties, and excellent boots.

He continued to read a good deal, sometimes in current authors like Stevenson or Kipling, but mostly sticking to his old favorites—Thackeray, Tennyson, Parkman. Needless to say, the successive intellectual and literary revolutions of the early twentieth century passed him by, as they did most busy American men and most of their sheltered and conventional wives.

It is hard to tell whether or not the intense religious doubts and needs of May's youth survived into his middle years—if not, they returned later. Religious activity, however, played an important part in his busy life. Most Sundays he went to the cathedral, often sharply criticizing the sermon, but never when it was given by his close friend Dean Hart.* Sometimes he went to other churches—the Baptist, the Methodist, more often the Unitarian. Only in his first years in Denver does he mention attending Swedenborgian services.

In his few references to politics, it is clear that in these years May remained a cautious, moralistic moderate, stoutly resisting the right-wing hysteria that ran through the Denver clubs in the stormy nineties. Most of the time, apparently, the young attorney simply listened and withheld comments.

July 21, 1893: Silver argument at the club all evening.

August 20, 1894: I went to the business men's political but didn't stay long.

In the campaign of 1896, most of Colorado supported the cause of free silver, though some conservatives were frightened by William Jennings Bryan's fiery rhetoric and radical allies. May found himself unable to be either a silverite or a reactionary. A club man in private life, in both politics and religion he was usually unable to find a group he could join and wholeheartedly support. A letter to an eastern friend explains his divided feelings in 1896:

Oct. 24/96

My dear Mr. Parker

I wish I could be as cheerful as you seem to be about the prospect of McKinley's election. I think you have reason to feel pretty confident of it and I can't vote for Bryan to help prevent it. McKinley seems to me to stand for the classes that for the last 25 years have "stood in with" the Government for the favors it could and

---

*H. Mervyn Hart was an Englishman who, after visiting Denver for his health in 1878, returned as dean of the cathedral, and became a much-loved Denver figure.

did give them in the way of special privileges in return for their support. Those classes are I think mainly responsible for the corruption and misgovernment that we have suffered under and for the widespread feeling of discontent that prevails justly. McKinley's election will mean a further development of these abuses and further discontent which must sometime break out into very serious trouble if not allayed. On the other hand the time has not yet come for revolution—or nearly come—and I fear the supporters of Bryan. I am not yet convinced either that free coinage of silver by this country alone at any ratio would be wise or safe. So I can't vote for Bryan. If there were any Palmer and Buckner electors* here I should vote for them merely to help hold together the real Democratic party in spite of their single gold standard plank. The election of McKinley seems to me likely to bring about an immediate revival of business which will be felt here as well as with you and will of course be a relief to us all. Let us hope that the discontent may not grow and that four years hence something will be offered that will be a real relief.

Yours sincerely

H. F. May

One can learn something about May's brand of moralistic and moderate conservatism from his activities in the state bar association. This was a period in which many American judges and lawyers were moving sharply to the right. Reacting to strikes, populist gains, and innovations like the income tax, they saw the legal profession as the chief defense of the nation against anarchy and communism. Nowhere was this ultra-conservative tendency more vigorous than in the Colorado Bar Association. May, however, stuck to his old-fashioned moderation.

*John M. Palmer and Simon Bolivar Buckner were the candidates of the National or Gold Democrats, the group that broke away from the Democratic party in protest against the nomination of Bryan and in defense of the gold standard.

The bar association met in a rich and clubby atmosphere, often in the spacious magnificence of the Antlers Hotel in Colorado Springs. After debating legal reform and similar topics, they were likely to have an elaborate dinner (in 1900 it ran to clams, soup, crabs, beef, kirsch pudding, plover and bacon, ice cream, and assorted desserts). With this sort of meal under their belts, the lawyers listened to patriotic orations and reminders of the importance of law and property, duly leavened by jokes about Irishmen, Negroes, and rough western characters. In 1900 Henry F. May addressed the group on "the Office of the Attorney at Law." It was not enough, he said, that a lawyer be "an honest gentleman of fair learning and ability. Beyond that he is a holder of most honorable public office." The same year May was given the responsibility of bringing in a report deploring recent attacks by labor unions on the Colorado Supreme Court, which had, for the second time, invalidated an eight-hour law for mine workers. The report emphasized the danger of undermining judicial independence. This was not enough in Colorado in 1900, and critics moved to amend the resolution, substituting "denounce" and "outrage" for words like "regret" and "mistake." May answered, insisting that "labor organizations have been misguided rather than deliberately wrong" and that it was unwise to "shake a red rag at them." Unrighteous words and actions should be blamed on "agitators and professional politicians using the labor organizations" rather than on the organizations themselves.

May's moralistic and somewhat severe side is shown by his work on the bar association's grievance committee, of which he became a member in 1899 and chairman in 1901. The committee's main task was to publicize by name, and when necessary to prosecute, lawyers who violated the association's code of legal ethics. May sometimes prosecuted on behalf of the association, securing the disbarment of malefactors.

At one point this kind of activity involved him in one of the state's wildest and most spectacular incidents. The *Denver Post,* run by F. G. Bonfils and Harry T. Tammen, was anathema to respectable and conservative Denver. From the partners' red-walled office, known as the "Bucket of Blood," the paper supported populistic causes, published sensational stories, and occasionally at least skirted the edge of blackmail. A man named William W. Anderson, violently denounced by Tammen and perhaps threatened by Bonfils, shot and wounded both partners in their office. In the series of trials that ensued, evidence appeared that Tammen had attempted to bribe the jury to assure a conviction. Eventually, in 1903, Tammen and several others were forced to plead guilty to this offense, fined a hundred dollars and jailed overnight. At one stage of the trials, May was selected along with Platt Rogers, a former reform mayor, to act for the bar association in opposing an appeal by Bonfils et al. to the Colorado Supreme Court against a lower court's decision in the case. The appeal lost. I remember my father telling me, chuckling, that because of some episode (probably this one) the *Denver Post* had a rule that his name must never be mentioned, even in its social columns.

In the early twentieth century prosperity returned to Colorado's railroads, mines, industries, and farms. Denver itself grew fast in population, wealth, and civic amenities. The rising tide brought new demands for Harry May's legal services. Between 1900 and 1917, when he left Denver, he argued eleven cases before the Supreme Court of Colorado (obviously a tiny part of a very busy practice). Of these, all involved property, and in all but three his client was a corporation. Four were concerned with mining, and sometimes with extremely technical and complex matters such as underground trespass. It is not surprising that we find May occasionally reading hard in geology.

Dealing with mining and other corporations brought May increasingly into contact with Denver's top elite. In 1901 he began going to parties or playing bridge with the Crawford Hills. Mrs. Crawford Hill was regarded by the society editors as the queen of Denver society. In 1900 he was finally invited to join the Denver Club, the citadel of Denver power and wealth. He accepted, but his loyalty lay with the University Club, of which he became president in 1902 and 1903. Presiding at the club's many convivial functions, he occasionally drank a good deal, sometimes regretting it the next morning.

In 1906 he was invited to give the commencement address at Colorado College. He accepted, characteristically objecting to an announcement that the address would be given by "The Honorable" Henry F. May. In a letter to the college president, he says: "If you feel that there should be something more than the mere name, I suppose I may be entitled to have the word 'Esquire' printed after it, but I certainly have no right to the title that appears in this morning's paper."

He had always loved poetry, and in the speech the quotations are well-chosen, the language polished, and the occasional humor apposite. The attitude toward poetry is that of the Genteel Tradition. Poetry's sphere is that of the ideal. Especially in a new country, it is likely to take a second place to the practical business of life. Yet even here, it is of some practical use, maintaining one's ideals and stimulating one's best feelings. Besides, it is extremely enjoyable.

In these flush years May traveled ever more widely, often mixing business and pleasure. On his trips to the East he spent almost as much time in New York as in Boston, dining in good restaurants and going to the opera. In 1901, 1903, and 1904 he went to Mexico. In the Mexico of President Porfirio Díaz, well-to-do American travelers had it both ways. On the one hand, the railroads were manned and run by Americans, and American and British corporations owned immense mining resources. The government's strong hand protected foreigners, and American and British colonies in the major cities enjoyed the good life. On the other hand, the country, with its leisurely ranches and handsome ancient cities, was everything that could be wanted by the tourist in search of the picturesque. It is clear that May enjoyed his Mexican trips, despite the inescapable intestinal troubles and the occasional hot dusty journeys. He usually stayed with American acquaintances, conducted his business with American and Mexican lawyers, and spent a good deal of time listening to excellent bands in arcaded plazas.

In 1906, a period for which his diaries are missing, May finally went to Europe, traveling at least to England, Belgium, and Paris. In England he stayed with Henry Wagner, a close Denver friend who was a mining promoter and worked for the Guggenheims. Wagner had settled comfortably into London and employed a cook and a "man." I remember my father telling me how hard it was to get used to having his bath drawn and his clothes laid out.

In the early twentieth century Colorado, like the rest of the country, underwent a wave of progressive reforms. Some regulatory legislation passed the legislature, and the state adopted the new panaceas of initiative and referendum. Colorado had already become a pioneer in woman suffrage. In 1916, after a long struggle, alcoholic beverages were prohibited. Like others of his class—probably a bit more swiftly than most—May moved from moderate conservatism to moderate progressivism. Unlike many of his friends, he was not opposed to the organization of labor. As a matter of course he deplored the violence of both sides in the mining regions. He could not approve such Denver radicals as Ben Lindsey, the famous "children's judge" who created the juvenile court system. Lindsey's environmentalist attitude toward crime conflicted sharply with the belief May had inherited through Judge John Wilder May, that in law as elsewhere moral righteousness is the supreme concern. Like other moderate progressives, May believed that the time had come not to change the existing value system, but to realize it: to call the nation to its promised moral greatness, delivering it from crooks and swindlers, including the predatory rich. By this time he believed the Democrats more likely to accomplish this than the Republicans.

As May became better known there was some talk from time to time of his getting into politics himself. His sense of public duty and probably his ambition beckoned, but moral fastidiousness and perhaps lingering self-doubt stood in the way. He kept a copy of one letter, written in 1904 to a close friend who had urged him to run for the legislature. This was the best way, the friend had argued, for May to attract the attention of his political party and thus get in line for appointment to the federal bench. No document could better express May's character, with its almost too delicate moral scruples, than his answer to this suggestion:

I could see how I might be able to go into politics in some such way as you suggest if I thought a public end demanded it—if for instance I believed I could render a public service in the legislature better than others or even if my name on a ticket would help elect it and I believed it of great public importance to have that ticket elected I might feel it my duty to overcome my personal distaste for it all and go in. But I don't believe either of these things. There are plenty of men whose name would add more to the chances of the success of the ticket than mine and very many who would be able to do more good in the legislature than I could. Nor should I be able to submit to the things the party organization would expect of me or to the obligations that membership in the legislature would impose. So I can't go into politics. Even if I felt differently and believed that it was justifiable for me to go in—still if I had the feeling that the real actuating motive was my desire for a judgship [sic] and to get standing in the party with that end in view I should be so heartily ashamed of myself that I couldn't look my friends in the face. Really I can't imagine myself doing those things with such an end in view without losing my self respect and when a man has managed to keep that for 44 years he values it more than anything.

With this May undertakes the delicate task of reassuring his friend that politics are all right for *him:*

You are an ardent Republican and believe the success of the party is an important end in itself. You like the political game and have the tact to get on with the people you would meet in it and influence them to the accomplishment of some good without in the least smirching yourself. So it would be quite right for you to do the things you suggest my doing. For me it would be absolutely wrong and is quite out of the question.

He ends the letter with some friendly personal chat, assuring his friend of his appreciation and continued affection.

My brother, who is six years older than I am and probably heard more from my father about his career, clearly remembers that he did finally, during the Taft administration, receive an offer of the federal judgeship he so clearly would have liked. The only condition was that May would play down—not conceal—the fact that he was a Democrat. This, of course, he refused to do, so the offer could not be accepted. The story casts some light both on his legal standing and—

since it was the Taft administration—his continued conservative credentials.

I remember on my own that he disliked Theodore Roosevelt, his near-classmate at Harvard. He had always disliked the Harvard swells, of whom Roosevelt was one, and he was affronted by the ease with which Roosevelt, at several crucial points in his career, managed to overcome his own gentlemanly scruples and play the political game. Also, the style of the Rough Rider was far too flamboyant for May.

Not surprisingly, he was completely captivated by Woodrow Wilson, defending him with gusto in letters to conservative eastern friends and to his sister Hattie, who remained a Republican (the two disagreed about most things all their lives). Like May, Wilson was an eastern college graduate who had never been rich, a devoted reader of English nineteenth-century literature, and a moderate conservative who had turned moderately progressive. The idealistic language Wilson used so well was exactly calculated to arouse the fervent support of a lifelong idealist. May must have thought Wilson's forceful and neutral intervention in Colorado after the Ludlow Massacre exactly right. The only point on which I know he differed with the Wilson administration was on the appointment of Louis D. Brandeis to the Supreme Court. In this he agreed with his old friend Moorfield Storey. Of course neither Storey nor May would have admitted or indeed believed that their opposition had anything to do with anti-Semitism, and Storey was a lifelong enemy of racial discrimination. Still, Brandeis was not the sort of man they were used to seeing on the Supreme Court. In a letter to Storey, May says that Brandeis is not a genuine champion of the people and is not highly regarded by most lawyers.

On one Progressive cause May took a consistently and rigidly conservative position. In several letters he responds to queries from eastern friends about how woman suffrage is working in Colorado. He answers confidently that most women don't want it, that it is supported only by an articulate minority, and that married women usually vote with their husbands anyway. The women of the lower classes vote more than those above them and are more easily manipulated by crooked politicians. He does *not,* however, agree with some opponents of woman suffrage that the vote has coarsened woman's character.

The attitude toward women shown in these letters—formally respectful but patronizing and protective, pretty typical of his time and class—bears on an important new chapter in his personal history. Part of May's increasing involvement with mining and mining law was brought about through his association with a mining family—the Rickards. Since this association led to his surprising late marriage, and thus to this memoir, the Rickards need a chapter to themselves.

8

Mining
and Marriage

In the confident Victorian heyday British explorers, investors, and engineers sought mineral wealth all over the empire and far beyond it. By 1890 the United States attracted 17 percent of British mining investments—only a little behind South Africa, Mexico, and Australia. In London, much speculative attention was focused on the successive gold and silver booms in Colorado, from the fifties through the nineties. The enticing possibilities of Colorado mining were written up in London magazines, discussed in City boardrooms, and promoted in England by American salesmen, some of them picturesque frauds. Most of the golden promises led to disappointments, and most of the investments paid no dividends, but there were a few shining successes—mines that quickly paid more than 200 percent on invested capital.

In California and Colorado and wherever there were mines, Cornish miners soon appeared—rugged "Cousin Jacks" with little scientific training but a lot of mining savvy. These were followed by trained mining engineers from the Royal School of Mines in South Kensington. Unfortunately, this impressive-sounding institution did not train its students very well—not nearly as well as the best Continental and, a little later, the new American mining schools. T. A. Rickard, the Uncle Arthur of my childhood, was both a prominent mining engineer and a patriotic Englishman. He says of the British system of mining education that it was "but a small degree better than none." However, Rickard predictably adds, the faults of the miserably financed mining schools of the Empire were sometimes made up for by the "inherited ability" of the British engineers. The lack of support for this badly needed training was partly the result of the profession's low prestige in nineteenth-century Britain, where traditional prejudice often got in the way of economic advantage. Mining engineers, after all, were on the "scientific side"; they did not have to study the classics; there were no schools of mines at the ancient universities. To quote Rickard again (and many contemporaries bear him out), in the United States young women regarded mining engineers as "energetic explorers" and "resourceful technicians" engaged in finding "the minerals necessary for civilized life." Young Englishwomen, on the other hand, "had a vague idea that the mining engineer is a somewhat nomadic person connected with queer doings on the stock exchange." Herbert Hoover, one of the most successful American mining engineers, tells of meeting a charming young Englishwoman on a liner. She was shocked to learn of his profession. "Oh, I thought you were a gentleman," she said to the future president. Most mining engineers lived a rugged and strenuous life, subject to rapid ups and downs. Nothing could be much less like the sober and settled, though impecunious, life of the Mays of Attleborough and Roxbury.

Despite indifferent training and low prestige at home, there is no doubt that some of the British engineers in America were very able men who played a major part in developing the mining West. They were also an important ingredient in the society of mining camps and brand-new towns, where they sometimes combined a capacity for roughing it with a taste for good food, good wines, and even good books when these were available. Some made money by using their professional expertise to invest on their own in promising mines. One of the competitive advantages of British mining engineers was that British investors preferred to employ them. English capitalists were not popular on the American frontier. Promoters cheated them and courts often held against them. London investors liked to have a mine inspected by somebody they knew.

The Rickards of Cornwall, my mother's family, were typical of British mining engineers in America. At one time eight of them were members of the American Institute of Mining Engineers. The first to come to America was Captain James Rickard, himself the son and grandson of mining engineers. The captain came to California in 1850 and was one of the first trained engineers to play a part in the Gold Rush. Five sons followed him into the profession, enduring its vicissitudes and ranging all over the West. One of these sons was Alfred Rickard, my maternal grandfather.

Alfred was the manager of mines in California, Nevada, and Colorado. He married Hannah Humphreys, of Swansea, Wales, and brought her to Denver. According to family tradition, Hannah was a beautiful and charming woman, but I know very little about her. The Alfred Rickards had four children. Harold, born in 1875, eventually became a rather unsuccessful and hard-drinking mining engineer in Mexico City, where he died. Marguerite (my Auntie Margo), was born in 1879 and gave early promise of unusual beauty and charm. By her twenties she was a heartbreaker in the opulent, rather flamboyant turn-of-the-century style, given to expensive clothes, big hats, and harmless coquetry. Grace Madeleine, always known as Ninette, was born in 1877, and was said to be very clever. My mother, Mary Octavia Maria, in childhood known as Baba and later as May, was born in Idaho Springs, Colorado, in 1885. Her mother died in bearing her, and May spent an unhappy childhood in the shadow of her fascinating sisters. Not without resentment, she later remembered hearing people say that Marguerite was the pretty one, Ninette the clever one, and May—well, May was the good one. Her devoted half-sister, Nina, remembers her at this time as a bit of a Cinderella, shy and somewhat melancholy but distinctly superior in mind and character to her two dashing elder sisters.

After taking his three girls home to live with his sister Lydia near London, Alfred and his son Harold went back to Colorado. There he lived in a rented room, traveling incessantly to inspect mines, writing constantly to English relatives and friends, and acutely missing his "girlies," especially Marguerite. A brief surviving section of a diary gives the impression of a hard-working, affectionate, unpretentious man, neither reclusive nor clubby. He read such standard books as *A Tale of Two Cities, Ivanhoe,* and *The Story of an African Farm.* He was a serious and regular Anglican churchgoer, but not particularly devout or ascetic.

In 1891, the year for which I have his diary, things started going well with some of his mining ventures, and Alfred Rickard went home to see his daughters. He spent some time getting to know them, taking them to the National Gallery and the parks, and then went to Newquay, Cornwall, with all but Baba. There in Cornwall he met Lilian Gatley and swiftly became engaged. Lilian, my mother's stepmother, was generally agreed to be far less good-looking than Alfred's first wife, but an excellent manager, prepared to take on her new family and do her best by them, keeping within the budget provided by the ups and downs of a miner's life. She was the kind but formidable "Granny" I was to meet more than thirty years later in Bournemouth.

In August 1891 Alfred Rickard was offered a fairly good position by the directors of the California Mine, near Central City, and within a month Alfred, Lilian, and the girls went back to Colorado. They lived sometimes in Central City, sometimes Denver. Alfred was away from home a lot. Yet he notes in his diary how different his Lilian has made things for him and expresses his joy at being able to have Christmas with his girls for the first time in some years. In 1893, however, the family was hit hard by the panic. When things got a little better they went back to Surbiton, near London. In 1895 Alfred was offered a position at a mine in New Zealand. He accepted and decided to stop off in Australia to visit his brother Reuben, who had recently accepted a position in the mines of Coolgardie. When Alfred reached Australia he learned that his brother had suddenly died. Alfred hated Australia, finding it hot and unhealthy, but poor health compelled him to stay on for a few weeks. In March 1896 he died on his voyage home, I do not know of what disease, just one month after his brother. Their joint obituary in the *Denver Republican* says that no two mining engineers and managers were better known in the mining regions of Colorado than Reuben and Alfred Rickard.

Lilian, Alfred's courageous widow, had to take over the family. The two older girls were sent to Berkeley, California, where Reuben had lived and prospered before his disastrous trip to Australia. (He had been mayor of Berkeley three times.) There Marguerite and Ninette were looked after by surviving relatives and friends and sent to Miss Head's excellent school. Lilian Rickard went back to England with her own little daughter Nina Belle and May, now eleven, to face a difficult and straitened period of life in suburban London. Gradually she managed to nurse the investments she had inherited from Alfred back toward a modest prosperity. The two older girls came home from America.

#

The first connection between the Rickards and my father had nothing to do with the three sisters who lived in England. In Denver he met and formed a close friendship with their first cousin T. A. Rickard, the son of Reuben and Alfred's older brother Thomas. Apparently some of the less happy traits that I remember in my Uncle Arthur set in early. The best historian of his profession, Clark Spence, reports that T. A. was widely known as a man with a high opinion of himself, and one of his professional colleagues wrote his cousin Edgar Rickard that "If T. A. wasn't a relative of yours I am afraid I would have to say that he is a conceited ass." And yet there is no doubt that this same T. A. (he was usually called by his initials, sometimes Arthur, never Thomas) was a man of great ability, wide experience, and considerable literary talent. One possible explanation for his lifelong need to exalt himself may have been the lack of social prestige of his profession in his English youth. Another may be the fact that his mining career was blasted at its peak by professional mistakes that amounted to disasters, almost to scandals.

Since his father was an unusually successful mining engineer, T. A. had a cosmopolitan background. He was born in Italy and spent part of his youth in Switzerland, part in Russia, where his father managed a mine in the Urals. After attending a school in Somerset, which he describes in his memoirs as "middle class" (he deplores the existence of such categories and remarks on their absence in America), he went on to the Royal School of Mines. This institution was then attached to the Normal School of Science, whose dean was none other than Thomas Henry Huxley, the Victorian major prophet of science and evolution. Rickard ever after referred to Huxley as "my great teacher."

After graduation T. A. came to Colorado, where his uncle Alfred got him a job as assayer for one of the English mining companies in Idaho Springs. He quickly rose to the top of his profession and served as consulting engineer for mines in Australia, New Zealand, France, Canada, and California, as well as for some of the richest and most famous enterprises in Colorado. By this time he had passed through many dangers and trials—he used to say that at one time he was the only man in Leadville who did not carry a gun. By the turn of the century, a prosperous time when silver and then gold recovered strongly from the panic of '93, Rickard was established between travels in Denver. Since 1895 he had enjoyed the largely honorary title of Colorado state geologist. Invited to give an address in 1898 at the University of Colorado, he devoted it to "two prevailing delusions: that mines grow richer in depth and that men were born free and equal." He was about to learn the truth of the first proposition in a very hard way.

In 1899, at the height of his career, Rickard was consulting engineer to the wealthy and powerful Venture Corporation of London. He was sent to examine the Independence Mine, the most famous of the gold mines in the Cripple Creek region. Rickard turned in a glowing report, and when his favorable estimate reached London, the stock boomed. The mine was bought by Winfield Scott Stratton, a picturesque American speculator who lived in great style in "Little London" (Colorado Springs). Stratton then sold the mine for ten million dollars—as yet the highest price ever paid for an American mine—to a new corporation, Stratton's Independence, and in turn sold his stock in this company, very profitably, to the Venture Corporation.

Unfortunately, another estimate had been made by John Hays Hammond, perhaps the best-known mining engineer of the day. Hammond found that the veins of ore were shallow, and estimated that the mine was worth only a fraction of the sum named by Rickard. When this news reached London, the stock crashed. The Colorado papers exploded with abuse of "Rickard the reckless," condemning him as a mere Englishman who didn't understand Colorado mining. It was pointed out that the Venture Corporation was owned by a relative of Rickard. Some people suggested that the mine had been salted, others that it had been gutted by earlier comers. There is no reason either in the record or in T. A. Rickard's character to believe that his report had been anything but an honest—perhaps a careless—mistake. In a somewhat similar episode the following year Rickard made a highly favorable report on the Camp Bird mine near Ouray. Again Hammond, his nemesis, estimated the mine's value at half Rickard's figure, and Hammond's report was accepted.

These episodes made it necessary for T. A. Rickard to withdraw from the profession of consulting engineer. He became instead the world's leading editor of mining magazines, heading the most important of these first in New York, then (from 1908) in San Francisco, and also for a time in London. In San Francisco he fought the Hearst press and denounced the violence of mining unions. Mainly, however, he campaigned for the proposition that mining engineers were and should be scientists. When he retired from journalism he became a historian of mining. His history of American mining remains the standard work, and his *Man and Metals,* an ambitious work on mining in world history, is respected. Despite this distinguished career, the Independence episode continued to rankle. His comment on it in his autobiography is characteristic: "The truisms of a scientific man not unfrequently are anathema to the mob. *Magna est veritas et praevalebit.* [Truth is great and will prevail.] That is a saying Huxley was fond of quoting."

One of the episodes disastrous to Rickard was in the long run immensely profitable to his brother-in-law, A. Chester Beatty. At the time of the Camp Bird episode John Hays Hammond decided to hire Beatty, then a young engineer employed by Rickard for twelve hundred a year. According to Hammond's memoirs, Beatty said he managed well enough, since he had beer tastes, but hoped to get to champagne some day. Hammond hired him for twice his former pay. Beatty's examination of the Camp Bird mine confirmed Hammond, not Rickard. (One wonders what the relation between the brothers-in-law was like at this point.) Because Hammond was employed by the fabulous Guggenheim family firm, Beatty in turn became first a Guggenheim employee, and then, making daring investments, the rival and enemy of the Guggenheims. He was to end his life a British subject, a famous philanthropist, a knight, and one of the world's very rich men. During the Depression he sent my mother a small allowance that was crucially important. When I finally met him at his home in Ireland, shortly before his death, he was still telling, with great gusto, stories about his wars with the Guggenheims. When he died I was to discover with great surprise that he had left me, as well as my brother and sister, a legacy that has made a lot of difference in my later life.

In 1892, before his disaster, T. A. Rickard became one of my father's four roommates in Denver. T. A. describes his fellow lodgers as all lawyers and "all good fellows," and says that to them "I am under a friendly obligation: they Americanized me—somewhat." One typically American institution T. A. enjoyed, like his friend Harry May, was the Discussion Club, where he could associate with lively and intelligent young women in an informal manner still rare in England. Except for the smutty stories, which he found offensive, he also enjoyed the club life centering around the University and Denver Clubs.

The friendship between the complicated and inward Bostonian and the rather brash young Britisher seems an odd one. In my childhood my father and Uncle Arthur never seemed easy. Yet in these early Denver days the two not only lived together but played golf and bridge and went for walks.

May's friendship with Rickard helped to involve him in mining law at the time of his own peak of prosperity and success. His diary makes it clear that he was involved in the legal problems surrounding both the Independence Mine and Camp Bird, the two sites of Rickard's disasters. Apparently May maintained a lawyer's impartiality in these fierce disputes. His friendship with T. A. Rickard remained intact, yet he saw a lot of Rickard's brother-in-law, Beatty, and also of Beatty's employer and Rickard's nemesis, John Hays Hammond. He also mentions dealing with "the mining men from London," including Fred Baker of the Venture Corporation. In May 1902 on a business trip to New York he saw T. A., who was then editing the *Engineering and Mining Journal* there. On the same trip he dined at Delmonico's with Beatty and Samuel Untermeyer, the chief lawyer of the Guggenheims. Beatty and May both spent the night at Greystone, Untermeyer's famous estate on the Hudson. At least twice, the firm of May and Macbeth won important cases involving W. S. Stratton, who had spectacularly bought and sold the Independence mine.

The Rickard connection was important in May's professional life. Far more important in quite another way was his introduction, one after another, to the three daughters of an impecunious widow as they arrived in Denver one after the other, each of them marrying "well," one fabulously well.

In 1898, while T. A. Rickard was visiting England, he was given the duty of conducting his first cousin Marguerite, the oldest and most beautiful of Alfred Rickard's three girls, to Denver to visit friends and see her brother Harold. According to her half-sister, my aunt Nina, the real reason Marguerite was sent to America was the threat of an attraction between her and a married man. In any case T. A., her cousin and escort, could not resist her charm any more than anybody else. The cousins were married in the cathedral in Denver, with a number of mining Rickards in attendance and Harry May as best man. May's friendship with the Rickards continued close—in the years after their marriage he had breakfast with them every Sunday. The very next year the second of Alfred Rickard's daughters, Ninette, turned up in Denver to visit her sister. Harry May records calls and golf games with "Miss Rickard." But Ninette, like Marguerite, married a mining engineer, A. Chester Beatty, whose enormously successful career was already under way. At *this* wedding, Harry May was an usher.

In 1900 the third sister, by reputation shy and somewhat melancholy, turned up as well in Denver to visit the other two. She was only fifteen, but Harry started calling on her in turn. He spent Christmas Eve, 1900, with T. A., Marguerite, May, and no others.

From the beginning something about the shy, gentle English girl seems to have had a strong attraction for the prosperous and popular bachelor of forty. Since his youthful proposal to Margaret Worcester, Harry had from time to time taken eligible girls to the theater, never coming close (as far as one can tell) to a serious involvement. Beneath his success and popularity, I believe, lay unhealed wounds of self-doubt, inner struggle, and inhibition. May Rickard seems to have re-

leased in Harry May feelings that had never before come to
the surface.

In a manner at first avuncular, Harry saw more and more
of May, helping her with her Latin, reading aloud Thackeray
and Tennyson, and taking her to the theater and to concerts.
Occasionally she took him, driving the brand-new little elec-
tric automobile belonging to her sister Ninette Beatty. In
1903, when May was eighteen, Harry met her stepmother,
the formidable "Mater" who was visiting her stepdaughters in
Colorado. That same year, since his sister Hattie was keeping
house for him, convention permitted him to invite May home
to dinner and even to spend the night. Once when May stayed
in the house Harry took Hattie to the Denver Club Ball—
May was obviously too young for such grand grown-up
events.

Gradually, though obviously, the relation became less
avuncular. Harry's diary lapsed between 1904 and 1908, but I
know from May's half-sister Nina that May was sent to Paris
to study singing in 1905. One can guess that her sisters
thought it as well for her to get away for a while from the
attentions of a man so much older. My mother always remembered the Paris year as one of the high points of her life, but
she did not forget Harry and kept the letters he sent her.
These, while expressing his affection more and more openly,
maintained an arch and elderly tone a bit distressing to a
modern reader. They refer to the writer as "your poor old
uncle" who misses his young friend. When she came home,
Harry was on the pier in New York and any family objections
seem to have vanished. In fact (according to Nina), the Mater
was delighted, somewhat in the manner of Jane Austen's Mrs.
Bennett, to have disposed of all three girls, including the shy
youngest, to prosperous and prestigious suitors.

In October 1906 the Beattys sent out invitations to the
May-Rickard wedding at a small Episcopal church at Spring-

field Center, New York, near the Beattys' summer place, "The Wigwam," in the Adirondacks. The marriage was celebrated by the local clergyman and blessed by Henry Codman Potter, the bishop of New York, a man well-known as a protector of liberal causes. Chester Beatty unfortunately had to be in Paris, but Ninette was quite equal to presiding alone at a wedding breakfast for fifty. Most of the guests were Boston and Denver friends of Harry's. The long list of presents was headed by a Steinway from Harry to May and included a framed reproduction of a Raphael Madonna from "Miss Worcester." Among the telegrams were those of Daniel Guggenheim and John Hays Hammond, both at the time business connections of the Beattys, as well as one bearing a long list of Harry's single friends from the club. The event was described at length in the Denver papers, one of which had predicted that it would be the leading event of the social season. Miss Rickard was described as a particularly charming young woman, already known to Denver society. Undoubtedly that society was full of curiosity about the young girl who had attracted the prominent, conventional, hitherto impervious middle-aged attorney. After a honeymoon in Quebec and Montreal the Mays returned to Denver to face that curiosity.

Reading between the lines of Harry's diary, which begins again in 1908, one gets a clear impression of mutual devotion but also of trouble and tension in the first years of this unusual marriage. How could it have been otherwise? May, unusually shy and barely into her twenties, had to assume the duties of a hostess in the period's formal and opulent manner, ceaselessly entertaining her husband's middle-aged and well-established friends. Harry, for his part, found it impossible to change the gregarious pattern of life so long established, and all the conventions of the time demanded that his wife share this pattern.

In the summer of 1908 it was high time for May to be presented to Harry's eastern relatives and friends. Having rented their Denver house for three months, Harry and May, with their ten-month-old baby Elizabeth, took the train for Chicago, Boston, and Portland, Maine. There was a nurse waiting in Boston and a house rented on Peak's Island in Casco Bay. On the island, their life sounds idyllic—walking, fishing, blackberrying, taking the boat to Portland for shopping or to the other islands for picnics. Ninette was with them a lot, and Harry occasionally departed to see old friends and relatives in Boston or Buffalo.

The first time the couple went together to Buffalo there was a large family party, after which May went to bed with a severe headache—a pattern that was to become common. Long years later she remembered, in a joking but heartfelt manner, how she really didn't like the shore dinners—fried clams, steamed clams, lobster, and blueberry pie—offered incessantly by her new Maine relatives. At the beginning of September Harry went back to Denver alone, leaving May at Ninette's house at Magnolia, on Boston's fashionable North Shore. In Denver, naturally enough, he took up exactly his old life of work, clubs, golf, and calls, also buying a new house and dealing with carpenters and plumbers.

When May got home she found life very strenuous. The Mays had incessant trouble finding and keeping servants—a cook, two housemaids, and a nurse. (Mary Thompson, the "Mungie" of my childhood, who came as a nurse in 1914–15, became the cook, and stayed the rest of her life, was a welcome exception.) As a matter of course, the couple tried hard to keep up the busy social life Harry had long taken for granted. Very occasionally and deliberately they had dinner alone together; more often they went to the theater, were entertained, or entertained others. The usual social occasion was a dinner party for ten. Nearly all the guests were old friends of Harry's—old in both senses from his young wife's point of view. Once May had a young friend to stay, and once she gave a party on her own (Harry records) for a group of young girls.

Bridge clearly presented a major problem—Harry was a lifelong devotee and May did not know the game. Often after a dinner party Harry played bridge with his friends while May did picture puzzles—a current fad. Sometimes she simply came home early.

Through 1908 and 1909 May's health became steadily worse. The usual pattern was a "sick headache" that incapacitated her. Sometimes she fainted or became exhausted and spent a day or two in bed. Often she came home early from church or a dinner party, or postponed a party of her own. Harry notes sadly but patiently how often he went alone to church, or how seldom they could entertain together. Often he wheeled the baby on solitary walks. In a manner very common among married women in this period, May seems clearly—and quite unconsciously—to have been using poor health to withdraw from routines she found almost intolerable. Of course at these times Harry found refuge in familiar bachelor patterns—bridge at the club, golf most sunny afternoons, men's dinners, men's camping trips. If I read his diary—or understand his character—correctly, he carried on these activities feeling guilty and trying not to feel resentful.

After the birth of John, in July 1909, and after May's recovery (childbirth was regarded as a risky business in those years), things got a lot better. May had fewer headaches, though stress could still bring them on. Forbes and Helen Rickard, her cousins and at this point the couple's closest friends, made a point of teaching May how to play bridge, and she gradually summoned the courage to take a hand with the experts. Harry and May went for long walks together. On New Year's Eve, 1909, May sang at a party for the first time. (She had often sung for Harry alone.) Clearly, the young wife had learned to deal with her social duties, though she was never to find them easy. The stiffness and formality many people saw decades later, traits really foreign to my mother's nature, were defenses against shyness, defenses that had been absolutely necessary in her early married years.

The pattern of trips to the East continued, with Harry always spending a lot of time at club reunions, bridge with Harvard friends, and business in New York. In 1910 they went to New York together for a memorable week of opera, concerts, and singing lessons for May with the city's best teachers. In March of that year they made a splendid leisurely trip to Mexico, leaving the babies for a month with a trusted nurse. Like most American travelers they enjoyed the handsome baroque cities, the lush tropical scenery, and the picturesque crowds. Best of all, according to Harry's diary, were the frequent good dinners, outdoors, with fine bands playing. At no time during the trip, carefully recorded in Harry's diary, is there any mention of headaches or illness on May's part. It was he who suffered, not seriously, from the usual tourist complaint. The trip was remembered as a high point of their life together, and two large photographs of Guanajuato always hung on our dining room wall in Berkeley.

With the end of 1910 the diary was abandoned, permanently. Letters of Harry's that survive—there are none of May's for this period—give a strong impression that the remaining Denver years were a time of increasing contentment. Affection is expressed ever more easily and naturally. Harry May's severe and self-punishing side—the Attleborough heritage—is far less in evidence than ever before.

Childhood remembered: our house (1921).

My parents (1920s).

Mungie, indomitable at sixty-nine.

Author, about eight years old.

My English grandmother and aunt had expected me, they later admitted, to look something like the American boy in this 1927 Punch cartoon. (Its caption reads: "American millionaire: 'Say, Keeper, I'd like to have your Zoological Gardens for my lil boy.' Keeper: 'Thank you, Sir. And we'd like to have your little boy for our Zoological Gardens.'")

They were not so far wrong.

Discovering the link to the past
(see chapter 5):
Nathanael Emmons (1745–1840).

A

DISCOURSE

DELIVERED JANUARY 22, 1811,

IN ATTLEBOROUGH,

AT THE *FUNERAL* OF

Mrs. Esther Wilder,

WIFE OF THE

REVEREND JOHN WILDER,

WHO DIED JAN. 19, IN THE 42, YEAR OF HER AGE,

BY NATHANAEL EMMONS, D. D.

PROVIDENCE:
PRINTED BY D. HEATON.
1811.

DISCOURSE.

DELIVERED IN ATTLEBOROUGH,

AT THE INTERMENT OF

THE

HONOURABLE ELISHA MAY,

WHO DIED

NOVEMBER 19th, 1811,

IN THE

SEVENTY-THIRD YEAR OF HIS AGE.

BY JOHN WILDER, A. M.

PROVIDENCE:
PRINTED AT THE AMERICAN OFFICE, BY DAVID HAWKINS, JUN.
1812

Two funeral sermons. On the sermon for Elisha May's death in 1812, note the small upside-down signature, "Tully May." Tully May (1787–1871), who attended this funeral, was my father's uncle. My father knew Uncle Tully in his youth.

John Wilder May, 1819–1883.

Elizabeth Farnham May,
1832–1878.

The house in Dorchester.

Harry May as a child. (Boys wore
dresses until they were about six.)

Harry May as an adolescent.

*As a collegian—he is probably wearing
the new suit that he found "more stylish than
I have a right to wear or wish to."*

Harry May (second from right) on a camping trip in the Rockies.

May Rickard as a child in England.

May Rickard May, probably about the time of her marriage.

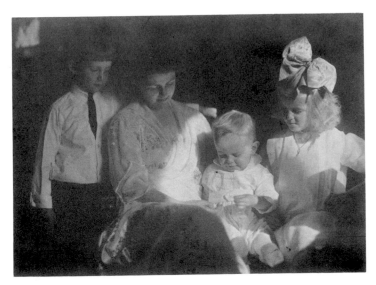

With her children, in Denver, about 1917.

Harry May at the height of his Denver career, probably about 1910.

In Berkeley, November 1921, shortly after his dismissal from his government post.

Author in high school.

In Marin County (author on the right, wearing a pack).

Just arrived. Author and roommate T. D. S. Bassett on the steps of Widener Library.

Learning about winter.

Professor A. M. Schlesinger Portrait by Gardner Cox that served as a frontispiece for the program of the annual meeting of the American Historical Association, 1942.

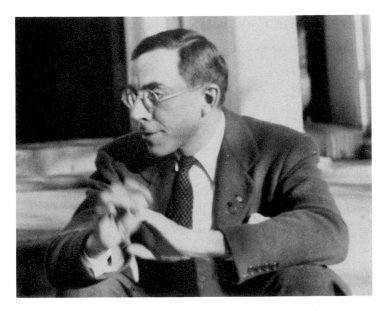

Jack Rackliffe. Photograph courtesy of Mary Rickard.

Jean Terrace, 1941.

Doing my best, Lawrence College.

With friends, Phib Group 12 (author on the right).

Our "unpretentious" house in Claremont.

Back in Northern California (early 1950s).

Most of Harry's surviving letters for the next few years were written from Denver to his wife and children in La Jolla, a small resort town in southern California. A number of Denverites spent the coldest part of the winter there, and John's delicate health seemed to make this necessary. (In those days parents worried a lot about tubercular tendencies in their children.) Harry misses his family acutely, and struggles to express his feelings: "I wish I could write you a good letter—one that would do you good and make you realize how much I love you—I can't do much more than tell you of my own doings which are not particularly interesting."

After a visit to the family in La Jolla he writes from the St. Francis Hotel in San Francisco that "I can't remember ever having lived a month more satisfactorily and happily than the month we have just had at La Jolla. We shall look forward to doing it again some day but can the babies be as fascinating that some day as they are now?" In a later letter he refers to the latest family addition: "What dear children they are! and Henry bids to be as dear as the others.* It's due most of all to you my dear dear wife."

In letters to his children while they were still small my father was able to unbend—not all the way, not very far by modern standards, but farther than I can remember his doing. This was especially so when he wrote Elizabeth. Once, after saying what a good time she seems to be having, he goes on: "I wish I was only 6 or 8 years old. I wouldn't like to be as small as Henry though for he can't do much of anything for himself and has to be kept from doing the few things he would like to do such as creeping up to the stove."

In two letters to Elizabeth in 1916 he mentions the war going on in Europe: "You know a great many soldiers are

---

*It is perhaps significant that the three children were named after my father's sister, his brother, and himself. John was given Rickard as a middle name.

being killed in this war and some of them have little children who have no fathers to take care of them." He explains that many people in this country are contributing small sums of money to help French orphans. In a more cheerful vein he tells her about a movie of the French army that showed airships, big guns, horses, and automobiles as well as all the generals and two kings.

Harry's surviving letters of late 1916 and early 1917 are not about family matters, but about the war and the reelection of President Wilson. When his sister Hattie wrote, right after the election, assuming that like all decent men Harry must have voted for Charles Evans Hughes, he took some sardonic pleasure in disillusioning her:

At your heat on the matter of the election I can hardly help being amused. At least you will have to add one more to the list of two on your black-list among the men who voted for Wilson. May voted for him too, and entirely from her own reading of speeches on both sides without any urging on my part; but evidently you do not expect much from women, so she need not be added to the black-list.

Though he was passionately pro-Ally and said he would have volunteered in France had he been younger, Harry defended the president against eastern friends who were furious at his policy of neutrality. Some of them blamed it on the materialism of the West, which Harry patiently denied. He argued that public opinion was simply not ready for war either on general principles or in retaliation for German atrocities. The submarine issue could provide the necessary unity and Harry ardently hoped for a German action that would bring the United States into the war. He got his wish, and on April 2, Wilson, in the most stirring of his speeches, reluctantly called the people to go to war "for the things we have always carried nearest our hearts." He asked Americans to

148

dedicate their lives and fortunes to the great objectives of democracy and justice. Harry May responded without reservation and never doubted the President's wartime leadership. Almost immediately we find him writing letters to the *Rocky Mountain News* urging food conservation. Yet May, never one to give in to popular emotion, avoided the war hysteria that swept Colorado and refused to accept some of the stories of German atrocities.

In the summer of 1917 a letter came from Washington, D.C., that was to bring an end to the increasingly cheerful and contented Denver life of the May family. Attorney General Thomas W. Gregory wrote asking whether May would be interested in becoming his special assistant in charge of the litigation concerning the government-owned oil lands in California and Wyoming. It was clear that the special assistant would be involved in one of the most bitter and complex struggles of the Wilson administration. The compensation was correspondingly impressive. May was offered a very handsome salary of $12,000 a year (current buying power would be at least ten times that), and further compensation was possible at the discretion of the attorney general. Moreover, though May's official headquarters were to be in Denver, he would actually be working in San Francisco, and he would be paid four dollars per diem when away from headquarters. Assistants would be selected by May, and office and other expenses furnished.

After a trip to Washington to meet the attorney general, May accepted as of September 1 and the family prepared to move to San Francisco. May's Denver friends were astounded and some thought he was making a great mistake to leave a place where he was so well established. In this they were to prove right. At the farewell party Harry was so overcome by feeling that he could not make his prepared speech. The affection and respect of his Denver friends was most eloquently expressed by his law partner, John S. Macbeth, in a letter he was moved to write the following Christmas: "you were the finest and truest partner that any man ever had on this earth . . . I respect and esteem you more than any man in the world . . . I am not delivering a eulogy or might add something as to your talents and many qualities of head and heart that all men admire."

Why did Harry May leave Denver, where he had spent twenty-seven years, where he was admired and loved, where he had achieved success and prosperity? I think it is doubtful whether the handsome salary that went with his new position was an important attraction—he was doing well enough where he was. I would guess that patriotism, the desire to be of service in wartime, and his devotion to the administration played a major role. So too, no doubt, did the challenge and prestige of the position. Wartime Washington, a center of power in a great struggle, was attracting a great many ambitious and able men. A friend wrote May that he was sure that Attorney General Gregory had him in mind for an eventual appointment to the federal bench. Conceivably some such possibility for further government appointment entered his mind, though he had long refused any maneuvers for such objectives. Finally, a dramatic change often appeals to men in their fifties, and often proves to be a mistake.

The other question, why the government had selected Harry May for this position, will take us briefly into the political history of the Wilson administration. History—together with his own character—was to force the Denver corporation lawyer into a fierce struggle with some of the most ruthless and powerful corporations in the land.

9

Fighting
the Good Fight

By the late nineteenth century, oil had become an essential fuel, a major industry, and the chief focus of the battle between unscrupulous big business and progressive reformers. During the early twentieth century oil became a pivot upon which world history turned. In America the automobile, once exclusively a rich man's toy, was becoming a means of transportation for masses of people. In Europe the armies, preparing for possible major war, were turning toward motor transport, and the principal navies were being converted from coal to oil. No one knew the extent of oil resources either in the world or in America. Many experts believed, wrongly, that American resources might soon be exhausted. Some therefore viewed government control of oil resources as a matter of national survival.

In 1909 the Taft administration, much maligned but actually carrying on a good deal of the Roosevelt conservation tradition, made the first move in the federal oil battle by withdrawing the oil lands still owned by the government from the time-honored process of private claim, occupation, and development. In 1911 the administration established two special naval oil reserves, Elk Hills and Buena Vista, in the rich oil-bearing lands of California.

Taft's withdrawal orders produced consternation among the oilmen, hundreds of whom, ranging from mighty companies to individual prospectors, were busily searching, locating, and drilling on the public lands. To many people the withdrawal orders were a bureaucratic brake on progress and a step toward socialism. Opponents of withdrawal included zealous apostles of free enterprise, businessmen who believed that unlimited exploitation was necessary for an adequate supply, westerners who thought that their states were being deprived of their rightful revenues by Washington, callous exploiters who intended to keep right on drilling no matter what the government did or said, and some plain crooks. Some lawyers honestly believed that Taft's withdrawal orders were illegal, at least until 1915 when the Supreme Court approved them. To many Progressives and conservationists on the other hand, Taft had taken an honorable stand in the struggle to reclaim for the people reserves that were being grabbed and exhausted, often illegally, by ruthless monopolies.

The question was anything but simple. Some oilmen were legitimate occupants fully engaged in drilling before the withdrawal orders, others brazenly started their work afterward. Some rich oil lands were contained within vast railroad grants of alternate sections, forming a checkerboard pattern with lands still in government hands. Some were parts of grants already made to states, though both state and railroad grants clearly excepted known mineral lands.

In Congress and within the Republican administration opinion was violent and diverse, ranging from diehard conservationists like Gifford Pinchot, head of the U.S. Forest Service, and Senator Robert M. LaFollette of Wisconsin to extreme believers in free development. The lobby organized by the oil industry to influence government action was believed by many to be the most powerful such effort ever mounted in Washington.

When the Democrats took over the government in 1913 after sixteen years of exile, nobody knew what oil policy to expect from the new administration, since conservation had been mainly a cause developed by progressive Republicans. In the beginning the Wilson administration inclined to moderately conservationist policies, but both the administration and the Democratic party were internally divided on the matter. The government oil lands were under the direct control of the secretary of the interior, Franklin K. Lane, a vigorous and eloquent man who was regarded as a progressive. He was also, however, a Californian, a strong believer in rapid private development of the resources of the West, and a personal friend of California senator James D. Phelan, a multimillionaire and a leading spokesman for the oil interests. More and more, Lane was to side with the oil developers and to undergo the fierce attacks of conservationists, Democrats as well as Republicans.

Lane was strongly opposed by two other members of Wilson's cabinet. One was Josephus Daniels, the picturesque, somewhat populistic North Carolinian who served for eight years as secretary of the navy. Daniels was widely caricatured by Roosevelt and other sophisticates as a landlubber and hayseed, concerned mainly to prohibit drink aboard navy ships. Whatever else, he was a doughty fighter, determined to secure and defend a safe supply of oil for the navy and inclined toward a policy of government development and production. In his fierce antagonism to what he saw as crooked and rapacious oil interests, he was generally backed by Attorney General Thomas W. Gregory. Gregory, a Mississippian by origin and a Texan by residence and career, is chiefly remembered for his tough policies toward wartime dissent, but he had a strong record of antitrust activity and a real dislike, based on solid

Texas experience, of the corrupt rich. A cautious conservationist, Gregory hoped to recover control of government oil lands, which he believed to be illegally occupied by railroads and oil companies, until the Congress could develop a sensible policy for operation under a system of leases and royalties. One of his principal aides in his battle with the oilmen was his special assistant, appropriately named E. J. Justice. Justice was an ardent conservationist, who instituted thirty suits for the recovery of California oil lands, won some of them, and in other cases settled out of court on favorable terms.

In his first administration Wilson seemed to side with the Navy and Justice Departments against Interior. In 1915 he established a third naval oil reserve at Teapot Dome, Wyoming. As the election of 1916 drew near, however, the president became more attentive to the wishes of the western Democrats, many of whom echoed the free-enterprise opinions of the oilmen. California, the headquarters of the biggest oil interests, turned out to be the crucial state in Wilson's reelection. During his second term Californians could count on speaking with a loud voice in the capital.

By 1917 the battle between Lane, on the one hand, seconded by the western states and the oilmen, and on the other Daniels and Gregory, applauded by Republican conservationists, had become fierce and uncompromising. The approach of war gave new arguments to both sides. Lane and the many dollar-a-year men drawn to Washington from the ranks of big business argued that patriotic necessity demanded the maximum supply of oil, without regard to petty arguments over past illegalities. Daniels and his friends argued with equal patriotism that oil should be nationalized as an essential wartime resource.

In July 1917 the redoubtable Mr. Justice, special assistant to Attorney General Gregory, suddenly died. Conservationists were dismayed, and Gregory quickly appointed Henry F. May of Denver to take Justice's place. I have been unable to discover any correspondence giving reasons for this appointment, so we can only conjecture what Gregory wanted. Clearly the new special assistant had to be an excellent lawyer with knowledge and experience in the complicated field of mining law. It was also essential that he be a Wilsonian Democrat and a westerner, since the administration was being widely accused of a pro-southern and anti-western bias. Beyond this we can guess that Gregory would have preferred a sound but moderate conservationist, neither a tenderfoot who could be suborned by the oilmen nor an extremist of the Pinchot type who would embarrass the government by shrill fanaticism. Doubtless Gregory looked into May's record and concluded that a man whose clients throughout his career had included railroads and mining companies would hardly be a boat-rocker.

What he got was perhaps a little different from what he expected. May was certainly neither an enemy of free enterprise nor any kind of radical. He had little sympathy for the Republican progressives who formed the conservationist spearhead. An ardent supporter of the war and the administration, he distrusted the isolationism of these men. He had, however, a deep feeling for the public interest, a long-standing suspicion of the very rich, and a fierce hatred of any kind of skullduggery. He was also a man who combined scrupulous personal integrity with some strictly controlled ambition and a good deal of fighting spirit.

In fall 1917 Harry May reported to his new San Francisco office, leaving his young wife to take care of the children and to pack and dispose of the house. In October he wrote to the house agent, characteristically asking him to tone down his advertisement. It was simply not true that the Denver house had an upstairs ballroom—"large attic room" would be more accurate.

May liked San Francisco but missed his family. He wrote Elizabeth about military parades, the opera, and especially about seeing a lot of "Auntie Margo and Uncle Arthur," the T. A. Rickards who were by then long settled in Berkeley. Berkeley was a quiet, attractive university town, only an hour by train and ferry from his office. When the house next to the Rickards on Ridge Road became available, he bought it and sent for his family, worrying as often about the strain on his wife. (This was the handsome house with a large garden always missed by my sister; I can barely remember it.)

May's office was in the Department of Justice section of the San Francisco Post Office, but he frequently made the long train journey to Washington, D.C., to consult with his superiors. In September 1918 he writes Elizabeth that he has seen the Washington Zoo but (there is no conscious humor here) has not yet seen "the President or any of the big men except the Attorney General whom I'm working under."

A few surviving letters show that at first the new special assistant advocated compromise and had to be prodded in the direction of militance; but as he learned what was going on, he changed his mind. According to Leonard Bates, the excellent historian of the oil battle, May "came to believe no less passionately than Justice in the righteousness of the cause" and acquired quickly a deep knowledge of the complex problem, partly by inspecting actual sites. Of the cases in which he represented the United States in the federal courts in California (district courts and the circuit court of appeals, ninth district), he won a respectable half, fighting the best legal talent oil could buy. He came to see his work as part of a battle against gigantic fraud and corruption, fought under the banners of an administration that represented the hope of the nation and the world. In his own and other departments of government he found colleagues who shared his beliefs and encouraged his efforts.

By the time May took office, however, history was preparing the downfall of Wilsonian idealism in general and progressive conservation policies in particular. In the congressional elections of 1918 Wilson made an unwise appeal for support on patriotic grounds, and the people responded by giving the Republicans control of both houses. From here on, bitter hatred of the president was more freely expressed by conservatives, westerners, and people tired of the Great Crusade. Some of May's Boston and Denver friends shared these strong anti-Wilson feelings. After the armistice in November the president spent almost all his waning energy in a desperate effort to save the treaty and the League of Nations, which he was sure embodied all the hopes of the world for peace and justice. Concessions to the interests of the western states seemed clearly necessary if the administration was to get Senate support for its lofty objectives. Moreover, the administration sincerely believed that wartime controls over business and industry should be rapidly relaxed. On January 19, 1919, Wilson sailed for Paris. From there he sent instructions to Attorney General Gregory to go easy in opposing congressional leasing legislation that would give considerable relief to the oilmen.

In March 1919 Gregory resigned from the cabinet, which surely disquieted his special assistant in charge of oil disputes. The president did not appoint Gregory's nominee as his successor, but rather A. Mitchell Palmer of Pennsylvania, an important politician from a crucial state. This is the Palmer who gave his name to the famous anti-radical roundups of 1919. He is also remembered for securing tough injunctions against postwar strikes. It says a lot about this period of progressive decline that Palmer up to this point had a considerable progressive and even pro-labor record in Congress.

Two events gave important clues about the prospect for the oil fight under the new leadership. First Francis J. Kearful, the assistant attorney general and May's immediate superior in the department, a man who was known as a fierce enemy of the oil interests, was pushed out. Second, Palmer refused to appeal a major suit against Standard Oil that the government had lost in district court. Secretary Daniels and Gifford Pinchot protested violently, and oil and rail stocks shot upwards on the market.

In the fall of 1919, Wilson, exhausted by his uphill battle for the treaty, collapsed in Pueblo, Colorado, and on his return to Washington suffered a stroke. From this point on the administration was clearly coming apart. Some of its members, among them Secretary Lane, resigned to enter the employment of the increasingly powerful oil companies, and the Republicans were confidently sniffing victory in the approaching election of 1920.

Yet the fight to regain government control of the oil lands, still passionately led by Josephus Daniels, had so much momentum that a few important victories were gained by the government even in 1920. In that year Congress at last established a sensible leasing procedure and also strengthened government control of the naval reserves. And in 1920 Special Assistant May won his own major victory.

This was in the Honolulu case, perhaps the bitterest of all the disputes between oil claimants and the government. Within large parts of the Buena Vista naval reserve, claims were held by the Southern Pacific Railroad, Standard of California, and the Honolulu Oil Company. The last-named company had been headed, until his death in 1917, by Captain William Matson, who badly wanted the oil for his shipping line and his

Hawaiian sugar plantations. Daniels, Gregory, E. J. Justice, and May each believed that these claims were fraudulent. In 1915 Clay Tallman, the commissioner of public lands, had approved thirteen of the Honolulu claims and denied four, and this decision was upheld by Secretary Lane, who seemed to be the final authority in the matter. Secretary Daniels, however, appealed to Wilson, who prevented the issuance of patents to the company. The case remained open until 1920, when the new secretary of the interior, John Barton Payne, was directed to give the argument a final rehearing. The stakes in this hearing seemed to both sides to involve the entire future of the naval reserves. Henry F. May, who had earlier defeated the Honolulu Company in a California district court case, presented the argument for the government.

On June 19, 1920, May, who had returned to San Francisco, got a telegram of congratulation from the attorney general. Payne had denied the Honolulu Oil Company's claims. This was a crucial victory in a long hard fight. One of May's Denver friends wrote expressing his delight: "How did you feel? Chesty, I hope." Even more important, Francis J. Kearful, the man who had been eased out as assistant attorney general, wrote May from Tampico, Mexico:

You must be very happy over it, as I am, for it is a vindication of the department's fight against the most powerful political lobby that ever appeared in Washington. This case was the storm centre and more than once it seemed to hang by the merest thread. I wish that you and Ernest [Knaebel, former assistant attorney general in charge of public lands] were here where we could have a round of "three rousing cheers."

In his answer May almost admits that he is pleased and proud: "The flag was kept flying during all Ernest's time and yours, and since, to good purpose and, as you say, the result is a vindication of the Department's fight." He reviews the other pending oil cases, as to which "we are having our fair share of ups and downs." He ends the letter with a jocular touch: "I join in your wish that you and Ernest and I could be together in Tampico or at some point not affected by the amended Constitution of the United States to celebrate the result of the Honolulu case." (The prohibition amendment had been in effect for a year and a half.)

This victory was probably the high point of May's professional life, and I can picture him in Berkeley happily celebrating with his family, perhaps opening one of his few hoarded bottles. This is almost surely the last possible glimpse of him as a successful and happy man, confident, well-to-do, proud of his work and his home life. I can see this man in my imagination; I never quite saw him in reality.

In 1920 May was deeply distressed by the widespread vilification of his hero, Woodrow Wilson, that took place during the presidential campaign. Bitter and sick, the president hoped for a third nomination, but Democrats shunted aside him and Palmer and other members of his circle, nominating the inoffensive governor of Ohio, James M. Cox. The Republicans chose a pliable and affable senator, also from Ohio, Warren G. Harding. Some have said that this nomination was engineered by oil interests. Whether or not this is true, it is quite clear that corporate wealth had a strong voice at the Republican convention. Such was the height of anti-Wilson passion that Harding was supported by some of the diehard Republican conservationists, who thought that Harding could be educated. One of them, Amos Pinchot, entertained hopes that he might be appointed secretary of the interior. Actually this position was to go to Albert B. Fall, a leading congressional defender of western oil interests.

Through this stormy time May passionately supported his president. When Senator Henry Cabot Lodge, in a Harvard commencement speech, referred to Wilson as a fake visionary, May wrote the alumni bulletin protesting (his letter was not published). Late in the campaign Joseph P. Tumulty, Wilson's devoted private secretary, made a highly emotional speech in Baltimore saying that Wilson had been "as violently misrepresented as anybody since Washington," and was "the greatest man of the age and the greatest force for public good in all the world at the present day." May wrote Tumulty expressing his relief that at last somebody had spoken out for the truth.

In his work May continued the losing struggle, even in the lame-duck spring of 1921. Obviously the Republican victory ended for the foreseeable future any hopes he may have had for a federal judgeship or other reward for his hard work. Yet somehow or other, he had persuaded himself that his actual position would be permanent. To me this suggests that for all his fighting experience, his grasp on political reality was not strong. He was hardly the man that Harry M. Daugherty, the new attorney general and the Harding administration's chief fixer, wanted anywhere near the oil lands.

On April 22, 1921, perhaps on the train on his way to work, May picked up the *San Francisco Chronicle* and read the following story on the front page:

One of the choicest plums in the gift of the national Administration, that of Assistant Attorney-General in charge of oil investigations for the Pacific Coast, has been given Ray Benjamin, chairman of the State Republican Committee during the recent Presidential Campaign, according to well-founded rumors afloat yesterday in the Federal Building.

The office pays $12,000 a year, it is said. Benjamin will have charge of all litigation concerning oil lands for the Pacific Coast. The office has been in charge of Henry F. May, who yesterday admitted that "sooner or later a change might be made in this office."

161

Actually May had had no notice of the change. On the twenty-seventh he received from Daugherty the following curt telegram:

Your services as Special Assistant to the Attorney General terminated effective close business April thirty. Please turn over all official property papers and files to Raymond Benjamin who has been appointed to take charge of cases heretofore assigned to you.

In his answer May could not help saying that "the suddenness of the termination and the notice somewhat surprised me," though he had by now read the newspaper reports and received a phone call from Benjamin requesting an appointment.

Conscious that his personal future looked uncertain, May called the attorney general's attention to the clause in his original appointment that provided for additional compensation at the discretion of the attorney general. In a prolonged correspondence that he must have found humiliating, May pointed out that his Denver practice had been lost. He had saved the government many millions of dollars. In similar cases in private business and in one recent government termination, handsome supplementary payments had been made. In a hostile and grudging letter Daugherty informed him that all requests for further payment were denied. Finally, and very briefly, he expressed appreciation for May's "efficient" service and admitted that very large sums had been involved. He went on to point out that May had been one of the highest-paid attorneys in the service of the government and that many others entrusted with equally important litigation were paid less. Therefore, he concluded, "I look with marked disfavor upon your request, which I think ought not to be granted." In this letter Daugherty appears in a most unaccustomed role, as careful custodian of the public funds.

During the next few years May read in the papers constant

reports of the reversal of all his work. Important suits were dropped, carefully worked out leasing procedures ignored. The Honolulu Company got leases to all the land for which patents had been denied. Most spectacular of all, at about the time May was fired, Harding shifted control of the naval oil reserves from the Navy Department to Interior, that is to Albert B. Fall. Fall hastily leased Teapot Dome to the Sinclair Oil Company, and most of the California naval reserves to the oil interests headed by Edward L. Doheny. Perhaps May found some ironic satisfaction when the western progressive Republicans—for whom he had never had much sympathy—forced the Senate to investigate the handling of the oil lands. Investigation led to the Teapot Dome scandal—the worst in the Harding administration's sleazy history. Secretary Fall was imprisoned for bribery. Attorney General Daugherty, indicted for conspiracy, was acquitted but forced to resign in 1923.

Somehow the unjust and humiliating end of Harry May's government career dealt him a blow from which he could not recover. It would, of course, have been a terrible experience for anyone to be summarily punished for doing excellent work. Yet I cannot help thinking that a more realistic man might have seen it coming and might also have recovered better. Some might have been borne up by sheer physical gusto, others by contempt for the sorry crew that sold public resources, still others by a cynical understanding that this was the way of the world.

What made it hard for May to accept his harsh treatment was, I think, a very old-fashioned idealism that had somehow survived his considerable worldly experience. Despite his fastidious distaste for politics, the record makes it clear that he could enjoy a good fight and accept occasional defeat. But fundamental injustice somehow was incompatible with his picture of the world. If he had been a real Calvinist like his immediate forebears he would have taken worldly injustice for granted and kept his confidence in the righteousness of God's ultimate plan. May's uneasy post-Calvinist mixture of doubts and hopes could not yield this sort of comfort. Yet enough remained from his Attleborough ancestry and Dorchester upbringing to incline him to melancholy brooding. This strain, obvious enough in his youth, had been recessive in the cheerful Denver years and the challenging struggle of his government work. It was brought out again, stronger than ever, by defeat and enforced idleness.

Unemployment is a scourge few can handle. May found a partner and an office and announced that he would practice law in San Francisco. (In his papers there is a similar announcement from his defeated hero, Woodrow Wilson, announcing the opening of a law office in Washington.) Clients did not come. It is tempting to guess, though this can never be proven, that a new practice started by a man who had worked mainly for corporations in the past might not develop easily in a place where many of the leading corporations, particularly Standard of California, Southern Pacific, and Matson Lines, had good reason to resent him and all he stood for. One wonders why he did not go back to Denver. Surely among his host of professional friends there, some place could have been found for him. But he was a proud man, and in returning he would have had to admit that friends had been right when they warned him not to accept the government offer.

Physically, May was a vigorous sixty-one when his government career ended. According to my brother's memory, when he came home with the news of his dismissal he said,

"Now I will devote myself to my fine family." I am sure he tried to do this, but it was not enough. In the twenties he gradually turned into the melancholy, brooding, and tense old man I remember from my childhood. One can perhaps see him as the representative of an old America with its own faults and virtues, defeated by a new America it could not understand. One may also see him as a man partly destroyed by some aspects of his own personality. Yet both these visions may well be lacking in charity. If one considers not only the defeat, the reversal of his public work, the absence of new work, the rising financial insecurity and fear, the responsibility for a young family, and the complete absence of any pension or "safety net," one should be surprised not by the prevailing unhappiness but rather by the courage, pride, and frequent intervals of good cheer.

When I went to church as a child I first encountered the text "Blessed are those who hunger and thirst after righteousness, for they shall be filled." I understood immediately that this was about my father, whose hunger and thirst were obvious. He knew, however, that the righteous are filled only with righteousness. In his more sardonic and cheerful moods he was fond of quoting a New England saw, based on another biblical text:

> The rain it raineth all around
> Both on the just and unjust fella.
> But mostly on the just, because
> The unjust hath the just's umbrella.

Easy to say and savor; hard to accept in its full meaning.

Part III

Slowly Growing Up

10

Democracy and
University High

I turn back at this point from history to memory, from what I have learned about my parents from their papers to what I remember about them and about my own growing up. These years of late childhood, adolescence, and early maturity are for everyone the time when each experience is poignant and meaningful. One is even more self-centered than at any other time of life, and perhaps properly so: one's chief business is building a self.

My memories of my parents at this time are enriched and explained by what I have since learned about them. I saw that my father was often tense or gloomy, and that he had not enough to do. Now I understand better that he was smarting from what he saw as bitter injustice. I have learned that tension and self-doubt were always part of his character, but that there were other parts as well. I had caught glimpses of him as a man capable of vigorous action, a man happy in his family, his friends, and his career. Those glimpses help me to remember better that even in his unhappy old age the more cheerful part of his personality could emerge—for instance, when he took my brother fishing, walked and talked about books with me, listened to my sister playing the piano or to my mother singing, or read aloud his favorite books.

My mother also had two different personalities. Within the family she was sometimes strong, often contented, and always loving. Outside it, dealing with tradesmen, giving parties, talking to friends on the telephone she was rigid and over-polite. I now realize that a great deal of the time she was playing the role of a society woman, a role she had never liked or felt at home in, one she had been forced to learn as the timid young bride of a prominent and successful middle-aged man.

Their mutual affection was never in doubt. A letter my father wrote my mother on some special occasion in the twenties expresses his feeling for her with real eloquence: "Everything you say so well is true except as to my greater wisdom and that is far from true. I may have a calmer way of looking at things but not half the real best kind of intuitive wisdom that you have. God bless you and give me a thankful heart that he has given me such a wife." I think he meant every word of this and also that he was right about her intuitive wisdom and its ultimate importance.

In 1931, the fiftieth anniversary of his graduation, my father wrote a stoical report for the *Harvard Alumni Bulletin:*

Attorney General Daugherty, soon after taking office, removed me from my position and work in recovering and protecting the government oil lands. I then took an office in San Francisco in the hope that professional work might come. But I found that it did not come in sufficient quantity to make it worth while; so in the spring of 1926 I gave up my office and took my family abroad for a year—drawing on my savings to do so.

"I took my family"—convention demanded that all decisions had to be his. My brother thinks, probably rightly, that the big trip was my mother's idea, and that its purpose was to give my father something cheerful to think about. If so, the effort was only partly and temporarily successful.

Reading between the lines of my parents' letters and drawing on many fleeting childhood memories, I can sense, beginning by the time of our trip to Europe and accelerating thereafter, a gradual change in roles. The vigorous and long-dominant man was beginning to be dependent, the shy and gentle woman finding it necessary to become stronger and more in charge. It could hardly be otherwise; in those days, even more than now, a man who was not working and earning money lost much of his power.

One day in September my father took me to the Key train to see me off to school. Rather awkwardly, he told me that I would undoubtedly hear a lot of nasty talk but should ignore it. I knew what he meant, but I was only half listening. This was the beginning of a period when my parents seemed to become gradually less important, my peers more so. My job was somehow to come to terms with both, and with myself.

＃

Over the stage in the auditorium of University High School, gold on black, was inscribed Giuseppe Mazzini's definition of democracy: The Progress of All, Through All, Under the Leadership of the Wisest and Best. I had to look at those words for six years, since I went to Uni High for both junior high and high school. Though they amounted to a somewhat idealized version of what went on in the school (or in American society), they made a noble symbol of the purposes of both. The whole vast public school system had taken on as its main job the inculcation of the quasi-religion and way of life of Democracy. Nobody—teachers, students, or supporting community—questioned the rightness of this purpose. That made the school, as an indoctrinating agent, extremely formidable. Initiation into an intact and strong culture, as ours then was, has always been a strenuous business. This was not— especially in intent—a brutal or rigid initiation. Everybody did not need to be exactly alike. As the slogan over the stage implied, there was a place for leaders and followers: success was admired—perhaps especially in athletics and civic leadership. Mediocrity was tolerated. What was not tolerated, and given the all-important purposes of the system could not be tolerated, was real dissent from the system's goals or real rejection of its methods. Those who did not accept or understand democratic values simply had to learn to do so.

In many parts of the United States, the main purpose of the schools had for a long time been the Americanization of immigrants. But in the Bay Area in the twenties there were no great masses of new immigrants, and perceptions about ethnic groups were different from those in the rest of the country. Jewish and Irish Americans did not seem to most Anglo-Saxons nearly as alien as they did (I was soon to learn) in the East. Japanese and Chinese Americans were respected but kept at a slight distance. There were only a handful of blacks in our school, and most people leaned over backward to show that they had no prejudice against them. One popular and able black boy was constantly elected to class offices. At school dances, however, he danced only with black girls.

The school was located on Grove Street in Oakland, in a neighborhood largely poor and Italian. This fact brought into play the real class division in the East Bay region, which was based on geography, specifically on altitude. Poor people then lived—and still do—mostly in the flatlands, middle-class and up in the hills. Because of the school's reputation and its connection with the University, hill people, especially professors but also naval officers, doctors, lawyers, and business-men, often petitioned to enroll their children at University High. (In the Bay Area then, only a few girls and still fewer boys, even of the rich, went to private schools.) Everyone in school knew there was a difference between the kids from the hills and the neighborhood kids, but of course no one referred openly to this difference. Those from privileged backgrounds took care not to refer to large houses, big cars, or vacation travel. In the schoolyard everybody talked the same lingo— laconic, colloquial, among the boys often obscene. Junior high classes were seldom divided according to academic abil-ity. Such a division would have segregated students by home culture and training, and therefore by class. As we moved into high school, certain subjects were elected by those whose parents expected them to go to college. The student body was still undivided in homerooms, gym classes, and the student government.

University High took student government very seriously. Students were pushed by teachers to take part in some activ-ity and received points, to be announced at graduation, for serving as everything from student body president to vice-chairman of the stamp club or head of the cleanup committee for the ninth-grade dance. Half a dozen top officials—in-cluding the student body president, the commissioners of fi-nance, special events, and the like, and also the yell leader— were elected annually. They ran campaigns complete with buttons, posters, and an assembly at which the candidates proclaimed their platforms. Winners were often athletes, al-ways genial and modest in manner, and more or less in sup-port of school spirit and school authority. I remember one boy solemnly pledging that he would stamp out smoking in Griffin's Store. Griffin's, right opposite the school, sold very greasy sandwiches and very thick milk shakes and refused to bother backroom smokers. It stayed in business year after year while competitors who cooperated with school authorities failed. Smoking was not stamped out.

For some purposes the student government had real authority. The president appointed a chief justice, who headed a student police force named—with unfortunate reference to California history—the Vigilance Committee. Members of this committee could impose mild penalties, usually after-school detention, on students who ran in the halls, pushed on the stairs, or on girls who did not wear the required kind of middy and skirt. The student government managed a fairly sizable budget, collected from student dues and admissions to school events. Students who had to attend important committee meetings were excused from certain classes—it was a matter of competitive prestige how often one was called out of class. Of course, there was some mild corruption—elected officials often chose their friends for appointive offices and expected some cooperation. There was also an informal ethnic and class balance: if somebody named Stanley Jones was elected student body president, he might well appoint as chief justice somebody named Louis Gallo. Even more than was intended, the student government was a training ground for the realities of the American system.

When I came home on the Key train from Grove Street in the flatlands to El Camino in the hills, I returned to a different world, with different customs and a different language. My parents neither opposed nor supported the influence of the school. I now think that they did not understand it. Uni High, after all, was not much like Roxbury Latin in the 1870s, let alone English girls' schools. Once in a while my mother visited school, as was expected. Friends I brought home were reasonably welcome. My parents thought nothing of taking me out of school when it was convenient for family trips or other reasons; unlike parents of my friends, they never supervised my homework. This relative aloofness had its advantages—the two powers of home and school were separated. It also meant that I had to live a double life. It was the school life that demanded and therefore got most of my emotional energy.

It is no exaggeration to say that for the first two years I had a hell of a time. This particular hell of early adolescence is familiar in hundreds of novels and autobiographies. One gets over it, but it is no fun while it lasts. Remembering grammar school, I expected some trouble, but this was a lot worse. In many ways I was an ideal target for hazing: I was skinny, ill-coordinated, and rotten at sports. After a year in Europe in grown-up company, I talked like a book. In class I was articulate enough to be admired by teachers, and during my first term a teacher appointed me chairman of the homeroom. Because of the school's democratic traditions, however, she could do nothing when I was deposed, to loud applause, in a perfectly constitutional revolution. As I remember it, that time I did manage to control my feelings enough to make a brief farewell address. In the schoolyard, there was never much serious physical brutality. Books were knocked out of my hand, gravel poured down my neck, the buttons of my fly skillfully ripped open with a single darting gesture just as I was about to walk into class. What mattered far more than all this was ostracism and derision. I learned the utter falseness of the saying that sticks and stones can break your bones but words can never hurt you. Words can hit fourteen-year-olds right where it hurts—in the fragile center of the ego.

I wish I could report, along the lines of the best school novels, that when I was pushed too far I responded bravely by socking one of my chief tormentors in the nose. I did that only in my fantasies. In the real world my responses, especially at first, were evasion and conformity. When I could work up a minor illness I stayed home. Confused and preoccupied with my troubles, I constantly lost my books, leaving in the boys' bathroom or on the schoolyard even the binders containing weeks of assignments and homework. When these did not turn up soon it was a disaster, deplored by teachers and ridiculed by students. At least once when this happened it seemed all too much and I went home in the middle of the morning. No one there said much, but my father gave me *Tom Brown at Rugby* to read. This book, written in 1857, was of only limited relevance. I had not, after all, been half-roasted in front of a fire, nor did I go on to become a manly Christian and head of the school. When I went back to school, to my surprise, neither teachers nor students made much of my having gone home. I think both were taken aback, my action was so extreme. All this reached its worst stage in the eighth grade, when I became so unhappy and ashamed that I got very poor academic grades—the only time in my life.

Fortunately, even in these bad years, there was a third world, better than school and more helpful than home. This was the world I lived in with my best friends. John, my closest companion, was the son of a neighbor who was a naval officer. (He was to follow his father's profession and was killed in World War II.) John was a relaxed and tolerant boy with an excellent sense of humor. He had no special status at school—he was neither popular nor unpopular and didn't seem to care. On Saturdays, with our two dogs and bag lunches, we would set out for all-day hikes in the hills. When we got past the last houses and into what seemed to us deep lonely forests (the pines planted not long before by the water company), peace descended. School did not seem to matter. We talked about metaphysical problems, as adolescents often do: Can you imagine infinity? When did time start? Is there a God? We had little use for conventional religious answers to these questions. Of course, we went on to sex, on which our information was as yet limited and somewhat inaccurate. Exactly how do they do it? Can you imagine your mother and father—? How about old Mr. and Mrs. Smith?—a delightfully funny picture.

At home with John and a couple of other friends I played endless formal games with lead soldiers. Sometimes there were battles, and we splashed broken soldiers with red paint to look like casualties. Quite as often there were ceremonial reviews. Coming home from school, I would throw down my books and dash upstairs to get into this more interesting world. Later, reluctantly giving up soldiers as too childish, we turned conventionally enough to stamp collecting. I got the idea of writing to postmasters in tropical British colonies and obscure native states of India. A surprising number sent price lists, and I enjoyed getting envelopes On His Majesty's Service from Gwalior or Trinidad. And there were always books—I could become a knight of Walter Scott or a brave Jacobite of Stevenson.

After the first two years of junior high, things got better—by tenth grade distinctly tolerable. By then I knew the lingo and the customs. I had begun to learn something even more important—that one got along better if one did not try too hard to be just like the others. There was room in the system for tolerated eccentrics. I was taken for granted, and the persecutors gradually laid off. Some I even began to like, though I think I was left with a prejudice against people who are handsome, popular, and self-confident.

At sports, though never good, I learned the necessary minimum of competence with two exceptions. I could never learn to hit a ball with a bat, and when it came to tumbling could no more do a somersault from a trampoline than fly out the window. On the other hand I liked basketball well enough to play in pickup games after school, and found some new friends with whom I would toss a baseball or football. In gym classes we took up boxing, and I found I didn't particularly mind getting an occasional bloody lip and thoroughly enjoyed inflicting one. The gym teachers encouraged us to challenge enemies to supervised grudge fights, with gloves of course. I duly picked a quarrel with a boy just as inept and even skinnier than I was, and we solemnly buffeted each other in front of an ironically applauding crowd.

When I think of the seventh to ninth grades, what comes back most clearly is certainly not the classrooms, probably not even the schoolyard, but the locker room of the boys' gym. My feelings toward it are not really hostile. I remember acutely the smell of jockstraps and socks very seldom brought home to be washed. I remember the steam from the showers and the wet towels, snapped skillfully at bare behinds. I remember boys singing obscene parodies of the latest hits. It is the gym that symbolizes for me the grubby jungle of junior high, the democracy in which I had to learn to survive.

By the tenth grade we were all emerging into the more interesting world of late adolescence, and we had more on our minds than persecuting one another. One new major interest was girls. We had always, of course, sat in classes with girls, but at least pretended to take no interest in them. This changed suddenly and sharply. It became allowable, even prestigious, to walk around the halls holding hands with a girl. It was absolutely necessary to learn to dance. At school dances and at radio dances organized by parents, couples paired off and sought dark corners for mild experimentation. I was more timid than most and handicapped for dates then and later by not knowing how to drive. (During one of the intervals when we had a car, my brother had tried to teach me, but I proved both rebellious and inept.) Yet I managed to find one girl who was very pretty, as bookish as I was, and somewhat responsive to my shy advances. We exchanged poems, notes, and—very awkwardly—kisses. We walked around the school corridors holding hands and were expected to dance mostly with each other at school dances.

Another important change was that for those who elected college preparatory classes, intellectual skills became important. To be a star student was not as good as to be a star halfback or student body president, but it was something. I have said nothing so far about what went on in classes because through junior high I can't remember that anything important *did* go on. From the tenth grade on, some classes were really interesting.

The women (and the few men) who taught senior high classes at University High were all competent and some were talented and devoted. Most were proud of the school's special standing. Some had doctoral degrees and seemed to know everything in their subjects. Some were highly sophisticated, quite ready to handle the most difficult students with a combination of toughness, humor, and understanding. One red-haired English teacher that I got to like quite a lot was expert at waking the drowsy or daydreaming student by throwing chalk with accuracy and force.

University High was where the University of California then trained all its student teachers—the senior teachers were members of the Department of Education. This meant that we were exposed to a great variety of beginning teachers—or rather they were exposed to us. In junior high some of them had a worse time than I had. It was common knowledge that if student teachers failed to get along with their classes or had to send many pupils to the principal it counted heavily against them. I joined in hazing them, probably partly to fall in with the other students, partly out of adolescent thoughtlessness. Recalcitrance and rudeness were common, organized semirebellion not unknown. In music class, where we sang in four parts unbearably boring songs about spring flowers or sailing voyages, the boys whose voices had changed sat in the back of the room in the tenor and bass sections. Some of them had real talent at making dirty parodies. If the teacher pretended not to hear, he or she was lost—the offensive singing got louder and louder. Faced with this sort of treatment, some student teachers broke down, hopelessly begging their students to be nice just this once, because the regular teacher was just outside the door. Others, by sheer force of personality, controlled their classes without trouble from the first day.

In senior high we largely lost interest in hazing teachers and realized that some of the student teachers were remarkable people. It was the Depression, and first-rate graduate students working toward higher degrees at the University sometimes got a teaching credential as insurance. I remember with real appreciation a number of senior and a few beginning teachers, but will concentrate on only two.

Miss Caroline Power taught creative writing. She was full of enthusiasm for literature, especially the New Poetry, which had begun to appear in about 1912. From time to time she held little award ceremonies at which she read poems and stories aloud. She especially encouraged us to send our work to magazines and brought in copies of writers' magazines that listed possible markets. Every year a few poems and stories were accepted. I had a light poem published in the famous "Conning Tower" column in the *New York World*. A little later a couple of my poems written in Miss Power's class were accepted by *Poetry,* the leading magazine in the poetic revolution of 1912 and in Miss Power's opinion still the best in the country.

As I look back at my poems of this period, I think that they were praised far too much by most teachers. I read poetry a lot and had a knack for accurate meter and rhyme. When I kept the poems light they were tolerable, but too often they were portentous. I tried to like the modern poets Miss Power admired, but my head was too full of the *Oxford Book of English Verse*. Nevertheless, her special kind of encouragement was very valuable. In those years most adolescents with any literary skill cherished secret dreams of writing the Great American Novel or Poem. Miss Power showed us a bridge between these dreams and the actual work of getting pieces published. If she made this career seem easier than it really was, at that point it was all to the good.

I also encountered in high school my first real academic intellectual. I kept on taking Latin year after year. Remembering the temples and arenas I had seen in Provence, I knew that real people wearing real togas had once talked this language. I liked the way Latin sounded and even enjoyed the grammatical tangles, with their sure, subtle, and complicated solutions. Miss Claire Thursby, the senior Latin teacher, was a good specimen of the old-fashioned teacher. Latin had long been on the defensive, and Miss Thursby considered it her job to prove that studying it was practical, necessary, and progressive. She constantly posted on the bulletin board instances of mythology used in advertising, or testimonials that Latin helped people understand English grammar. What she really loved, however, was Virgil, and the summit of her career came when Mussolini's government in a very clever propaganda gesture subsidized a trip for American teachers to Italy and other Mediterranean lands. Miss Thursby's Christmas card was a photograph of camels "on the road to Troy."

I started Latin in the seventh grade, and by the time I was a senior had plowed through a good deal of grammar and then the usual sequence of Caesar, Cicero, and Virgil. In my senior year only four of us elected Latin 9, and the small class was organized by DeForest Rodecape, a student teacher and a graduate student in classics. Rodecape, with his pince-nez, his longish yellow hair, and his sardonic manner, was like no one else I had ever met. He scoffed at Virgil, much to Miss

Thursby's horror, and put together for our use a reader of his own. This included, among others, a lot of Horace and Catullus, some Martial, and even a few pages of Lucretius, the only poet we found almost too difficult. In this little class there was never any mention of the practical uses of Latin. Rodecape did not present any set pieces of Roman history as "background" but simply explained events that we came across in our readings. All that really mattered was the poems themselves— subtle, polished, immeasurably graceful, mildly erotic (his syllabus excluded the truly erotic ones), and above all worldly. We usually read more than was assigned. I tried my hand at the demanding job of translating Horace into English verse, not realizing that I was following a Renaissance tradition. Though my Latin is largely gone, I can still recite some of the poems we read. I think I may have never again found myself in so pure an atmosphere of uncompetitive scholarship, pursued for sheer love of the text. I found I could even talk about Latin authors with my father. He gave me an old edition of Horace's *Odes* to give to Mr. Rodecape on the last day of class.

By the time graduation approached, I found myself pretty much at ease in the school, popular in some circles and tolerated as a familiar oddity in others. I had run once for elective office and lost by a margin less than disgraceful. I had been second lead in the alternate cast of a school play. As president of the Latin Club, head of the Honor Board, and so forth, I had accumulated a decent if not outstanding number of activity points. I got excellent grades, and people no longer held this against me.

It was still true that I looked forward to approaching freedom as we rehearsed our graduation ceremonies. The important one was not the evening commencement, full of idealistic oratory for the benefit of parents, but the morning assembly, when awards were given, the Senior Farce presented, and finally the graduating seniors marched down the aisles for the last time to a Sousa march, played very slowly and rather badly by the school band minus its best players, who were graduating. Five times we had seen classes march out to the same tune and now, unbelievably, we were actually leaving ourselves.

#

While things were getting better at school, disaster hit at home. Financial worry had become a constant. Feeling guilty about not helping, I tried several business ventures. I learned from a wax company a new technique of polishing and waxing cars, then sent out some business cards offering my services. Either the process or my performance was partly unsuccessful, and the finish usually came out streaky. In this period my feelings toward my father improved as he exerted less and less authority. It began to occur to me that he was old and not in very good shape.

One day he politely knocked at the door of my room and said he had something to tell me. This was that Mother had a lump in her breast and was about to have an operation. Ever since I was a little boy I had thought that the worst thing that could possibly happen was for my mother to die, and now I realized that this might happen. It did not, but for some months after the operation she was not only very ill but plainly terrified. At one point I learned that the scissors had been removed from the dressing table in her bedroom for fear she might try to kill herself.

She finally recovered, and it was twelve years before she again was to face death, this time with superb courage. But I learned from this episode once and for all that the very worst can happen—no guardian angel can be summoned to prevent it, even by one's utmost concentration.

I had learned a lot in these six years, not all of it salutary. Fears and self-doubt, present from as far back as I can remember, had been intensified both by this overwhelming home event and by hostility encountered at school. I had learned to get along—a necessary but not always admirable skill. I was left with a divided attitude toward democracy and majority rule. On the one hand, I felt a passionate sympathy for those who were different and a hatred for compulsory conformity. On the other hand, University High had done its work well and I recognized the legitimacy of the majority. I had even learned to like some of its ways. The resulting ambivalence, never resolved, was to prove a valuable beginning for the study of American culture, in and out of books. One can learn a lot about the problems of individual freedom in democratic culture from reading Tocqueville. I learned about it first at University High.

Despite failing family finances, I knew that I was going to go to the University of California. It was tuition-free and I could live at home. I had been brought up in its shadow, and the idea of becoming a part of it was thrilling. Looking forward, I wanted at the University to be a radical, a dissident, a poet. I also wanted to be popular, successful, and happy. Such was the nature of the University of California at that time that I seemed for a while to be able to follow both these paths at once.

Sunshine at Cal

My four years as an undergraduate at the University of California were a time of happiness and partial liberation. After my nineteenth-century upbringing, I was suddenly introduced to the culture of the twentieth century at a particularly stirring time. Struggling like my father in his college days against deeply imbedded fears and inhibitions, I achieved like him only a partial victory. Like him, I remained a worrier. Aside from minor worries about such matters as term papers and examinations, I worried about two major questions of equal importance—why I was not a Communist and why I was a virgin. But a lot of the time I was having too good a time to be entirely obsessed even with these all-important concerns.

As with my father in his college days, my emancipation and growing up were slowed by the fact that I still lived at home. Money troubles were pressing the family hard, and the cost of a dorm or fraternity seemed prohibitive. I did not have the kind of trouble with either parent that my father had had with his father the judge. For one thing, my father's energy and power were slipping fast. Also, I think, my parents made a great effort to be tolerant and understanding. They did not care how late I came home at night. Even when once in a while I came home full of beer, staggering to bed after noisily vomiting in the bathroom, nothing was said the next morning. Yet the house with its familiar standards and routines inevitably registered its silent judgment.

I felt no hostility to my parents but could not really talk to them about most of my new experiences and ideas. At least they were not Republicans. I knew that they experienced a good deal of hostility and ostracism in some of their social circles for sticking to FDR. (They lost very little this way; their real friends were sorted out from their acquaintances.) I respected them for this. Yet I discovered that Wilsonian idealism, which remained at the center of my father's loyalties, was seen on the campus as a failure if not a hoax. When my mother picked up a volume of Dos Passos that I had brought home she was deeply shocked by its language. Once when my parents' closest friends came to dinner, Mrs. Briggs was mildly upset by a recent poll, I think at staid little Mills College, that said that Marx, Freud, and Darwin were the greatest men of the past century. Nobody I knew on the campus would have questioned this. I remained on friendly terms with my parents, dismissed their ideas rather too easily, and did not realize how much I still reflected their influence.

I received no allowance. My father simply told me to ask for what I needed. When I absolutely had to I asked him for five, ten, or twenty dollars and received it immediately and without question. Since I hated this procedure I tried to save, to get scholarships, and to earn money at odd jobs through the University's Bureau of Occupations. Reading aloud three hours at a time to a rich old man in Piedmont who was mainly interested in biblical prophecy brought in a whole dollar. Assisting in a puppet show that performed for schools was far more fun, but the eccentric lady who owned it hardly paid at all. At Christmas time the postmaster, a family acquaintance, saw that I was taken on as helper on a mail truck. One summer I answered a help-wanted advertisement for Campbell's

Soup. As one of the fortunate few who passed the interview, I attended an indoctrination film about the worldwide romance of Campbell's, paid for my own smock, and worked weekends for thirty-five cents an hour, handing out samples at the largest groceries in the East Bay. I had to learn to say, when a lady asked about mock turtle, that it was my favorite kind. I acquired some skill at throwing the cream of tomato down the toilet when it curdled. (It wasn't supposed to curdle, and one had to be sure to get rid of it between visits of the company's inspector.) I can't say that I learned from my various jobs much about the great world outside the campus. Nor did I want to: the campus was my world and I loved it. In the 1930s the Berkeley campus was the University of California, except for what was still called the Southern Branch in Los Angeles and the Aggy school at Davis. The campus was spacious, dignified, as yet uncluttered. It swept down from the hills toward the Bay; from many points one could see both the hilly horizon and the broad sheet of water with the City glittering beyond it. There were plenty of broad lawns for sleeping and talking. Between the stately white buildings flowed a stream of lively chattering students, swelling to a roar at hours when classes were changing.

With about 15,000 students, graduate and undergraduate, Cal was large enough to provide a certain liberating and urban anonymity and diversity, but not so large that one could not acquire, gradually, an understanding of its dominant customs and ideas. In good and bad ways it was a provincial university. The faculty did not feel bound to compete every minute with the great universities of the East. Some were distinguished and brilliant, some went in more for elegant living than intense scholarship, quite a few were distinctly mediocre. Among the students there were still plenty who followed their predecessors of the twenties in living for football, dates, and drink. Few undergraduates altogether neglected any of these, but times were changing: it was becoming more fashionable to be interested in learning—mostly outside one's classes—about life, politics, literature, and the arts. Quite a few students openly or secretly cherished literary ambitions. Once a week in the student union classical records were played. Students lay on the floor with soulful expressions listening to the César Franck Symphony or Beethoven's Fifth. Student publications were becoming both more highbrow and more political, and by the time I graduated the fraternities had lost control of the student government to more or less radical intellectuals. But between the beer-and-football crowd and the arts-and-politics crowd there was no sharp gap, rather something of a continuum, and very little hostility either way. For a week in November, just before the Big Game, intellectual pursuits went underground while football rallies took over. For a week in April, just before the annual Peace Strike, liberal and radical propaganda took center stage.

Some students who came to Berkeley from small towns found the campus huge and impersonal. To me it seemed welcoming from the start. Growing up in middle-class Berkeley, I had heard a good deal about the supreme importance and difficulty of making a fraternity. To my surprise, during rush week I was invited out to lunch and dinner every day and treated with the greatest friendliness. On the second or third visit to the same house I found myself invited into a back room and seriously invited to pledge brotherhood. The first time this happened I was immensely touched and flattered. After a few more such episodes I realized that I was riding a seller's market. Most of the fraternities were having a hard time paying off the mortgages on the handsome new houses they had built in the twenties. They needed me quite as much as I needed them, and this fact removed much of the glamour. I accepted an invitation from one of the fraternities to become a pledge without either living at the house or paying dues, to see whether I proved able to afford initiation. For a year I enjoyed the pleasant company and odd rituals. With the others I stood up at dinner while the lights were turned off and we sang our mystic song. Like the other pledges, I was occasionally beaten on the behind for not doing enough work around the house or not knowing some of the fraternity lore. But by the end of the year, despite my friendly feelings to my prospective brothers, I decided that I did not really need the fraternity and did not want to ask my parents for the necessary money.

By now I was spending my time with several quite different sets of acquaintances. One centered around Edith, a red-haired girl whom I had known at University High. There she had turned up, a fish much farther out of water than I was, straight from an upbringing in Paris and Vienna. Edith and her very young and attractive mother served green tea on Thursdays in an old house on Ellsworth Street. Edith was a— in fact *the*—Sanskrit major, and some of her friends went in for similar exotic interests and also for harmless affectations. She was a warm-hearted, generous, and rather shrewd person, however, and her circle included a few who never strained after Wildean epigrams. One boy had an inexhaustible stock of obscene limericks concealed in his engineering notebook; another, a bit stiff, was a top officer in the ROTC unit. Edith and her mother were very poor and had to give up serving cookies with the tea. Twice they had fancy dress parties—one to which everybody came as a character from *The Three Musketeers* and another based on the *Arabian Nights*. As far as I remember there was nothing to drink—it was beyond their means. Yet both parties went on with great hilarity until four in the morning.

Another set of my friends, centered around some sons and daughters of professors, went in for high seriousness. They were bright, cultivated, and a little exclusive. Most were musically trained, some had traveled. Their politics tended toward the far left and their tastes toward the austere. They liked to listen to chamber music or discuss philosophy while eating graham crackers and drinking milk. Their sport tended to be soccer, not American football. I admired them greatly. Still another set, overlapping only slightly, consisted of students with literary ambitions, people who admitted that they, like me, wanted to be poets or novelists. Gradually I formed half a dozen close friendships, drawing from these groups and going beyond them. The people I liked most tended to combine some intellectual seriousness with a lighthearted ability to enjoy themselves. Most of our pleasures were simple and inexpensive. Going dancing in a San Francisco hotel—the traditional gaiety of the fraternity crowd—I tried a few times but could not afford and did not need. Talking, walking, and drinking beer were almost enough. An acquaintance of my mother's who gave music lessons and had two daughters in college had the idea—just right for my group—of having recitals, in which anybody was welcome to sing or play an instrument, followed by radio dancing. These parties, held about once a month, became very popular. We enjoyed equally the serious music, the dancing, and the large and shadowy garden where the less musically inclined were free to go in for off-color stories or a little mild necking.

My best times, though, were the long weekend days when a group of us—usually about a dozen boys and girls in easy camaraderie—went hiking in Marin County. We would catch an early train and ferryboat to San Francisco. From the Ferry Building we would take a longer boat ride to Sausalito, where we would board a train, full of middle-aged German hikers, to Mill Valley or Fairfax. From there we would walk, sometimes twenty miles, through the green or golden-brown hills, up and down gorges, through deep fragrant woods of madrone, bay, and pine, or on flowery bluffs over the ocean.

190

As we walked and as we sat and ate our sandwiches, we talked, seriously or lightly, about books, war and peace, each other. Sometimes we got lost and had to crawl through the chaparral and poison oak. At the end of the day, dirty and disheveled, we would take the train and boat again to San Francisco and have dinner at one of the many cheap French or Basque restaurants near Broadway. Nobody seemed to mind our dirty clothes. Once when we were singing with our veal and red wine, a waiter approached ominously. It turned out that he had no threat but a message for us: a gentleman in the bar would like to keep on buying us wine as long as we were willing to sing. Of course we exhausted our repertory. After dinner we would spend another hour, tired and happy, on the boat and train to Berkeley.

Within the hiking group it was a point of honor not to refuse to spend a Sunday hiking even though there were term papers or examinations coming. And indeed one of the virtues of Cal at this time was that students were not pushed too hard—there was time for the kind of education that took place outside the classroom, for instance in the Morrison Library, an elegant room for recreational reading in which students were not supposed to study and forbidden to take notes. A picture that comes to my mind is of one of my friends sound asleep in one of the Morrison's upholstered chairs, Spengler's *Decline of the West* open in his lap. Open at the middle—he had read some of it.

The system of teaching that generally prevailed at the University, especially in the freshman and sophomore years, was that which was the rule (and in part still is) at all large American state universities. A professor gives three lectures a week to a class of several hundred students (Econ 1A had a thousand). The class is divided into small sections meeting once a week, in which graduate assistants try hard to stimulate lively discussion of the lectures and the assigned reading, while most of the students try to get useful tips about the examinations. In the thirties, the reading in elementary courses invariably consisted of textbook chapters, often written by the lecturer and sometimes duplicating the lectures. Two midterms and one final examination, together with an occasional short quiz, were supposed to keep the students on their toes. The examinations inevitably tended to demand repetition, with some comment, of material drawn from the lectures. For the student this system put a premium on feats of memory, for the lecturer on dramatic power and a kind of paternal geniality, for the graduate assistants on the adding and subtracting of points. Some teachers and some students resisted the demands of this intellectually deadening system; I conformed to it too much. Determined to snare some of the small scholarships and also compulsive by training and nature, I worked too hard to become a master of the sterile technique of getting A's on examinations. Yet I learned some things. In my sophomore year, like all students majoring in history or literature, I was required to take two half-courses in natural science. Consulting my friends and the class schedule, I chose elementary paleontology and a survey of zoology. To my surprise, both were interesting. Together with the reading I was doing in modern literature, the science courses brought on what surely must have been one of the last recorded nineteenth-century religious crises.

At this time I did not consider myself religious, and my occasional attendance at St. Mark's was only to please my parents. I needed, however, to believe in a meaningful and friendly universe. Temporarily, I had solved this problem without realizing it by becoming a nineteenth-century liberal optimist. Like many in my father's generation, I used this position to keep at bay underlying doubts and fears, of which I had plenty. Like my father, I took for granted evolution and vaguely assumed an upward direction for it. It was staggering to learn, in Paleo 1, about the endless ages of geological history before the appearance of life, and after that the hundreds of millions of years of apparently random appearance and disappearance of species. In Zoo 10 I remember a lecture in which Professor S. J. Holmes, a mild and gentle teacher and also a famous biologist, discussed the practically indistinguishable border between life and nonlife. Just like a student at Oxford or Harvard in the 1880s, I asked myself how any human preferences, ideals, or values could possibly have any meaning whatever in the face of this staggeringly indifferent universe. For a few weeks during my sophomore year this question stayed with me day and night, preoccupying me as I swam in the pool at the gym or walked by myself in the hills. I found no answers. Gradually it dawned on me, to my immense relief, that I wasn't likely to find any and didn't really have to—at least not right yet.

I was equally attracted by English and by history. The English department, to its great credit, had partly broken from the lecture-and-quiz pattern. In the freshman year one wrote themes and book reviews—hardly an exciting procedure but better than taking lecture notes. After that there was one series of literature courses and one of writing courses. I took none of the former but all of the latter that I could.

The center of my sophomore year, and the real beginning of my encounter with modern culture, was English 51, whose clumsy subtitle was Writing in Connection with Reading Certain Great Books of the Nineteenth and Twentieth Centuries. This was taught by Professor Benjamin Lehman. Lehman's dress and speech were careful and elegant, his manner slightly

193

jaded. Yet he was an apostle of expression and feeling. Early in the course he told us that most undergraduates were reasonably advanced intellectually for their years, but emotionally sadly undeveloped. It soon became clear that his interpretation of literature was mostly Freudian. In a lecture on *Alice in Wonderland* he posed a dramatic rhetorical question: "Where did the rabbit go? [*Long pause*] Into a hole. Back [*short pause*] to the womb." In our later college years we were to consider Mr. Lehman a bit old-fashioned and deplorably lacking in modern social consciousness. He was, however, an enormously effective teacher of sophomores, and for many an important liberator.

English 51 was designed to stimulate our feelings and imaginations. In each session Lehman lectured, often eloquently, on a single great writer—the first term these included Darwin and Newman, Tolstoy and Whitman; the second, Yeats, Eliot, and Lawrence. We were given a list of important books. Every few weeks we had to read one of them, and then write about two thousand words on whatever the book had suggested to us. The connection could be minimal. Essays, stories, and poems were equally acceptable—for poems we received liberal length equivalents.

In this class the professor-and-assistant system worked wonderfully well. Lehman provided the enthusiasm, and then our writing was subjected to sharp and careful criticism by two graduate students whose approach was far drier and more skeptical. Part way through the first term about a dozen students received formal invitations from the two assistants to come to tea and bring some of their work to read aloud. For this fortunate group, the course and the informal meetings became the center of their college life that year. I still have some of my papers, and they seem to me by far the freshest writing I had done so far. My style was becoming less stilted, its model more Hemingway than Stevenson. I experimented with poems, stories, and sketches, confident of enthusiastic appreciation from Lehman and demanding criticism from his assistants—an ideal combination. Both assistants became good friends of mine and pillars of the Marin hiking group— older equals from whom one could learn a lot about literature and life.

After Lehman's course I took a poetry course in which the instructor made us experiment with French forms like triolets and ballades but told me that my verse was sicklied o'er with the pale cast of thought—a trite quotation but a valid comment. Then I went on to take two successive courses in critical writing from T. K. Whipple. Whipple was one of the professors most admired by students of an intellectual bent, and his classes were full of the most ambitious undergraduate and graduate student intellectuals on the campus. He was a man of seamed and genial face, dry wit, and no professorial pomposities. At Princeton he had been a friend of Edmund Wilson, who once called Whipple's *Spokesmen* "the best book about the contemporary writers." Whipple regarded himself as primarily a writer, and warned us with a grim smile that if we wanted to follow that path we must at all costs avoid becoming professors. We commented on each other's essays, he commented on ours, and occasionally he brought in a piece he was working on for our criticism. One of his essays that I remember was called "Literature in the Doldrums" and was about to be published in the *New Republic*. We all thought it splendid and tried to make it our model. Whipple was, like most of the students in his classes, a socialist with Popular Front leanings. Yet at one point when we were all arguing about proletarian literature and the fascist unconscious, he made us read James Thurber's essay "What the Leftists Are Saying." This sounded embarrassingly like a session of our class. At another point, when we started saying that some contemporary novel was a great book, he made us read a Greek play and *Samson Agonistes* to revise our standards.

Whipple was a wonderful teacher, and his dry, witty style a fine contrast to Lehman's easy flow of sentiment. Yet as I read over what I wrote in Whipple's classes I find my work conventional and pretentious. This is partly because I was awed both by Whipple and by my classmates, some of them older and all of them in my judgment more sophisticated than I was, and was trying hard to write and think like them. It is distressing but true, moreover, that when I look now at Whipple's own essays I find them flat and dated, full of the standard correct sentiments of the day. "Literature in the Doldrums" proclaimed that the literature based on Proust, Joyce, and Eliot was dead, along with the blood-thinking of Hemingway, Faulkner, and Jeffers. What was needed was "plain simple, direct writing about individual American workers." I suspect now that this choice was for Whipple a matter of painful duty; his real loyalties were with the tradition he condemned.

After having taken all the writing courses I could, I went back to history. I liked history for two reasons. I had begun to think about such matters as wars, changing societies, and revolutions, and history dealt with these. More important, though I never would have admitted this to myself, was the old fascination with the past because it was the past, because it was different, because it had or seemed to have a structure and a story. In the more advanced history courses I heard some good lecturers and acquired a lot of factual knowledge about the Middle Ages and modern Europe. (The history of the United States was starved at Cal because of the influence of Herbert Eugene Bolton, who thought one should study the Americas as a single unit.) I was exposed to some teachers who had done some thinking about war and revolution and their origins, and to

196

some who had not. I ended with a very conventional but arduous research paper on an obscure recent treaty, and with a lot of reading, both wide and shallow, for a comprehensive honors examination on European and American history.

I think now that I took far too much history; I should have roamed around the campus, sampling for instance its excellent offerings in anthropology. Fortunately, even for a determined A student there was time for education beyond classes. What was going on in my mind, in class and even more outside, was a sudden immersion in two very different cultural movements, those of the 1920s and 1930s, both at once. Some books many of us read were powerful examples of each of these two movements; a few brought them together. Among books of the twenties, Joseph Wood Krutch's *The Modern Temper,* published almost at the end of the decade and read by me in Lehman's course, epitomized the elegant disillusion of the postwar period. Krutch described the successive failure of all the illusions man had tried to live by—religion, humanism, the beneficence of nature, the ability of science to answer human needs, finally love and art. "There impends for the human spirit," Krutch announced, "either extinction or a readjustment more stupendous than any made before." Krutch was not hopeful about the possibility of such a readjustment; his own conclusions were stoical. In passing he admitted, without seeming to care much, that the world might be taken over by some kind of childish and confident barbarians—perhaps the Russians—who had not yet realized the hopelessness of any struggle.

In a very different style, Hemingway's novels and stories, then universally admired, taught part of the same lesson—the indifference of nature to human needs. The poetry of Jeffers made nature not indifferent, but malign. Another part of Krutch's message—the failure and collapse of modern culture—was marvelously conveyed in the early poetry of Eliot,

"Prufrock," "The Waste Land," and the shorter poems, whose musical cadences I dearly loved. Dipping back to an earlier kind of decadence, I also drew a sensual pleasure from A. E. Housman's bleak, elegant evocations of youth, illusion, and death. Some of us considered it our duty to plow through Spengler, who told us that among the most beautiful colors were those of the inevitable sunset through which we were living. Reaching strenuously toward all the sophistication of which we were capable, we read (without fully understanding) the stories and novels of Thomas Mann, some of them profound parables of cultural decline.

On the other hand, many students I knew also read John Strachey's *The Coming Struggle for Power* (1933), a boiling-down of Marxism and Leninism that went part way with Krutch. Strachey too was concerned to demonstrate the decline of culture—in his terms, of bourgeois culture. Capitalism was dying, rapidly and inevitably, and with it the culture it had created. Most current writers and artists were conscious apologists for dying imperialism. Of these the worst were those who considered themselves liberals or socialists. This was just before the development of the Popular Front: social democracy was "by far the most formidable obstacle" to the victory of the workers. But Strachey was a man of the thirties, and the outcome was not a matter for either despair or doubt. Certainly the victory of the revolution would entail much bloodshed and suffering, but once it was achieved man's prospects were unlimited. Art and science, at last in the service of all, would reach new heights. Among the strong possibilities was, in the end, the "indefinite postponement" of death itself.

Not many were able to believe that the revolution would abolish death, but some said that individual death would simply become unimportant. A poem of Stephen Spender, whose first slim volumes together with those of Auden I bought at

the Sather Gate Bookstore, expresses this view so typically
that it is worth quoting at length:

THE FUNERAL

Death is another milestone on their way.
With laughter on their lips and with winds blowing round
   them
They record simply
How this one excelled all others in making driving belts.

This is festivity, it is the time of statistics
When they record what one unit contributed:
They are glad as they lay him back in the earth
And thank him for what he gave them.

They walk home remembering the straining red flags,
And with pennons of song still fluttering through their blood
They speak of the world state
With its towns like brain-centres and its pulsing arteries.

They think how one life hums, revolves and toils,
One cog in a golden and singing hive:
Like spark from fire, its task happily achieved,
It falls away quietly.

No more are they haunted by the individual grief
Nor the crocodile tears of European genius,
The decline of a culture
Mourned by scholars who dream of the ghosts of Greek boys.

Certainly nobody I knew, probably not Stephen Spender
himself and perhaps no human being anywhere, was able
fully to reach the new consciousness proclaimed by this
poem. Yet the basic message of hope coming from the movement for drastic social change affected us deeply and gave
some support for the natural cheerfulness of youth. Things
were terrible, but they were going to get much better. Perhaps this conclusion was not so far after all from the nine-

teenth-century optimism my father had learned (and only partly believed) at Harvard. For the thirties, however, the inevitable forward movement was to come through cataclysm and not through orderly evolution. In any case, cynicism was regarded as old-fashioned, associated with the bygone and self-indulgent twenties. Hope and even—without its old religious supports—morality were part of being truly modern. Morality did not mean a return to Victorian sexual standards—about such matters we were somewhat confused.

Our belief in cataclysm and our effort to believe in a new social dawn were fed not only by books but also by our reading of current events. The deepening depression made many doubt that capitalism could recover. Some hoped for peaceful change through the New Deal, but the left was able to point to Roosevelt's failure to make a major impact on unemployment. In Europe fascism, moving from one triumph to another, was plausibly interpreted as the last struggle against socialism: "Capitalism plus Murder." Somehow, hostility to fascism and support of China and the Spanish republic had to be combined with the most powerful legacy of the twenties, the nearly universal hate and fear of war. These sentiments continued to be fed by novels, plays, and emotionally powerful movies. Signs carried at campus demonstrations called for SCHOOLS NOT BATTLESHIPS but also urged us to SUPPORT THE SPANISH PEOPLE. The paradox was resolved by Marxist analysts: all opposition to war was good, but war would finally be ended only by the triumph of socialism everywhere.

Nearly all young people I met were in favor of labor organization and social reform, and against war and fascism. Middle-aged conservatives were regarded as benighted and pitiable; young conservatives as monsters. Campus political argument was carried on between New Dealers on one side and Marxists on the other. Communism, fully accepted only by a small minority, tugged effectively at our Protestant or Jewish consciences (I did not know many Catholics). The Communists were the people who really cared, who moved from words to action, who had guts and were willing to suffer if necessary. They had, moreover, a theory that seemed to make sense of all human history. I remember that when a Communist acquaintance told me that the social revolution was the only thing worth thinking about today, I answered—fresh from my history courses—that this was just like saying, in the Middle Ages, that all that mattered was the church. "Of course," was the answer, "that was *right* then." The books we read challenged the view of history taken for granted in many of our classes, a view that took for granted the progress of Western civilization from the Middle Ages through the Reformation and the rise of liberalism to American democracy. R. H. Tawney associated the Reformation with avarice, Harold Laski linked the rise of liberalism with exploitation, Charles Beard was powerfully ambivalent about the triumph of America. Part of our anticapitalism was aesthetic in origin. Sinclair Lewis had taught us to hate Babbittry. Now we found a theoretical basis for this emotion. Babbitt, the symbol of American commercial culture, whose face we could see all around us in the magazines, whose voice we could hear on the radio, was not only repellent, he was also doomed by history.

When I came to college in 1933 the Communist parties of the world were still in their "third period" of ultra-militance. Much of their effort went into attacking the socialist parties of Europe and the American New Deal as "social fascism." Liberals were the most subtle and therefore the most deadly defenders of the status quo. In 1934, of course, following the disastrous triumph of German fascism over Communists and socialists alike, this line was sharply changed to that of the Popular Front. Socialists, liberals, New Dealers, religious reformers, and pacifists were all courted and, up to a point, approved. On the Berkeley campus this change was dramatically reflected. The old, uncompromising Social Problems Club had disappeared. The characteristic new organization was the American Student Union, which invited everybody to join together who was against war, for civil liberties, and in favor of student aid. Who could oppose any of these positions? Few students, in the earlier period, had been able to believe that Roosevelt was an ally of the Fascists; now they were free to see him as a valuable leader whose reelection was crucial. Those who hesitated to join the Communists—by far the majority—were told that as long as they were against fascism, history would inevitably lead them along the right path.

There have been many arguments about the degree of power attained among intellectuals in the thirties by the Communists, and I do not want to exaggerate it. On the Berkeley campus there were still lots of students who gave little thought to politics, but the politically conscious minority was steadily growing both in numbers and prestige. Even within this minority only a few went all the way with the Communists. In college I never seriously considered joining the Party, nor did my friends—I and some of them were to come closer a few years later. Doubtless caution played a part in this: so did style. The Communists we knew were too serious, intense, and sectarian for most middle-class young Americans, and most Cal students came from the middle class. Yet the questions raised by the Communists powerfully stirred our tender consciences. One had constantly to explain, to others and to oneself, why one would not accept the Communist demand to join the group that meant what it said, that went in for action and not just talk. Self-doubt comes easy to adolescents. Was I, in hanging back, really a fake, a coward, a careerist?

It is curious, and something I cannot explain, how little

Russia meant to most of us. Russia had solved unemployment; Russia was against war. Of course there were blemishes in the beleaguered country of revolution. The purge trials, then bringing down in bizarre self-destruction most of the Bolshevik heroes of the past, were explained and justified with truly surprising facility, though lingering doubts remained in the back of our minds. As I read now the memoirs of contemporaries brought up in radical New York, for instance Alfred Kazin and Irving Howe, I am conscious of one important difference between their political education and mine. In New York, in circles with a long tradition of radical argument, the Trotskyists and other left opponents of the Communist party were strong contenders; in Berkeley these were surprisingly weak. My friends and I hardly realized that such powerful intellectuals as Edmund Wilson had already moved in and out of the Communist orbit. In the period of the Popular Front (1934–39) there were in my student circles two possible political choices—to remain a liberal or New Dealer, the choice to which most of us uneasily clung; or to move on in what seemed the same direction, through socialism to Communism, the final, serious revolutionary commitment that demanded the whole person.

The appeal of Communism was heightened by the nearby radical culture of San Francisco. This centered around the waterfront unions, which had dramatically demonstrated their power in the General Strike of 1934. It had its own folklore and its charismatic leader, Harry Bridges. The Communist party played a major part in San Francisco radicalism, but the tone of the movement was both less intellectual and less rigid than that of Communism in New York or Chicago. From the newspapers, as well as from Steinbeck's *In Dubious Battle,* we learned that in the agricultural towns of California vigilantes beat up trade unionists and Communists alike.

On the campus the Movement, which meant Communists, socialists, left liberals, and sometimes religious pacifists, centered its efforts on the annual Peace Strike. For weeks before the day of the strike, leaflets distributed at Sather Gate appealed to students to leave their eleven o'clock classes on a certain date and attend a mass meeting against war and fascism. The strike was unintentionally promoted by the San Francisco press, alert to the menace of student radicalism and eager to report its every manifestation. The university administration of Robert Gordon Sproul played an uneasy middle role, preaching the importance of free speech but also arguing for balance and restraint, bargaining with student radicals about such matters as the number of speakers, trying to limit the damage to the University's support among conservative legislators. Professors were urged to take roll in lecture classes scheduled for the hour of the strike. Roll-taking was against university tradition and most did not comply; a few supported the strike by finding some reason to dismiss their classes. In 1936 and 1937 the strike became a major campus event, drawing more and more support from the official student government. On the Day a good crowd of sympathizers and the curious—perhaps three or four thousand—gathered at Sather Gate to hear the powerful voice of Norman Thomas. Cameras flashed, taking pictures of the crowd for small-town newspapers that wanted the University divided into a number of small colleges, all to be located in towns outside the Bay Area. We were convinced that our faces were also being recorded, for possible reprisal, by university cameramen. Many cheered, a few heckled. Once the loudspeaker cable was cut— we believed at the instigation of the ROTC instructors.

Compulsory ROTC furnished the ideal permanent issue for the movement. There were those who suggested that the boring hours spent in sloppy close-order drill or listless classes in map reading or military history had a valuable pacifist effect. Most, however, disliked anything military and anything compulsory. The board of regents unwisely and, as it turned out, inaccurately insisted that the University's land-grant obligations included compulsory ROTC.

An incident in 1936 brought liberals and radicals together, and brought me to my first real participation in protest. The city of Berkeley suddenly decided that an ordinance hitherto believed to regulate the distribution of door-to-door commercial literature made the distribution of leaflets illegal. Eighteen students were arrested for handing out peace pamphlets at Sather Gate. Since there were few other means for publicity available, this seemed clearly to raise constitutional issues. A Communist I had argued with, who was also a very attractive and intelligent girl, called me up at home that night and urged me to be at Sather Gate the next day to distribute more leaflets in defiance of the ordinance. I did not want to get arrested, but could see no way to turn this down that would not show me up as a weak-kneed liberal who did not mean what he said. The next morning I appeared at Sather Gate, got my leaflets, and handed one of the first to a policeman who, to my surprise, did not arrest me. So many people were handing out leaflets that the ordinance became unenforceable. It had been denounced by liberals throughout the state and its constitutionality seemed clearly in question. The city council repealed the ordinance and the case against the eighteen was dropped. This victory, stirring at the time, was remembered by some almost thirty years later when restrictions on political activity at Sather Gate brought on the massive revolt of the Free Speech Movement.

On a loftier literary level, the clash between activists and old-fashioned liberals disrupted the English Club, a more or less bohemian honor society within which students and faculty associated on easy, almost equal terms. I was elected to the English Club in my junior year and enjoyed the meetings, at which red wine and Monterey jack were served in faculty

houses, and the annual banquet, when professors made mildly
ribald speeches. The English Club took pride in putting on art
exhibits and Greek plays. Why not, somebody suggested, put
on socially radical plays and exhibits of antiwar posters. To
some of the older members this seemed humorless and inappropriate, contrary to the Club's nonpolitical traditions. Nothing could have dramatized much better the clash between two
literary cultures, identified by many with the twenties and
thirties respectively.

Conservative opponents of the movement talked a lot
about Americanism. Actually, the radicalism of the Popular
Front period helped to lead me and many others into a lasting
love affair with this country. At the beginning was the powerful voice of Walt Whitman, encountered by me in Lehman's
course. An undiscriminating love of nature, of the people,
and of romantic democracy was strong medicine for my generation of inhibited middle-class youth, as for many before
and after. The United States in the thirties was still a country
of diverse regions, and distinct folk cultures persisted in some
of them. These were described in some of the guides published by the WPA. American folksong and folk art had been
discovered by scholars in the twenties, and now radicals,
among others, learned to sing the songs of cowboys, railroad
men, Kentucky mountaineers, militant Wobblies, and op-
pressed blacks. First-rate novelists and poets in several regions
brought new landscapes and lifestyles into literature. Jeffers
showed us the Big Sur as a coast "crying out for tragedy,"
Steinbeck brought alive the richness and latent violence of the
small coastal valleys. In California as elsewhere young people
of a literary bent, hitherto obsessed with the glories of Europe, realized with pride and excitement that their own country had its culture also, a culture still open to exploration.

As I think over my first exposure to political radicalism, at
Cal in the thirties, I find little in it to regret. I was never to be

a serious Marxist, though for years I tried hard to become one. I think that I never had the kind of mind that could find the key to human motivation and behavior in any single social—or for that matter psychological—theory. My natural tendency was both eclectic and romantic—I did not have the passionate need for full understanding that may be the hallmark of the real intellectual.

In the particular positions taken by Berkeley radicalism there were plenty of contradictions and some supreme foolishness, topped by the easy explaining away of Stalin's cruelties, then at their height. Yet the intent and spirit of the movement at Cal were humane and libertarian; even the Communists went in more for positive emotional appeal than for bitter denunciation. There is no question that the movement broadened our education. Everything that was happening—in Spain and Ethiopia and Detroit, in American politics, in literature and the arts—was important and relevant. Each of us was a responsible citizen of the world, with the duty of making up his mind, joining with others, taking action. Each person's decisions and actions would make a difference, however slight, in changing the world. This was more than a theory, it was a faith and a way of life. Even those who could never quite believe it all still remember its powerful attraction.

Of course social concerns never entirely displaced individual ambition. I was still trying hard to become a writer. Following the high school advice of Miss Power, I continually sent manuscripts to magazines, and among a host of rejection slips received a few acceptances. The *American Scholar* accepted two long poems, and *Poetry* two short ones written in

Miss Power's class. Perhaps better, I got a letter from Robert Penn Warren at the *Southern Review* telling me that though they weren't accepting my work it was "on the right track." My poems had become somewhat less vague and moony. Still a romantic at heart, I tried to be rougher, more realistic, more of the thirties. Auden, whom I most admired of thirties poets, was far too difficult a model for me to imitate. I think I sounded, instead, all too much like Archibald MacLeish in his brief radical period, or when I wrote about my new excitement about America, like Stephen Vincent Benét. I tried hard also to write short stories, most of them autobiographical. One, dealing with a hesitant middle-class student confronting the Cal radical movement, was nearly accepted by *Scribners.* But I realized I had little talent for fiction.

In my junior year, to my great joy, I was suddenly invited by the staff of the *Occident,* the campus literary magazine, to become editor. This gave me an office in Eshleman Hall and a salary of fifty dollars a year from the Associated Students, which also paid our printing bill if ads and subscriptions were insufficient. Football receipts and student activity fees could cover the costs of literary experiment almost without anyone's noticing. The *Occident* had been ultra-highbrow and had lost circulation for several years. I tried to make it into something like a campus review, printing experimental student work but also a few essays on campus issues. I also tried to put the magazine in touch with the outside literary world. We published a letter from John Steinbeck, an interview with Lincoln Steffens (a great hero of young California radicals), and an account of study with Diego Rivera by a student painter. A freshman on our staff, later a well-known poet, was an acquaintance of Gertrude Stein, and she was kind enough to send us an unpublished story—and a good one. We were printed on good paper and illustrated with woodcuts.

We worked hard, had a wonderful time, and I think reached a circulation of eight hundred.

The *Occident* staff overlapped with that of the *Pelican,* the college humor magazine, which was of course far more popular and, as I sensed even then, had more talented writers. I was pleased to get some light poems in the Pelly and became friendly with its editors. Through a girl friend (I'll come to her later) I also had some acquaintance with the Little Theater crowd, whose annual Mask and Dagger Revue in these years reached a high standard of cleverness. Meantime, plugging hard in classes, I got excellent grades and was elected student president of Phi Beta Kappa. I was one of the University's candidates for a Rhodes scholarship, which was won by one of my best friends. By my senior year I was, in a special way, almost a prominent student, though too bookish quite to be accepted among the Big Men on Campus. I was very pleased with myself in most ways.

What I was not pleased with was my progress in the quest for sexual liberation, a topic one could talk about only with good friends, preferably late at night. The mores of the time are hard to explain to people who have lived through the sexual revolution of the 1960s. On the surface all of us tried our best to seem liberated. One could tell most jokes in mixed company. We had at least a second-hand knowledge of Freud and believed that repression was evil. And yet the popular songs to which we danced were mostly about longing and frustration. They expressed our feelings, even about the girls we held in our arms as we shuffled solemnly around. Of course, some students I knew achieved an active sex life. For many, however, theoretical liberation was a thin layer over accumulated shyness and self-doubt. I had a long way to go to overcome the puritanism in which I had been brought up—if I may be a bit fanciful, the Attleborough inheritance. Something we learned about in books and talked about freely was homosexuality. Nobody admitted homosexual leanings, but I knew a couple of boys who were generally believed to belong in this category. I was subject to strong emotional rushes of feeling directed toward contemporaries of both sexes, and sometimes I worried about my direction or destiny.

In my junior year I met Jane. She was active in Little Theater. She was also cheerful, warm-hearted, popular, and pretty. Very intelligent and interested in literature, she was a bit anti-intellectual—at least she disliked the pompous campus intellectuals and tried, as we got to know each other, to get me over my tendency to wordiness and conceit. Once, lying on a hill overlooking the campus, we talked about maybe getting married some day. She thought she probably would like this, if only I was not going to be a professor. We were together a lot and everybody in my circle assumed that she was and would remain my girl.

Suddenly Jane told me that she and her parents had decided she was going to spend her last year at Occidental, a small college in southern California. Whether this decision had anything to do with our involvement, I am not sure. Her letters from Los Angeles are full of affection. They indicate, as I read them over now, that I was important to her but that she was still troubled by my bookish side and my tendency toward making complicated critical judgments of everything—including her. She gave me a lot of good advice—to move away from home, not to go to graduate school right away after college but to get some temporary job and knock around a while. She was taking mostly commercial courses, had and enjoyed a part-time job at an excellent Los Angeles store, and was thinking of going to the New York School of Merchandising. We wondered how it would be if I was in New York too.

When it came time for graduation I asked her to come up for Senior Week, a time of incessant festivities—dances, barbecues, and so forth, culminating in the all-night Senior Ball. She came, and we had a splendid time, but the constant parties provided little time for real intimacy and, far more important, I was not yet ready to break through my self-imposed barriers. After the Senior Ball my friends and I took her to the Southern Pacific Station in San Francisco to catch a morning train back to Los Angeles. Almost my last memory of her is her gallant walk down the platform, her long dress sweeping the dust and the gardenias on her bosom a rich brown. She carried it off well and the commuters laughed and applauded. Somehow, over the summer our relation failed to define itself and gradually lapsed.

Almost any young person today would ask why we did not try living together. That was not an option open to any but the very boldest spirits then. Perhaps if we had both gone to New York, she to merchandising school and I to pursue my writing ambitions, something like that would have developed—perhaps not. If I had boldly decided to follow that road, I might well have found some job, and I probably would have had more pieces accepted for publication. Eventually, however, I think I would have decided that I belonged in graduate school, and she would not have gone with me. What is certain is that I would have grown up faster than I did. My only real regret is not that I did not take this road but that, through indecision and sheer immaturity, I gave something of a bad time to an excellent girl.

Thinking hard about going to graduate school and inclining toward Harvard, I discussed the matter in letters with Bill Leary, whom I had met at the San Francisco interviews for the Rhodes scholarship. He had been a candidate from UCLA, a first-year graduate student and a teaching assistant in English. After the extremely tense interviews, waiting for the decision, we went to see an art show and struck up a friendship. His advice to me has so much good sense and realism, and was so well borne out by my later experience, that I want to quote it.

I once had a romantic idea about teachers and their profession. My common sense told me that it couldn't be true. This year I found out for myself that it isn't. But the worst of it is that every other profession is exactly the same. Since this is true, and since we all insist on living and consequently eating, the only thing to do is to find the thing you like to do most, or—and I'm not sure that this isn't closer to the truth—the thing you dislike to do least. I feel that I should apologize for this sententious blah; undoubtedly you know all this as well or better than I do. [Here he was wrong.] But here is something that you may not fully realize. I am sincerely convinced that the teaching profession is, when undertaken seriously and honestly, the hardest job in the world. This is especially true today when the preparation for the job is continually being made longer and more difficult. There are only two types of people who can take a Ph.D. at a major institution: a really brilliant man, and one who has an infinite capacity for hard work. And then, worst of all, presuming that you fit into one of these types and get your degree, you are by no means assured of a good job—OR OF ANY JOB. And while I'm throwing on the water I may as well tell you this. According to those men in our English department who are Harvard men, that venerable institution seldom (they say never) grants a scholarship to a man from another school until he has been in residence at Harvard for a semester or two and has proved his worth—then the school is his. If this is true, it means that you will have to have enough money to support yourself for a year if you decide on Harvard. Furthermore (the tale becomes increasingly dolorous) you may as well go to Harvard if you entertain any desire to find yourself with a job after getting your Ph.D., for, no matter what you hear to the contrary, this school holds the key to 99 out of every hundred worthwhile jobs in the U.S. This is the sum of the bitter tale. It obviously throws the impecunious students (which is I—is it you?) into a bad dilemma.

Bill, wrestling with this dilemma, decided to take a master's degree at UCLA with enough units in education to qualify him for a job in a junior college. There, he thought, he would either settle down to a pleasant enough humdrum life including marriage and children or save all the money he could and go to Harvard later, where, he predicted, "I shall undergo the same unpleasant existence for a number of years—years that will undoubtedly complete the ruin of my stomach as well as my temper, and wind up with the coveted mealticket, a Ph.D., and the vague hope that it will get me a plate of beans once a day. Then, if I am not too old and the hormones are still making themselves heard, I shall marry etc. etc." This was much too realistic for me, and apparently my answer slightly irritated Bill. His next letter took me to task:

. . . my boy (I am feeling damned paternal these days—my brother just got married) you billow like a goddam Don Quixote about things you don't understand. I refer, of course, to your effusions anent careers, life, and other sundries. Henry, you are young, romantic, and an undergraduate. Apparently you are such a guy as forgets that the most essential thing in this lousy 20th century world of ours is security. Very well, tilt your lance vs windmills and you may pull the old shack down and be a hero.*

Despite Jane's preferences and Bill's realistic advice, and despite my own romantic hankerings to try my hand at free-lance writing, I decided on an academic career. History, after all, was a kind of writing. It was also, I convinced myself, relevant to the social crisis. Yet my ambivalence about this

*Bill Leary, much as he had predicted, had a harder struggle than I did because of his early lack of funds, but achieved a distinguished teaching and writing career. He gives me permission to quote these letters with some reluctance, because he is embarrassed by their slightly world-weary tone—in my opinion entirely forgivable in a very young man.

choice was to last a long time. I now think that it was the right one for me, though it might have been a good idea to go to New York and try writing for a while. I would probably eventually have found myself in graduate school, but I might have learned a lot about myself and my abilities in the meantime.

Bill had convinced me that Harvard was the best bet. It also had a glamorous sound, and perhaps I was influenced more than I knew by my father's example. I set systematically about the dreary business of applying for scholarships and taking tests. I was admitted but received no financial support. Unlike Bill, I was not quite without resources. My father, in richer days, had set aside for me a bond that was now worth nine hundred dollars. (To have used this simply to live on while I was trying to write would have taken a much more liberated spirit than I could muster.) The Harvard Club of San Francisco, after an embarrassing ceremony in which they hung a pink ribbon around my neck (in token of immaturity? a start on the way to crimson?) gave me a scholarship of two hundred dollars. With the eleven hundred, I had what Bill said was needed—enough to pay the tuition and to support myself frugally for a year.

Very excited about the prospect of actually seeing the romantic and exotic places indicated on my long green train ticket—Ogden, Omaha, Council Bluffs, Chicago, Albany—I set off in company with my friend Bruce, who had won the Rhodes and was on his way to Oxford. My mother managed not to cry. A good crowd saw the two of us off at the Berkeley Union Pacific Station, singing the songs of our Marin County hikes.

The four years that ended that morning had been good ones. I had encountered twentieth-century culture, sharpened some literary skills, and even got a good grounding in European history. (I had decided to get my degree in American history, about which I knew much less, because of my new infatuation with the U.S.A.) Probably more important, I had had a good time, made some friends, and begun—only begun—to dispel some of the fears and self-doubts I had accumulated at University High and earlier. Yet the welcome sunshine and geniality of Cal, and the fact that I lived comfortably but unadventurously at home, had blunted some of the necessary lessons of growing up. What Lehman had said about Cal students in general, and what Jane had fully understood about me in particular, was quite true. For my age, I was reasonably well-developed intellectually and very immature emotionally. No doubt my father or his father would have said I needed some adversity to toughen me up. In the next chapter I got it.

12

Cambridge Winters

It was during my four years at Harvard Graduate School that I finally began to grow up. Instead of the reassuring and badly needed geniality of the Berkeley campus, Cambridge provided me with a series of intense experiences, bad and good. During my first two years, when I lived at Perkins Hall, I learned to survive in what seemed to me a hostile environment. My second two years, in Dunster House, were probably the most exciting and important of my life, and ended with a major transforming experience.

My new life started in September 1937 with five days on the train, sitting up in the chair car. I was to make six such trips in the next three years, each time by a different route. A round trip, Berkeley to Boston, cost ninety dollars, whether one went by Chicago, New Orleans, or Kansas City. These names stirred my imagination as much as though my ticket had read via Venice, Paris, or Peking.

The first night or two on the train I always tossed and twisted, trying to find a comfortable position. One way was to stick your suitcase diagonally into the aisle and put your feet on it. Inevitably the conductor, making his rounds, stumbled and scolded, but one did get to stretch one's legs. Another far more sophisticated trick was to occupy one of the leather couches in the men's lounge outside the toilet at the end of the car, holding it against all comers from late afternoon through the night. In any case, after the first two days I always stopped caring and dozed groggily on and off, day and night.

On the first trip, following the standard Union Pacific route, I remember dawn over the rolling prairies of Wyoming, rushing to the Art Institute between the two Chicago stations, the green and domesticated scenery of upstate New York and the Berkshires, with their small white houses and red barns. On other trips I saw the cactus on the Arizona desert, the dizzying splendors of the Royal Gorge, the huge new Grand Coulee Dam in Washington State. Most exotic of all was the South, with its brown rivers choked with blue hyacinths, its hillside cotton patches and shacks. I spent three days learning the sights, smells, and tastes of New Orleans, seeing in the Cabildo the exhibits about the horrors of Reconstruction and the great accomplishments of Huey P. Long, even plucking up my courage to dance, belly to belly, with the girls in tight black dresses who poured your beer in every bar in the Vieux Carré.

For all the people on the train, I felt a warm, facile, Whitmanian affection. People shifted around in the coach, forming congenial groups, sometimes passing a bottle. Coach passengers were allowed to eat in the dining car, and though you were not supposed to use the club car, usually nobody bothered you if you ordered a drink. Among my choicer companions I remember a gnarled Czech woman going to visit the old country (it was 1937 and I later wondered what happened to her), a New Mexico student who taught me some southwestern folksongs, and a very friendly man just out of San Quentin for robbery. He lent old ladies his pillows and everybody liked him. In the middle of the night he got off at some small stop, accompanied by a pretty girl he had just met. The next morning the police came through the car looking for somebody's missing wallet. Middle-aged ladies told me about their troubles with their daughters-in-law. The wife of a jazz drummer was going home to her mother because she couldn't stand all the dope. In Alabama a young man agreed with me about oppression by big business. He had once, he said, even been in favor of the Spanish loyalists. Then he had met one, who told him that he would just as soon have dinner with a nigger as a white man. My companion hit this crazy bastard, and since then he had had no use for the Spanish Republic. From him and many others I got an inkling that America's problems were more complicated and less tractable than my Berkeley friends had thought.

My first impressions of Cambridge were entirely favorable. The late September weather was sunny with a hint of crispness in the air that was quite new to me. The red brick Harvard buildings *all* seemed old and beautiful to my untrained eye. The sights of Boston—the Old State House, the Old North Church—now seemed almost up to my childhood memories of Europe. Perkins Hall, with its long stone corridors and iron steps, did indeed seem a bit forbidding. Yet since I had not been away to college, it was interesting to buy second-hand furniture and hang red curtains. I was rooming with Seymour, the son of a classics professor at the University of Vermont, who as a Yale graduate knew the eastern ropes. I had met him and liked him in Berkeley, and he knew many of my Berkeley friends.

Forewarned by my mother about the requirements of calling cards and party calls (perhaps a bit out of date in 1937 even in Boston) I set out dutifully—far too dutifully—to meet my father's surviving relatives and friends and their children in Boston. I did not know how any of them fitted into his life, and I could not ask him. It would have meant a lot to both of us if we could have talked about Harvard and Boston. This was impossible: for the last couple of years his mind had been failing ever more rapidly. During one of my summer vacations from Harvard he was to ask whether I had met the wonderful old man who lived in that big white house. By that time I had learned enough Harvard lore to know that he meant Charles Eliot Norton, professor of fine arts from 1873 to 1897.

Though I didn't know who they were in terms of my father's life, the cousins and friends were all kind and hospitable. They were hardly the companions I wanted and needed, but their houses were a contrast to Perkins Hall and their ways taught me a lot about upper- and middle-class Boston, still stubbornly Bostonian. One of my first calls was on Mr. Worcester and his still unmarried sister Margaret, about whom I was much later to learn so much from my father's diary. In letters home I describe Mr. Worcester as the handsomest old man I had ever met, with a strong face and long white hair. He enjoyed talking about my father's Cambridge days, and I wish I could remember what he said. *Miss* Worcester did not talk about my father. Mrs. Lane was the widow of my father's other close friend, Will Lane, who had become the Harvard librarian. She lived in a big house very near Perkins Hall. There were hospitable cousins in Boston and the Newtons.

The Boston connection I saw the most of, however, was Miss Gertrude Baker, the daughter of still another of my father's classmates, Ezra Henry Baker. Miss Baker lived on Marlborough Street with her friend Miss Mary Lothrop. She had just closed her own house and insisted that I "store" some of her furniture in our Perkins rooms. I accepted this offer, and a truck delivered a huge and appropriately shabby sofa and Morris chair, both upholstered in royal blue. These additions made our room far the most comfortable on the hall.

The Misses Baker and Lothrop lived in a handsome house in the heart of Back Bay. From the entrance one took a little gilt elevator up to the bay-windowed living room on the second floor. In the dining room a portrait of President Kirkland,* a Lothrop relative, looked down at us gravely as Sunday dinner was served by a pair of elderly maids in deep red uniforms with white aprons. In spite of Miss Lothrop's kindly efforts, dinner conversation with a young man from the unimaginable West could be a little stiff. Miss Lothrop and her other guests were experts on who used to have what box at the opera. Once, when people were discussing what would happen to Groton after Peabody left, Miss Lothrop tried to include me: "And where did *you* go to school, Mr. May?" "University High School, Oakland." There was no possible answer but "Oh, I see." John P. Marquand's *The Late George Apley* had just been published, but Miss Lothrop and her friends could not see why anybody would want to read it: "It's just what we've always known." Harvard was always "the college," as in "What year was Mr. X in the college?" "He didn't go to college, he went to Yale." It was hard for Miss Lothrop to understand just what I was doing at the college. "Not the law school, not the business school, surely not the divinity school?" "No, Miss Lothrop, I'm studying history." "Really; is that *all?*" This was an answer I treasured and repeated in Cambridge.

Miss Lothrop said she was tired of her Packard, which she described as "something between a truck and a hearse," and thought of changing to a Buick. The ladies were an impressive sight, however, sitting in the Packard as I once saw them on their way to a North Shore vacation. In the back seat were Miss Lothrop, Miss Baker, and Miss Lothrop's little dog; in the front the chauffeur and a maid holding the cat. Miss

*John Thornton Kirkland, president of Harvard from 1810 to 1838.

Baker, whose conversation was always both lively and tactful, often took me to the Chilton Club to dinner and once to opening night at the opera. I, of course, wore the tuxedo I had bought for the high school senior prom. We had orchestra seats for *Falstaff*, and I wrote home that mine was the only black tie below the fourth balcony. I added some details:

There was a woman in a pink dress with a green wig and a woman in a green dress with a pink wig. I thought that was a bit un-Bostonian, and Miss Baker explained that since the Opera had reopened, every sort of person came, the people one did know and the people one doesn't know. I thought hurray for the people one doesn't know; what Boston needs is a little more green and pink hair, but it turned out the next day in the paper that they were sent out by some store to advertise their clothes.

Of the other family friends I will mention only Mrs. Pinckney Holbrook, who frequently invited me to her evenings of reading Shakespeare aloud in her Cambridge apartment overlooking the Charles. Mrs. Holbrook read Cleopatra and Lady Macbeth, while her patient husband covered several parts such as Second Porter. The arbiter of questions of interpretation was Miss Charmian Kittredge, the daughter of the great Professor Kittredge, my father's college friend.

All this was educational if not exactly hilarious, but my real life those first two years in Cambridge ran on a very narrow track between Perkins Hall and Widener Library. My first impression of the graduate school was how hard people worked—far harder than anybody in Berkeley. It seemed to me that the norm was to get to Widener when it opened at nine, interrupting one's work there only for classes and meals, leaving at ten at night when the library closed. The senior graduate students were full of warnings about how dreadfully demanding the doctoral program really was. Later I noticed that those loudest in their warnings had been at it six years and more, which suggested that their advice was hardly very useful.

Ambitious for scholarships and recognition, I tried hard at first to fit into the strictest possible pattern. I gave up reading anything that was not history, even the daily papers. I never listened to the radio. I had no time for literary experiment. Politics receded to a minor place in my life. Most Perkins Hall students inclined toward the left, though to my surprise there was a sprinkling of declared Republicans. My hallmates, students of everything from classics to traffic engineering, were not an uninteresting lot. Like me, however, most of them were new to Cambridge, scared, and hell-bent for success. Among American history students, conversation tended to center around rumors about who was likely to get the one straight A given each year in the seminars of Mr. Schlesinger and Mr. Merk—the lucky fellow might well get a course assistantship. On Saturday night there were often gatherings, all male of course, in somebody's room—drunk, noisy, and depressing. A student proctor tried to keep the noise down for the benefit of those who studied even on Saturday night. His ally was the hall's porter, known to many as Honest John the Bastard, who treated the students with a semisubservient hostility.

Seymour, my roommate, was in general congenial and considerate. He was also, however, an extremely frugal Vermonter. For breakfast he insisted on having a mixture of oatmeal, prunes, and toast, prepared several days in advance and eaten in a soggy mixture. Not only did I refuse to share this, I soon decided that I could not even bear to watch *him* eat it. Most mornings I went out for coffee and a "dropped egg" (to me a poached egg) at Hayes-Bickford, whether I could afford it or not. Our other meals we took at the Episcopal Theological School on Brattle Street. These unreligious years were very hard ones for all divinity schools, and the ETS refectory kept going by serving meals to students from the law school and some other graduate students as well as the theologs. The food was substantial, satisfactory, and not very expensive. The law students, aiming at positions on the *Law Review* at least as fiercely as we at our seminar A's, spent most of their mealtimes arguing cases.

As I learned the ropes of graduate school life, things got a bit better. I realized that the students who spent the most hours in the library were not really those who got the best results. I loved the snow and made people laugh by rushing to the window whenever it started. Sitting in a carrel in the library, I spent precious minutes away from my note cards watching the big flakes drift and swirl. I learned to take the subway to Washington Street for the movies, and afterward to drink beer at Jake Wirth's. It was not until January that I discovered the Boston legitimate theater, where New York shows often opened. For fifty-five cents one could get a gallery seat, and in the next years I saw everything from Ethel Merman in *Panama Hattie* to Maurice Evans in *Hamlet*. This, at least, my father would have understood fully.

Occasionally some benevolent institution, concerned for lonely students like me, put on graduate student dances. Most, not all, of the girls were those with nowhere else to go, but they were the only girls most of us ever saw.

Best of all, and always crucial for me, I began to make some friends at the refectory and Perkins Hall. Several happened to be students of literature who had gone to Bowdoin College, in Brunswick, Maine. I could barely imagine what such a college was like—small, proudly traditional, and in Harvard's shadow. It was clear that my Bowdoin friends thought a place like Cal huge, crude, and comical. They were not at all like Berkeley intellectuals. Just as bright, they went in for cynical wit and even sometimes for Tory-aesthetic poses rather than for political idealism. They did, however, experiment with verse, and after a while we formed a group that met once in a while to criticize each other's poems. My new friends educated me in the ways of the Mysterious East. Once, for instance, when we were in a bar in Boston, a group of young men approached and asked us whether we were from Harvard. "Hell, no," one of my friends immediately answered, "We're from Holy Cross." He explained to me later that if he had told the truth we would have been beaten up.

However much I was learning, it remained an unsatisfactory life. My letters home repeatedly deny, in a revealing way, that I was unduly lonely or depressed. As winter came on, my colds tended to turn to flu or bronchitis, and I made frequent short stays in Stillman Infirmary. These I enjoyed. Most of the patients were undergraduates, less desperately serious than the inhabitants of Perkins Hall. When a newcomer entered the ward, he would be greeted by a horrible chorus of hacking or gurgling coughs. When he said he just had a cold, somebody would whisper hoarsely that that was what they had told *him* when he had come in two months ago. Girl friends would visit, and people would get out of bed and dance to the radio while the nurse wasn't looking. At worst I could lie peacefully and look out the window at the frozen Charles and the black trees, trying hard not to think about unwritten papers and approaching exams.

Inevitably, that first winter my academic struggle for success was affected by minor illness, still more by depression and loneliness, and perhaps most of all by the worst part of my own temperament, which led me to try too hard in the wrong way. The work was heavy but not impossible. One was supposed to give half one's time each term to a long research paper for a seminar, most of the rest to three courses, and whatever was left over to preparation for the all-important qualifying exams in four fields. It seemed that there were always papers due or course exams coming up.

The three major figures in American history were Professors Samuel Eliot Morison, Frederick Merk, and Arthur M. Schlesinger. My first American history seminar was with Mr. Merk, a fragile looking and saintly man who taught a famous undergraduate course on the westward movement that he had inherited from Frederick Jackson Turner, the father of the frontier theory of American history. In the Merk seminar, students worked on almost any topic, since Mr. Merk seemed to know everything about American history. One student turned in a paper of more than two hundred pages on a second-rank statesman of the 1790s. Another worked on the growth of the milk industry around Bellows Falls, Vermont. I remember that when this report was read, Mr. Merk was less gentle than usual. As often happened when he was excited, his voice rose almost to a squeak when he complained that the paper was *trunc*ated, because it stopped in 1900. My own topic, chosen after long discussion with the professor, was the attitude of the Democratic party in New Hampshire toward the Civil War. I enjoyed getting to know my way around the Granite State—in libraries; I had never been there. As I learned how doggedly the leading Democratic politicians tried to evade the great issues of slavery and union I could understand what Emerson meant when he wrote in one of his best poems:

The God who made New Hampshire
Taunted the lofty land
With little men.

I tried hard to understand how people felt, reading the changing battle news coming in daily from Virginia and the West. In true Merk-Turner style I made maps, charting the relation between poor soil and Democratic votes.

As almost any topic would have, this one awakened my dormant political feelings. Of course the abolitionists were right, and the Republicans the party of capitalist development and therefore of the future. Yet I hated war and sympathized with the citizens of Manchester or Concord who got their windows smashed because they wanted peace or because they were loyal to the party of Jackson. Since this was the spring semester I spent the Easter vacation in Worcester, living in the YMCA and reading New Hampshire newspapers all day in the library of the American Antiquarian Association.

In the first weeks of the seminar, before the papers were really started, we spent part of the time discussing the theories of Charles A. Beard. These greatly upset Mr. Merk, as they did most professors then. What shocked him was not *An Economic Interpretation of the Constitution,* which had shocked the general public in 1913. Nor was it *The Rise of American Civilization* (1927), whose rich prose and sweeping synthesis had opened for many 1920s intellectuals the possibility of a quasi-Marxist interpretation of American history. It was rather Beard's recent presidential address to the American Historical Association, "Written History as an Act of Faith." This was an essay, neither very original nor very tightly argued, in historical relativism. Following Benedetto Croce and many others, Beard suggested that there was no such thing as an objective approach to the past, and that it was best to admit and understand the "frame of reference" through which one saw and arranged the facts. A little reminiscent of William James's *Will to Believe,* this approach could enable a historian to put his faith in the future he hoped for—in Beard's case a future of democratic collectivism.

226

Democratic collectivism, like the economic interpretation of history, was probably perfectly acceptable to Mr. Merk. His own views, which he seldom directly expressed to students, were progressive and pacifist in the Wisconsin tradition. Like his teacher Turner and like most of his own academic contemporaries, Mr. Merk took it for granted that economic interest motivated most political action. What horrified him about Beard's address was the suggestion he thought he read there that the effort for historical objectivity, to which he had given his life, was futile.

When students tried, as some did, to corner Mr. Merk and ask him what history was for or why he thought it was important, he could not understand what they meant. He *loved* history, and what he loved was to get the facts straight—the precise topic did not matter at all. Jonathan Edwards would have understood. Mr. Merk was filled with what Edwards considered the only real kind of virtue—the disinterested love of being in general. He loved history for itself, not for what he could do with it. He was—nobody who looked at his face could doubt this—a nearly selfless and truly happy man.

Mr. Schlesinger, who was to be my major professor, was perhaps the most influential American historian of his day. His subject, which he more or less invented, was called American social and intellectual history. This meant the history of everything except politics. In his courses and in the massive *History of American Life* that he edited, American history was chopped into periods, in each of which all topics got equal treatment: religion, science, literature, the arts, education, sports, city transport, family life, the status of women, high society, race relations, and much more. There was little time for analysis and not much subordination of one theme to another. This last was, I think, deliberate: Mr. Schlesinger believed deeply in democratic equality and all topics, like all people, were equal. Despite the bewildering multiplicity, his courses and books told the same story: the gradual broadening of democracy and its slow but sure solution of problems. Slavery, crime, the slums, and corruption were not neglected—all these were serious faults that had been or would be gradually corrected. Nothing could have been more sharply opposed to the view I had heard among some Berkeley radicals, that reform was a palliative, designed to fool the masses. If someone had suggested this opinion to Mr. Schlesinger, I believe he would have been tolerantly amused, sure that a joke was intended.

One must admit that Mr. Schlesinger's lecture style was not exciting. One of his most admiring students, my friend Wallace E. Davies, could imitate it so well that you could almost see the five-by-eight card flipping over as he made a transition: "If the bicycle craze had reached its height and begun to decline by 1895, public libraries were just beginning to become familiar." Anyone who listened to Mr. Schlesinger's lectures learned a lot. The knowledge was chaotic and confusing, but so was American culture. It was up to the student to extract or invent a pattern.

When I got to know Mr. Schlesinger better and began to turn in thesis chapters, I found that he had an eagle eye for inadequacy of research or inaccuracy of language, but made few substantive criticisms. Yet no one in the country had as many students who turned out to be creative scholars, and each was entirely different: there was no Schlesinger pattern. His great gift was for gently guiding each student to a topic that fit his interests and abilities and then leaving him alone. Many more-exciting teachers are so passionately committed to their own ideas and methods that they can't help turning out students who imitate them, usually without the passion and without developing their own styles.

Like his other students, I was always a bit afraid of Mr. Schlesinger and had to stop, pull myself together, and swallow hard before I knocked on the door of his office in the

Widener stacks. A truly kind man, he was unable to unbend. I was pleased when, at a certain stage in our acquaintance, he began to use my first name. (To use his was unthinkable, even for well-established professors who had been his students twenty years earlier.) The next step was to be invited to tea on Sunday at his house in Gray Gardens East. We all sat in a circle and while Mrs. Schlesinger poured, Mr. Schlesinger would ask each of us serious questions about the political situation in our home states. Schlesinger was a devoted New Deal Democrat, active and effective in state politics. Later I found out that in his youth he had been a socialist. His political style, by the time I knew him, was one of sober practicality, in both history and politics.

Years later, when he came to my house in Claremont and sat with my little daughter in his lap, I caught glimpses of the warmth beneath the shyness. Whenever I asked for recommendations, his response was not only immediate but truly supportive and encouraging. After his death in 1965, when I wrote to Mrs. Schlesinger, she answered that "nobody knew the love and pride" with which he followed his students' careers. By then I knew something about the teacher-student relationship and its problems, and I knew that her statement was precisely correct. The love and pride were real, and nobody did know.

My own performance in these wearing years was mixed. I did well in seminars, where there was a premium on literary skill as well as sheer hard work. In course examinations I did badly at first. The student readers who graded papers demanded a rigorous memorization of detail and discouraged the sort of venturesome interpretation that had been acceptable at Berkeley. I tried harder and harder to remember exactly at what date cable cars were introduced in New Orleans, but always got some things wrong. In the middle of the year, when decisions were made about scholarships, my grades were not good enough for me to get one. This seemed a major disaster. I realized with a sinking feeling that I would be left with very thin pickings for the rest of my graduate career. The blow to my self-esteem was even worse. Top grades were something I had long been able to take for granted. A letter home, written on my birthday in March 1938, shows that I had hit a low point. I had a bad cold, had just got a barely passing grade in an hour exam, and came close to admitting that I really didn't like Cambridge.

The coming of warm weather helped. By spring, also, I began to learn how to handle the system and how to take time off in spite of its pressures. After a recuperative summer in Berkeley I came East again in the midst of the great New England hurricane and the Munich crisis. Stuck in a friend's house in Westchester County, I was glued to the radio to learn whether there would be war or disgraceful surrender in Europe, and when the rail lines would be open to Cambridge. My feelings about both were divided and confused. I hated Hitler and hated war. And I was not really eager to see Perkins Hall again.

I came back to Cambridge with two hundred dollars. That fall of 1938, though the work went well, I came near running clear out of money. The dean gave me the proctor's job at Perkins, which meant a free room. Now it was my turn to try to quiet down the Saturday night parties. At one of them, in the room of an acquaintance of mine, people started rolling beer cans down the metal stairs. It made a satisfying racket, and the inevitable student studying for his orals promptly complained. After a long and slightly drunken argument the party's host and I came to an agreement that saved the honor of each. He would roll one more can to show he would not take my orders, and then, entirely voluntarily, he would stop.

At the ETS I asked for a waiter's job, but found I really could not enjoy wearing a white coat and waiting on my friends. I managed to get transferred to the kitchen, where I wiped dishes as they emerged, by no means clean, from a primitive dishwasher. The refectory served a lot of peanut butter, and I have never been able to eat it since—it *always* stuck to both plates and towels.

In my classes I met two new major figures. The first was Samuel Eliot Morison, then at the height of his career. He was a splendid narrative historian, a passionate navigator who followed the course of Columbus and later explorers in his own boat, and a Boston aristocrat. It is hard to say which of these roles he took most seriously. Lecturing on the great navigators in his undergraduate course, he deplored the fact that he had to explain the elementary laws of navigation—in his day every Harvard man had known how to sail a small boat. Going over the class list with his assistant, a friend of mine, he asked whether I came from the Boston May family. My friend, who had no idea, said yes, and I found myself invited with some other students to an elegant dinner on Brimmer Street. Mr. Morison passing the cocktails—polite, charming, and only a little condescending—was quite different from the aloof, imperious lecturer. Of course, when he greeted me in class the next day his manner was exactly the same as always.

Like Schlesinger, but in his own Bostonian way, Morison was a liberal Democrat. On his office wall hung a framed letter from Bartolomeo Vanzetti. He highly approved of his acquaintance and fellow yachtsman, Franklin Roosevelt.

The other major encounter that year was with Perry Miller. As many have told us, he was a self-dramatizing, sometimes brutal figure who modeled himself after Ernest Hemingway and boasted his independence from dull academic models. He was capable of tormenting a student from the podium and then treating him as a comrade, even discussing in detail the sexual performance of his own mistress. He was also a brilliant and intuitive scholar, just then in the midst of his major enterprise—rescuing the Puritans from the writers of the twenties who blamed them for all that they most disliked in American culture: its thinness, its narrow opposition to sensuous pleasure, its morbid rigidity about sex. Denying or minimizing these faults, Miller, an atheist himself, admired the Puritans for their intellectuality and still more for the sheer courage of their theology. To Miller's Puritans, it was a logical necessity that God had decreed all that happens, including the damnation of most of the sinful human race. Sometimes envisaging their own damnation in all its graphic horror, they were yet able to delight in the full glory of God. As Miller put it, they stared straight at the great sun itself, knowing that it might blind them.

Perry Miller was a product of the literary twenties, when the tragic side of American life and literature had been rediscovered in Melville and Hawthorne and newly expressed by Dreiser, Hemingway, Jeffers, and many others. His version of the American past was thus the polar opposite of Schlesinger's, and without quite realizing it I was finding each a corrective for the other. Two years later I sat in on Miller's first course in the history of American religion, a bizarre and diverse subject then unknown to most academic historians. Once when I was sitting in the front row he made me uncomfortable—deliberately, of course—by discussing with the other students in detail the question whether in Jonathan Edwards's terms my soul was surely damned or not. Reading forgotten theological arguments once full of life and passion, learning how intellectual Calvinists and earthy revivalists battled for the nation's soul, I began to suspect that this might turn out to be the field for me.

By the end of my second year I had begun to get to know a few of the brilliant students in the brand-new field called American civilization—usually then a combination of literature and history with a little art and sociology thrown in. These, many of them products of the Harvard History and Lit program, clustered around such luminaries as Miller, F. O. Matthiessen, Kenneth Murdock, and Howard Mumford Jones. Their interests were much broader and their conversation far livelier than that of most history students. I wonder why I did not decide to join them. Perhaps because of some grim determination to fight the battle I had begun, perhaps because of some related penchant for dealing with the refractory materials of most historical research, I stuck to the history department.

One friend from the American civilization group who was to make a lot of difference in my thinking and my career was Henry Nash Smith. Henry came from Dallas and showed his southern origin in his soft speech and slightly formal manners. He was ten years older than most of my friends and far more experienced than any of us. After a first false start at Harvard as a student of English when the emphasis was on Anglo-Saxon and Gothic, he had gone back to Dallas for several strenuous years as a professor and local literary journalist. Now he had returned to Cambridge because of the American civilization program, in which he shortly got the first doctorate. I picture Henry, my other new and lifelong friend John Lydenberg, and others standing with Perry Miller on the steps of Widener Library, smoking and arguing and huddling into their jackets, with the winter sun gleaming on Henry's already partly bald head. They were, of course, taking a short break and would soon go back to their carrels in the stacks.

In the spring of 1939 I got wonderful news. First I learned that I was one of five students who were to be excused from taking the dreaded oral qualifying examinations for the Ph.D. This was part of an experiment, never repeated, intended to speed up the degree process. My friends, congratulating me, could not always conceal their jealousy. How this incredible exemption made *me* feel is suggested by the fact that I still dream about it. In my dream it is suddenly found out, after I have been teaching at Cal and writing books for years, that I never took the examinations and that therefore I do not really have a Ph.D. My colleagues have to examine me. Sometimes the dream carries through the frenzied preparation right into the examination, and quite plausible questions are asked and even—with much hesitation—answered. I wake up sweating, and it is a while before I can believe that I really do have a valid doctorate.

The other piece of wonderful news was that I was appointed something called a counsellor in American history, at the lavish salary of eighteen hundred dollars a year, and would be living in Dunster House. This meant goodbye to Perkins Hall, Honest John, and the ETS refectory. It meant a new and luxurious way of life, a new circle, and even more important, a new status. I had climbed aboard the Harvard gravy train just as my California friend Bill had said I could. But he had said this would happen after one year, and because of my own wrong tactics and inherent rigidities it had taken me two. And those had not been easy years.

With the huge cloud of the oral exams magically dispelled, I was ready to start a thesis, and after long discussions with Mr. Schlesinger decided it would have something to do with religion. Religion and slavery was being done by somebody else. "How about religion and capitalism?" he asked. "Only don't call it that; it sounds too left-wing." So that was it, and I was to spend a lot of time for the next two years, and then more after the war, turning through moldy religious newspapers of the 1880s and 1890s in the neglected and dusty basements of seminaries. It sometimes occurred to me that this was an odd way for a young man to be spending his twenties. Gradually, however, my imagination was grasped by the picture of all these men of good will, sitting in their golden oak studies in brand-new rectories attached to brand-new Romanesque churches, full of guilt and horror at the greed and vio-

234

lence burgeoning around them, wondering how far in the direction of socialism it was their duty to move, and how the bankers and lawyers in the front pews would react.

Despite all the good news, the two years of intense work, minor illness, temporary defeat, intermittent depression, and frequent exhaustion had taken their toll. For some time I had been frequently unable, night or day, to stop worrying. The immediate subjects of my worrying were simple enough—papers and their deadlines, facts I might forget, whether my dwindling money would hold out. Underneath these petty problems—I knew it even at the time—lay the deeper tensions of celibacy, frustration, and occasional deep self-doubt.

When I went home to Berkeley in the summer of 1939, I took a grueling and lonely ten-day bus ride through the Northwest, stopping most nights in YMCAs. When I got home I found that my mental torment got worse and not better. Talking with my mother, sister, and brother, going with them and my rapidly failing father to see the World's Fair on Treasure Island, even hiking in the hills with old friends, I had a hard time stopping my mind from whirling aimlessly about like a squirrel in a cage. I was frightened and wondered whether I was going crazy, whether I should tell anyone my troubles, and especially whether I should discuss my worries with my mother. In letters she had given me a lot of intelligent support in times of discouragement, never doubting my eventual success. On my visits home we were able to talk together with increasing frankness. Without a touch of modern psychological knowledge, she understood a lot about people she loved. But I did not want to scare her. This was before young people went easily to psychotherapists, and in the end I kept my fears to myself. Eventually, in the easy Berkeley summer, recovery set in. It was brought about, I suppose, by rest and the sense of trust and affection with which I felt surrounded. The sights and smells of home perhaps played their part also—the brown dry grass, the live oaks, the sparkling Bay.

As I think over these first two years in Cambridge, I ask myself what I had learned. First, to work very hard. Second, a great many facts and the beginning of a few insights— hardly yet formulated or understood—about American history. Third, a lasting and healthy ambivalence toward the American academic establishment and its standard procedures. No doubt a doctoral degree has to be demanding. But does one really get a grasp of a subtle and complex subject by passing doggedly through a long series of separate and rigid requirements?

There is no question that the Perkins Hall experience perpetuated and greatly intensified the worst traits of my character—self-doubt, fear, compulsiveness, rigidity. If these two years had been my entire experience of Harvard, I might on balance have ended by hating the place. Fortunately they weren't, and I don't. To be fair I must remember that whatever the deficiencies of the Harvard graduate program, my unhappiness came mainly from within. There were others who handled graduate school far more astutely. My troubles came from my character and upbringing. To stretch a point a long way, they came from Dorchester and Attleborough.

13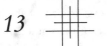

Springtime

In November 1939, well after the beginning of my new life in Dunster House, I got a telegram saying that my father had died of arteriosclerosis. This news affected me surprisingly little. For one thing, my father's mental decline, rapidly accelerating in the last few years, had been increasingly painful to the whole family. For another, as I have tried to explain, I had always been lacking in affection for him and had always felt guilty about this. Though I had at times briefly guessed at the warm feelings that underlay his sober exterior, and though I had always been proud of his integrity, I had known him only as an old man, in the days when circumstances had conspired to bring out the tense and gloomy side of his nature. Yet as I remember the lack of emotion with which I responded to this important news, I am somewhat ashamed of my callousness. A good man was gone, and that good man my father.

I did not even consider making the week-long journey home. When I telephoned my mother, she could hardly speak for tears, and when I saw her the next summer she still sometimes wept for her husband of thirty-three years. Yet it was soon apparent that for her this death had much in it of liberation. Her husband had always loved her, but in their early married years he had been dominant and formidable, she a timid schoolgirl awed by her own new position. Through the years of raising a family she had developed more and more confidence, without ever losing the shyness. Recently she had found herself in charge of a rapidly declining man at a time of rapidly increasing financial crisis. As her acute grieving passed, my mother was to find herself increasingly free and courageous.

For my own part, it seems clear that this death of a once-feared father helped to cut the links to my childhood, especially to its fears and compulsions. Talking to my friends, I later realized that I never had to deal as a grown-up with one of the most difficult human relations, that between a mature son and his vigorous, long-dominant father. For many reasons my links to Berkeley had already been gradually weakening. Before 1940 I had looked forward eagerly to long summers at home in Berkeley. In the summer of 1940 I went home a bit reluctantly and only for a month; in 1941, utterly absorbed in new emotions, I did not go at all.

Of course I duly answered the letters of condolence and made a few decorous and very temporary cuts in some kinds of social activities. Without anguish I declined invitations from Boston relatives, whom I had been seeing less and less in any case. When I turned down one of Mrs. Holbrook's Shakespeare evenings she predictably answered that she quite understood the need to "absent thee from felicity a while."

But it was not like that at all. I was having the best time I had ever had. The least important part of my new life was the job that supported it. A wealthy patriot had given a large sum of money for "the extra-curricular study of American civilization." In each of the Harvard houses an advanced graduate student had the job of putting on sprightly programs about Benjamin Franklin, the Spanish-American War, or the difference between the two Roosevelts. Most of these earnest efforts were a terrible flop. Obviously, the more serious Harvard students were busy with studies that counted in their records. Moreover, anything that even faintly smacked of patriotic zeal conflicted with the cagey and skeptical Harvard style. I made friends among the students and one night, when I had announced a meeting on some fascinating subject, I opened my door to find a group of my well-wishers using physical force to get me some recruits.

After a year on this program, in which I did no better and no worse than my colleagues in the other houses, I was appointed to a tutorship, a regular rank that usually carried a tenure of several years. I was also appointed assistant senior tutor, which meant that I was third in the house hierarchy. This put me in charge of the house when the master and senior tutor were away at meetings or skiing in New Hampshire. At this point—for a short time as it turned out—I felt far more successful and secure than I had ever felt before or was to feel again for some years.

The most obvious change from Perkins Hall was in the amenities. I had a comfortable furnished suite consisting of study, bedroom, and bath. In the dining hall in those days students and tutors were met by a smiling headwaitress, who presented a printed menu of the day. If one didn't like what was offered, one ordered something else. For breakfast, for instance, tutors might order eggs benedict, while undergraduates were likely to start with grapefruit covered with honey, washed down with chocolate milk. Upstairs in the senior common room was a cupboard well stocked with excellent liquor, for which one signed a book. As I remember a martini cost thirty-five cents, a cognac after dinner fifteen cents. The group of resident tutors proved to be so congenial that neighboring students, studying for examinations, complained that we were keeping them from sleep by loud singing late at night.

The house system had been established in the thirties in

obvious imitation of Oxford and Cambridge colleges, but the effort at instant transatlantic import of British tradition was not entirely successful. For house dinners our master tried hard to make us wear either caps and gowns (no support at all) or at least dinner jackets (support only from the former Rhodes scholars and visiting Englishmen). For tutorial dinners at the Harvard Club in Boston we did allow ourselves to be persuaded to wear dinner jackets with bright red ties. These minor efforts at instant tradition were a little embarrassing, and yet there were great advantages in collegial life. One was that the house system breached the very sharp status lines characteristic of American academic life. Within the house I found myself on first-name terms with famous scholars. On the other hand, the line between people like me and the undergraduates was fragile—so fragile as to cause some difficulties. To go from an undergraduate cocktail party straight in to dinner and then—with my two superiors away—to have to quell an outbreak of bread-throwing took more poise and tact than I usually had on tap.

By fellow tutors, and still more by students, I was initiated into the mysterious world of Harvard snobberies. I learned that the preferred costume was a three-button Harris tweed jacket and the darkest of gray flannel trousers, the more rumpled the better. The clubs at the top of Harvard undergraduate society were important only to that fraction of the students who were potential members. This was the period when Jack Kennedy came to college with his own servant but still failed to make the very top societies. In Dunster House, where there were few clubmen, jokes about the clubs were frequent enough to suggest some remaining envy. For a few, ties with Boston society remained. Once at a large and boring Boston party to which I had been invited by a relative, I was approached by a particularly snotty young aristocrat who said, "Sir, do you mind if I ask how you happen to be here?"

240

This sort of thing was archaic: ethnic and some kinds of class lines were another matter. Harvard had become far more cosmopolitan than the other major Ivy League colleges, but the process was not smooth. When I found myself associating with one group of students who seemed to me bright and attractive, one of them explained to me, as to an ignorant western hick, that I had joined the second-best Jewish set in the house—the best consisted of a few members of old eastern Jewish families. It still did not occur to me to think whether people I met were Jewish or not, but in this I seemed just about alone at Harvard. The Irish, with partial exceptions for people like the Kennedys, were the local subclass—including the "biddies" who cleaned the rooms and the hostile population just outside the house.

When I became assistant senior tutor I played a major part in the complex process of selecting students for the house. In interviews I sat behind a table, looking surreptitiously at application forms and scribbling notes while the student applicant answered questions. Applicants were divided into five categories: at the top were boys from "select" private schools—Groton, St. Paul's, and the like. Next came Andover-Exeter, then "other" private schools, finally graduates of public high schools (these were sometimes National Merit Scholars from the West). Students the interviewers believed to be Jewish had their applications marked with an asterisk and were referred to within the house hierarchy as "starred students." This repellent system was defended as a means of equalizing the houses—without it, it was plausibly argued, one house would get all the potential clubmen, another would be western, another Jewish. On the basis of interviews like mine, some of the masters bargained intensely. A master might offer to take two western high school students or one Jew in return for a good Groton man. The classifications were secret, but they obviously reflected lines that were quite real and well known both by those who indignantly rejected them and those who did not. Like everything else, ethnic discrimination was usually treated in undergraduate circles with a cool, sardonic style impossible for me to master or even quite understand. A student from Brooklyn, looking around him at a fake Georgian courtyard, would shrug his shoulders like a vaudeville Jewish peddler, saying "Nu, so this is Harvard!"

What principally delighted me in Dunster House was the constant company of a group of young tutors who seemed to me then—and still seem in retrospect—not only intelligent but often truly creative and characterized also by generosity of spirit and lightness of heart. Among my intimates were John Kelleher, who had come from industrial Lawrence, Massachusetts, with an inexhaustible store of Irish lore and song; Hugh Cunningham, an English tutor who went in, with some self-deprecation, for elegant amenities; and John Lydenberg, who lived next door in Leverett House and combined sharp intelligence with more self-doubt than most. We were all somewhat awed by Paul Sweezy, an assistant professor of economics who combined a committed and deeply informed Marxism with a cultivated aesthetic taste. I was joined in my second year in the house by my close undergraduate friend from California, Burr Overstreet. All these and others were likely often to meet in somebody's room for a relaxed evening playing poker, keenly but for low stakes.

I had learned to love New England. In the fall some of us, tutors and students, went cycling over country roads to Concord and beyond. I especially remember the landscape of November—gray skies, brown fields, bare black trees, and occasional brilliant piles of apples or pumpkins. In winter John and I would take long argumentative walks along the frozen river toward Wellesley. When spring came, leaves would appear, silhouetted at night against the streetlights. We left our topcoats home and walked briskly through the chilly streets to Jim Cronin's bar to drink bock beer.

The most important influence on my life and thought during most of my time at Dunster House was an extraordinarily gifted, eccentric, and in the long run tragic figure, John B. Rackliffe. Jack was a tutor in English, a Harvard graduate of New England and Canadian origins. He was a small man, whose clothes were always both correct and rumpled. In the depths of winter he wore over his jacket and flannels only a raincoat, which had to be of a precise shade of brown. His face was bright pink, his eyes somewhat prominent, his voice a bit raucous, especially when he sang Mozart or Verdi arias in a piercing falsetto. His language was profane and obscene, whether he was talking to a student or the stuffiest professor. His wit was formidable and his talents many. He could play the piano fluently, if a bit carelessly, in almost any style; he commanded, for instance, an authentic tinkly ragtime. His languages were fluent—he could declaim in French or swear in Italian. His drinking ranged from heavy to prodigious to disastrous.

Jack was an expert on the nuances of the Harvard and New England social system. Though he was poor and radical, he was ironically attached to the amenities and graces provided by the system for the enjoyment of the rich. He went to concerts at the Republican Women's Club in Boston, wearing a dinner jacket (with narrow and nonshiny lapels—he pointed out that mine, bought for high school dances, was all wrong). Once, when we were having a good dinner in Boston before going to *The Magic Flute* he looked around, sighed, and said a little defensively, "Nothing is too good for the workers."

Jack had long abandoned working on his thesis but was tolerated by his department and reappointed as a tutor because year after year one or two of his students won their degrees summa cum laude. A summa was a rare distinction, which demanded a thesis of top literary and scholarly quality. When a new tutee seemed at all promising, Jack always took over his entire education, not just in English literature but in the world—Jack's world. First the new student had to listen carefully to the Glyndebourne recordings of *Don Giovanni,* with Jack commenting between records. Then he might be taken to art shows, the opera, political meetings, or the worst dives on Scollay Square. Jack read lots of poetry and prose, especially Shakespeare, Yeats, and Hemingway. Each student's writing style was criticized with plenty of wit and no mercy. Jack's tastes and opinions were as intolerant as they were cultivated, and it was a rare student who did not do his best to adopt them.

Though I was only a few years younger than he was, I was much his junior in knowledge and sophistication, and as we became friends he took over my education in almost the same way as that of his official students. Part of his credo was political. He was a fierce radical and, I later learned, a member of the Communist party. He was, however, a very odd Communist—by temperament an anarchist, by deep conviction a despiser of all tactical compromise. He was saved from many of the cheery banalities of Communist taste in this period by a philosophic distinction, expounded often late at night. This was his distinction between the "system" and the "setup." The system was capitalism and could be changed. The setup was the tragic character of human life and could not. This was how Jack handled the conflict that had plagued me since undergraduate days, between a wish to believe in progressive change and a feeling that the great tragic writers were telling the truth about the human condition.

I soon learned that essentially Jack was a moralist, and a strict one. The most important thing in life was to be a Good Guy, and the requirements were very demanding. Like Jonathan Edwards, Jack scorned all virtue except the highest and most disinterested. A few anecdotes may help make this clear. I once went with him to visit his friend David Prall, a distinguished philosopher who was dying of cancer but continued to keep his door open to students. The students exhausted him, and after we left I suggested to Jack that Prall ought to see fewer of them. Jack disagreed: no Good Guy holds anything back. Another time after Jack had drunk far too much and I had helped him to bed, he asked me to get him another whiskey from the common room. Knowing that remonstrance would get me nowhere, I got one. When I brought it back Jack, sitting up in bed pale and shaky, near vomiting, asked me whose name I had signed for the drink. "Yours," I answered. "Not good, Henry, not generous—you should have signed your own." I agreed and was awed by the deep dedication, even in the worst circumstances, of a passionate moral teacher.

One day when we were walking in front of Dunster House, Jack told me he was about to marry Mary Douglass, a tall, humorous, very charming woman who was house secretary. They moved to 359 Harvard Street, an apartment building a few blocks from the house. Their apartment became for me a refuge, always freely available, from every tension or anxiety. We would play shove-ha'penny, read P. G. Wodehouse aloud, or Jack would accompany me in his best whorehouse-piano style in verse after verse of "Frankie and Johnny." With Mary I formed a two-person club known as the Crappy Poetry Society. We would recite endlessly the sentimental anthology pieces we had both learned as adolescents, while Jack applauded and groaned. Whenever I wanted, or things at Dunster House seemed in any way stressful, I spent the night on Harvard Street, arriving back at the house in the morning not without causing speculation.

Looking back at Jack, I can of course see many flaws, then hidden by my dazzled admiration and my need for direction. His politics were an unworkable combination of passionate egalitarianism and passionate elitism. His need to feel that he was on the side of the workers sometimes made him forget his intellectual standards. He followed, with whatever inner provisos, the twists and turns of the Party line. When he saw a picture of the grandiose and ugly new skyscrapers of the University of Moscow he said that a people who had accomplished all that the Russians had were entitled to a little bad taste. A few years later he admired Joseph Davies's unbelievably sentimental *Mission to Moscow,* which made Joseph Stalin a gentle soul loved by children and dogs.

Jack's literary tastes are harder to fault, but he was sentimental about Hemingway, clearly less of a supreme Good Guy and also less of a perfect stylist than Jack thought. As I reread Jack's letters I find his own style sometimes admirably personal and expressive, sometimes a not-quite-successful combination of Hemingway, Wodehouse, and Evelyn Waugh. More important, it soon became clear that the drinking was a symptom of a desperate drive toward self-destruction. Very shortly Harvard was to find it could keep him on no longer. For a while he moved from one job to another in government and publishing, sometimes doing very well for a while but always eventually quarreling needlessly with even the most tolerant colleagues or superiors. In 1947 I was to hear with great distress that his marriage—to me an ideal example—had broken up, and not many years after that he died. I had learned by then that he had suffered from epilepsy and also that he had had strong bisexual tendencies (he never showed these to me or to his tutees).

Most of Jack's faults hurt only himself. I look back on him not only with affection but also with admiration and deep gratitude.* I am grateful most for his liberating vitality and for his central teaching. The cult of the Good Guy, in which the supreme value is generosity and the supreme duty is to follow one's generous affections wherever they may lead, is a dangerous one. It is not a good basis for the complicated decisions necessary in politics. It is not always a sound basis for artistic judgment. But for personal relations there is a lot to be said for it. And above all, its teachings were what I badly needed, to help me overcome the compulsive and rigid sides of my character, present since childhood and drastically re-inforced during my first two graduate years. I was able to resume a movement toward liberation and emotional maturity that had begun when I was a Berkeley undergraduate.

The extreme code that eventually proved fatal to Jack was beneficial to those he taught, who did not have to follow it all the way in every part of life. Though I spent many of my evenings at Jack and Mary's, I spent the days either teaching or working on my thesis, reading nineteenth-century religious newspapers in the libraries of the region. Jack never tried to induce me to follow him in giving up work for a degree. Indeed, his advice to his students and friends was often surprisingly prudent and sensible, so long as they did not fundamentally transgress against the ethic of the Good Guy. It proved possible, though not easy, for me to follow two wildly incongruous leaders, Mr. Schlesinger and Jack. When I was especially tired of reading *The Christian Union* or the *Independent* I would preach a sermon for Jack and Mary in the character of a liberal Protestant minister of the 1890s,

---

*I am by no means alone in this. Henry Nash Smith, older and far cooler-headed in these years, looking back at his Harvard experience once wrote me that Jack "taught me more than anyone else at Harvard: I mean chance remarks that explode two years later."

pointing out the spiritual benefits of the sufferings of the unemployed. I knew the tone and the lingo and could carry on
until Jack, laughing but revolted, begged me to stop.

Despite my prudential countertendencies, Jack's ethic of
passion and affection was sufficiently absorbed. It was to be a
major factor in enabling me, very shortly, to forget my
doubts and fears in making a quick emotional decision that
changed my life.

My political emotions and commitments, in abeyance during the hard grind of the Perkins Hall years, flourished in
Dunster House. These years when my life was rich and stimulating were the terrible years of Hitler's successive, apparently
unstoppable, triumphs. I remember one morning when, sitting over a late breakfast at Hayes-Bickford's, I read in the
Globe about the Nazis' entry into Austria. In Vienna Jewish
professors, on their hands and knees, were being forced to
scrub out anti-Nazi sidewalk slogans. What right had I to be
having a good time? While I was at home in Berkeley in the
summer of 1939 the Hitler-Stalin pact brought to an end the
easy simplicities of the Popular Front versus Fascism. Two
weeks later war broke out and my brother and I, listening to
the radio on our sleeping porch, heard that a British ship had
been sunk by a submarine. It seemed as though we were
somehow finding ourselves back in the time of World War I,
whose horrors had powerfully affected our imaginations during the antiwar thirties. This sense of *déjà vu* was to recur
often during the war just opening.

The comparatively benign political arguments of the New
Deal period did not immediately disappear. Harvard, and in

particular Dunster House, was one of the major world centers of the Keynesian revolution. In the Dunster House Economic Forum, deficit spending in particular was defended by Seymour Harris, the senior tutor, and New Deal liberalism in general by such stars as Alvin Hansen, one of the principal economic spokesmen of Roosevelt's program, Gottfried Haberler, and the young Paul Samuelson from M.I.T. Ranged on the two extreme sides of this vital center were two apparent opposites, both more interesting to me: Paul Sweezy, the powerful young Marxist economist, and Joseph Schumpeter, the brilliant, detached, skeptical, and pessimistic Austrian. Schumpeter, with black eyebrows and a hooked nose that enhanced his Mephistophelian manner, was the most dramatic of the speakers. At one point he announced with appropriate dramatic pauses that "the only difference—between me and my young friend Paul Sweezy—is that he is alife—and I— am deadt." What I think he meant in part was that they agreed in skepticism about the New Deal. Schumpeter believed that Roosevelt's measures were likely to injure the delicate process of cyclical recovery. Sweezy doubted that the capitalists would allow the structural changes, combined with big enough deficit spending, that would be needed to save the system. Even as they talked, this question was becoming moot. The enormous government spending that was to end the Depression was about to take place—not for social welfare but for rearmament and war.

Irving Howe, whose excellent autobiography deals with these same years in literary and intellectual New York, says that the Harvard English department (and by implication Harvard in general) was regarded with suspicion by the New York critics as "a nest of WASP gentility and literary fellow-travelling" (with the Communist party). This harsh judgment was essentially true, and the gentility was organically connected to the Stalinist susceptibilities. The New York friends of Howe or

Alfred Kazin, another critic of Harvard fellow traveling, were second-generation immigrant Jews. This meant that they grew up on the intense sectarian infighting of people who had long taken socialism for granted and felt entirely free to look with skepticism at the Russia of the great purges. Many of the leading figures of Harvard literary radicalism, in contrast, came from upper-middle-class backgrounds, felt guilty about their privileged upbringing, had a wistful and gingerly but sincere wish for solidarity with the workers, and were emotionally unable to break with the organization that claimed to be the workers' party. One example is of course Jack Rackliffe, another, Granville Hicks. Hicks, the fiercely polemical literary editor of the *New Masses,* had been appointed by Harvard as one of the first group of counsellors in American civilization, and held in Adams House in 1938–39 the same position to which I was appointed in Dunster House the next year. Hicks's openness about being a Communist caused a violently hostile outbreak in the Boston press, much of which was always delighted to jump on Harvard. Hicks bore the attack bravely and even managed to debate the local Catholic supporters of Father Coughlin without actual violence.

Hicks had been a candidate for the Unitarian ministry and continued to look and talk much like a minister. He had written a pamphlet, *I Like America,* in which the narrator explains to his little daughter why he is a Communist. This pamphlet, a perfect epitome of literary Communism of the Popular Front era, had moved me when I read it in Berkeley. In the fall after the Nazi-Soviet pact was signed, right at the end of Hicks's Adams House ordeal by vilification, he resigned from the Party with a public letter. During the rest of my time at Harvard he stood in front of a series of Harvard audiences, patiently, seriously, and honestly answering two questions, asked alternately in speeches of great length. One began "Mr. Hicks, would you mind telling us why you decided to sell out the only hope of achieving a just and peaceful world?"; the other "Mr. Hicks, will you please explain to us how you managed for so long to swallow the lies of the Stalin dictatorship?"

The most powerful and complex figure of the Harvard left was F. O. Matthiessen, who together with Perry Miller formed the creative center of the flourishing American studies movement at Harvard. In his rich and powerful writing there is no hint of Hicks's sort of doctrinaire Marxism. Indeed, during the period when Hicks was still a Communist, Matthiessen sharply criticized his work, considering it "thinly theoretical." (Somewhat paradoxically, when Hicks resigned from the Party, Matthiessen said he had been far more cogent before he had withdrawn to a rootless "neo-liberalism.")

Matthiessen's own major works are characterized, as Henry Nash Smith once pointed out, by a tense and agonized effort to bring together the democratic hope of Whitman and Emerson with the profound tragic insights of Melville and Hawthorne, or, in other periods, Henry James and T. S. Eliot. Almost alone among leading Harvard intellectuals of this period, Matthiessen was a serious and active Christian, a lay reader in the Episcopal church, a believer both in the central and transcendent place of love in the universe and in the necessity of redemption through suffering.

Matthiessen did not ever consider joining the American Communist party, which he regarded as both rootless and rigid. He did, however, after as well as before the Nazi-Soviet pact, participate proudly in dozens of Communist-dominated Popular Front organizations and take part in Communist-organized meetings. He refused to abandon individuals he loved or admired who came to different conclusions than he did, but was capable of expressing biting scorn for those he thought, probably sometimes mistakenly, to be motivated by careerism or cowardice. Longing for solidarity with the workers and unable to make easy contact with actual members of the American working class, he was moved by the geniality of a Communist picnic in the Bois de Boulogne to say that if French, he would have had to be a Communist.

Matty, as his students called him, was almost unique among Harvard professors in one way: he gave his teaching all the intense dedication he gave his writing. His students responded with deep devotion. Those of whom he was fondest were fostered in every possible way and entertained at his elegant house in Louisburg Square and at the unpretentious and charming country place in Kittery, Maine, that he shared with a friend. I was not a member of this circle but knew many of its members very well. Matthiessen was, I think, unsurpassed at bringing out the intellectual enthusiasm of the brightest undergraduates. With graduate students he was less successful. He gave them so much of himself that in some cases—not all—their independent personalities did not have room to grow. Sometimes, I think, he expected a great book from a person who had in him only a decent monograph. In terms of scholarly results, the aloofness of A. M. Schlesinger and also the abrasiveness of Perry Miller worked better.

Since his tragic suicide in 1950 it has become clear that Matthiessen was a secret, guilt-ridden homosexual. He carefully kept this side of his nature in check in his relations with students, but in that period even the most decent and well-regulated homosexual relations, like Matthiessen's with his housemate, had to be hidden. This was obviously a nightmare for a passionately honest and often combative man, used to facing down all sorts of critics. The resulting tension may explain much of the vitality of his teaching and writing, achieved at immense personal cost. He was an exact example of Jack Rackliffe's ethic of holding nothing back, and of the older sacrificial ethic he himself derived from the New Testament. Since I think that in the long run many of the positions he took were as mistaken as they were heroic, he is also to me an example of the limitations of passionate personal loyalty as a guide to political decision.

A number of the junior faculty agreed with Matthiessen in supporting many of the positions taken by the Communist party, and a few of them joined up. Later congressional testimony and individual memoirs have made it clear that the much-investigated Harvard Communist cell was by no means a powerful organ of the mighty Third International. Its members, usually about fifteen, were serious young intellectuals not really trusted by the Party, which knew better than to ask them to slant their teachings. Their main assigned duty was to try to capture the control of the Harvard Teachers Union. They also tried to recruit new Party members. Aside from this the group seems to have amounted to a Marxist discussion club. Nevertheless the existence of such a group, secret and in crises acting together, helped to embitter political argument at Harvard as elsewhere.

My own feelings, partly under Jack's influence, moved sharply to the left. I was trying hard to jettison the cautious reservations that had held me back at Berkeley. I wanted badly to be a Good Guy, and that meant of course to be a radical, and especially to stick to one's radicalism under pressure. I was invited to join in informal Marxist study group that met in Jack's apartment. The atmosphere was genial, and there was plenty to drink. Nevertheless, the discussions were serious, and I now know—I think I half knew even then—that the purpose of the group was to screen possible members for the Party. For each session all of us read a chapter of Stalin's *Essentials of Leninism* and one member reported on the corresponding Lenin pamphlet—*What Is to Be Done?, Imperialism, Left-Wing Communism,* and so on. I was a little disturbed when it was suggested that in order not to attract attention we not buy our reading matter in the same place. I could agree with most of what the group's leaders were saying but remember that at one point I asked an inappropriate question. Even if we grant, I said, that the present Russian government is not oppressive, might it not become so because of the lack of checks or opposition? The discussion leader looked at me disapprovingly. "If we're going to have *frivolous* questions we might as well quit," he said. I was not pressed to join the Party and was not ready to do so. I think I was held back, then and later, not only by a lingering opposition to all authority but also by a religious tendency, still unadmitted and unformulated, that prevented me from feeling comfortable with systematic materialism.

From the spring of 1940, as the Battle of Britain grew more desperate, the majority of the Harvard faculty organized to back with great fervor Roosevelt's efforts to aid Britain. This drive was opposed by pacifists, by many kinds of isolationists, some of them belonging to the far right, and by the Communist party and those it influenced. With the Nazi-Soviet pact the Communists had sharply reversed their early support of the United Front against Fascism and resurrected the antiwar slogans of the thirties—still full of power for young people brought up on them. Franklin Roosevelt, to Communists an essentially reactionary fake until 1936, and since then the chief American champion of the antifascist cause, now became a dangerous warmonger. A song began:

Oh, Franklin Roosevelt
Told the people how he felt,
We DAMN near believed what he said . . .

Britain and America were aiming at world hegemony, and believers in peace and progress were to oppose American intervention.

With many qualms and much complicated argument I

went along with this view. The real main reason for my stand was the influence of Jack and other people I wholeheartedly admired. I remember one ridiculous evening, after a Dunster House staff dinner at the Boston Harvard Club, when Jack, Paul Sweezy, and I, still wearing dinner jackets and bright red ties, stopped for drinks at an Irish bar in Central Square and carried on a somewhat boozy argument as to which was the worst—American capitalism, the British Empire, or the Roman Catholic church. It seems to me miraculous that we were not beaten up.

In addition to my strong feelings of loyalty to my friends, I was influenced by my western hostility to Harvard anglophilia, always much in evidence. Beneath the surface lay a wish to repudiate the Wilsonian loyalties inculcated by my father and sharply reversed in college. I could identify myself with the handful of people, heroes of plays and novels of the thirties, who had braved persecution to oppose World War I. I wrote an essay—always the way I tried to make up my mind—about what I saw as the ridiculous antics of some senior historians. Men who had been all-out Allied propagandists during World War I had repented in the thirties and taught that all nations had been more or less equally guilty of the follies of 1914. Now they were worrying in print whether they had played a part in corrupting the youth who might have to fight the Nazis. I felt, and still feel, that this amounted to an egotistical overestimate of the power of professors. I had absorbed at Berkeley a lot of the argument that America had been led into the Great War by munitions makers and British propagandists. I was sure that war would once again end civil liberties. I was attracted by Charles Beard's belief that America's mission was to preserve, as European civilization destroyed itself, an island of freedom. Finally—though I did not admit to myself that this was one of my motives—I dreaded having my own satisfactory life interrupted by military service, which I thought of as something like junior high school but far worse.

In the struggle against aid to England, a struggle I now regard as totally and disastrously mistaken, I was more active than I had ever been in a political cause. I was one of the five-man executive committee of the Harvard group on the antiwar side. (Two of my colleagues, I now know, were Party members.) We tried to answer every press statement by the aid-to-England faculty organizations. I found myself debating senior professors on the radio. Once at breakfast in Dunster House, Professor Paul S. Buck, very much a rising star in the department and the university administration, asked me whether I had been to the aid-to-England meeting in the Yard yesterday. "No," I answered, in the best Good-Guy manner, "but I was outside picketing." Well-intentioned efforts by friendly professors to persuade me that I was wrong naturally stiffened my resistance, and I began to feel less comfortable at Harvard.

#

The Dunster House period of my life had been a very good one, but neither relative success, amenities, nor intellectual stimulation had completely overcome the old tensions. This was shown in a number of ways. One, I now think, was my tendency from time to time to drink far too much. The general assumption in the period was that there was something robust and mildly comical about pouring down alcohol to the point of stupefaction. It was also a way to dispose of doubts and fears. Another indication that these persisted was my increasing insomnia. Some nights, lying in bed in Dunster House and hearing the hours chime in the Bow Street Catholic church, I would give up about four o'clock and go for long walks through nearby streets. Undergraduates coming home from an evening out would assume that I had been roistering. They would greet me in a friendly enough way but later make remarks. After a number of desperate nights I went to the infirmary for help. I was given more pills and less counseling than I needed.

What was the matter? No doubt it was less than easy to follow the very different banners of Jack Rackliffe and A. M. Schlesinger. No doubt I felt guilty—at times acutely so—for living so comfortably in a world of bombs and Nazi persecution. Despite the most convincing explanations, I could not help being uncomfortable with the political struggle to prevent the United States from helping my mother's hard-pressed country. At bottom, my doubts and fears came from a more immediate and obvious source, my badly blocked sexual drives and my constant worry about my failures.

The society in which I was living was nearly all male, yet some of the young faculty managed to form successful relations with girls, usually from Radcliffe. Three very attractive recent Radcliffe graduates lived in an apartment in Quincy Street to which I was often invited. One of the three became engaged to John Lydenberg, another to his old friend Carl Schorske, also a friend of mine. It was clear that it would have been acceptable to the group if I had followed their example, but neither the remaining girl nor I was inclined that way. As a matter of fact, I had met another extremely attractive Radcliffe girl, whom I regularly took to dances. I saw a lot of her, but the old inhibitions kept me from intimacy—in fact, to my despair, I seemed shyer and more awkward than I had been in Berkeley with Jane. Understandably, this girl got tired of our unduly tentative relationship and broke it off with a cutting letter.

One day in the early spring of 1941 I got a severe blow from an unexpected quarter. Crane Brinton, the chairman of the history department, called me aside for a talk. He started by saying how much the department thought of me and my

teaching. Unfortunately, however, they lacked funds to con-
tinue my employment as a tutor. Instead, they were giving
me a traveling fellowship of twelve hundred dollars. Since it
was wartime, I would not be expected to travel very far.

This meant the end of my very pleasant way of life and my
membership in a wonderfully lively society. It was also a hard
blow to my self-esteem, only recently recovered from earlier
setbacks. Usually, I knew, tutors served for several years, and
I was pretty sure I had been a good one. I could not but
wonder if there were other than financial reasons for the department's decision, and my doubts were to be sharply increased when, before the opening of the next academic year,
another graduate student in American history was appointed
to exactly the same position I had had and given most of the
same students to tutor. At the time, and for some years after, I
thought that perhaps I was being removed from the community because of my political activities and opinions, which
were certainly sharply opposed to those of my superiors.
Now it seems perhaps more likely that my way of life was not
quite what was wanted in an assistant senior tutor. A little too
much conviviality with undergraduates, nights away from
the house, rumors of heavy drinking and walking the streets
at night. Or perhaps it was true that they had run out of
money and then suddenly found some more. In any case this
blow fell far more heavily because of a new and overwhelming commitment.

In early March Dunster House had its winter dance. My
usual date was not available. I remembered Jean Terrace, a
girl I had met at one of the dreary graduate dances some time

ago. She had come with one of my Bowdoin College friends. I knew that she came from Portland and was living in Cambridge. I remembered her as nice-looking, tall, blonde, and witty, and felt that she would provide a pleasant evening and do me no harm with my friends. When I called up she accepted, and before the dance was over my feelings were intense and confusing.

We started meeting almost every evening and all of a sudden nothing else mattered. I kept up, perfunctorily, the teaching preparation that had until then seemed to fill every minute. I forgot about my thesis, about political concerns (though I still went to meetings). I forgot to worry about not sleeping. I even forgot that I had never been any good with girls.

It turned out that we had a lot in common. Like me, Jean was half British. She had spent several unhappy years in school in England and had come back to America, she thought, much less sophisticated than the other Portland girls her age. After a boring period in a Portland girls' school, she had come to Boston to find a job, and now worked as a secretary in a psychiatric social work institution. Like the other girls I had met, she lived in a Cambridge apartment with several roommates. She was in conscious revolt against the conservatism of Toronto, where her parents lived, and the stuffiness of Portland, where her grandparents lived—yet she went to Portland to see her grandparents almost every weekend. Her politics were liberal, partly because Portland's were not, and she was perfectly willing to be pushed farther to the left. She loved poetry—our current favorite then turned out to be e. e. cummings. In all sorts of ways she was, like me, a person of essentially traditional tastes who wanted very much to be radical and free.

By late March, about three weeks after we had met, I told my friend Hugh that I could stand this tension no longer and had to ask her to marry me. To him I rated my chances as 40 percent no, 50 percent maybe, and perhaps 10 percent yes.

259

Perhaps my instincts were telling me that things were a little better than this. The next evening I called for her at her Agassiz Street apartment, took her on the subway to Boston, wandered in a daze into the nearest place, a rather drab cellar on Tremont Street with a bar and sometimes music for dancing. We sat down opposite each other and I ordered two beers. I swallowed hard, told her I couldn't get along without her, asked her to tell me frankly what my chances were, and to be fair told her what a difficult person I was. Her answer was an absolutely unequivocal, definite, and shattering yes, she would marry me. It was still the same when I called up the next morning. I canceled my tutorials and walked into Boston for lunch with her. It was my birthday and the crocuses were out all through Back Bay.

I remember the rest of that spring as a time when I was overwhelmed and stupefied by emotion. Actually I kept up my usual activities competently enough. My letters seem to show even some effort at practical planning, with a strong emphasis on the moral superiority of taking big chances—the ethic I had learned from Jack.

Of course my first letter was to my mother. Part of it was as follows:

I suppose the only way one can answer such a letter as this is to say that I ought to take a lot of time and be very sure and think it over and so forth . . . OK, if that's what you think. But . . . if you'd seen her or if you'd seen me during the last few weeks I know you'd agree with me that it's the best thing that's ever happened to me and that I'm terrifically lucky and that you were all for it. You certainly know enough about this sort of stuff to understand what I'm trying to get across and I count on a letter of approval right away. How warm that approval is will make an awful lot of difference in my happiness for a long time, but I know that a sight-unseen judgment is asking an awful lot.

My mother knew emotional blackmail when she saw it, and knew me. She answered just as I wanted and immediately sent Jean a welcoming note and a little present.

The next assignment, Jean's family, proved more difficult. Her grandparents in Portland checked with Judge Sidney Thaxter. Thaxter was, I now know, the son by his second marriage of the man of the same name who had been the husband of my father's favorite aunt. He reported that he had indeed known Harry May and that though May had never made any money he always had lived well. Jean and I went up to Portland for the weekend, and I encountered her grandmother sitting at a card table working on a jigsaw puzzle and playing very effectively the role of a sweet old lady, which she was not. In reality she was and long had been the dominant figure in the whole family. Of Irish and German origin, she had married first a New England publisher, Jean's actual grandfather, and then an artist.

Jean's much loved step-grandfather, Alexander Bower, was a self-educated intellectual who had formed his opinions before and right after World War I. He admired H. L. Mencken and hated both William Jennings Bryan and Henry Cabot Lodge. He was now head of the Portland Art Museum and its school, and was accepted by Portland as a favorite eccentric. In company he usually kept his iconoclastic wit under control, but at home his conversation was full of barbs, usually directed at his wife. He was utterly devoted to Jean and repeatedly told me that "that goil's happiness means more to me than anything in the woild." I liked him immensely.

Jean's brother, already in the army, came to my room in Dunster House. He told Jean that I was pretty foolish, but that he thought this all to the good. Finally I had lunch with her Scottish father, who had allegedly come to Boston on business. I found a handsome, very conventional man who was—even I could tell—as nervous as I was; he immediately started talking about plans for the wedding. I exchanged pleasant letters with Jean's mother in Toronto, who was used to doing what *her* mother told her. So far so good.

The grandparents announced the engagement at a large party in their house on Cape Elizabeth. Back in Cambridge, accepted and reassured, we took up the pressing business of getting to know each other. I remember countless evenings in Boston with extravagant taxi rides back to Cambridge. After we dropped Jean at Agassiz Street, I always told the taxi driver all about it, and never got an unsympathetic reception. In the midst of all this euphoria, two blows fell, one practical, the other emotional.

Mr. Schlesinger had assured me that since I couldn't go abroad, I could keep my traveling fellowship and stay in Cambridge or at least Boston. With Jean's job this seemed to make sense. To confirm the permission to stay home, I went to see the appropriate dean, William Scott Ferguson, a professor of ancient history and an unsentimental Scottish Canadian. He treated my request as preposterous. Traveling was traveling, and I would have to go at least as far as New York. Temporarily staggered, we changed our plans. Jean would get a secretarial job in New York and I would write my thesis there. After all, the Depression was ending and there were jobs.

The second blow was far more serious. Jean's grandmother thought she had been generous enough in formally accepting the engagement and would as a matter of course—as she had in the case of Jean's mother—completely control the rest of the proceedings. She announced that it would be best to have a large wedding in Portland in September. This was as unacceptable to both of us as though she had said that we should wait five years. We politely said so, and she was immediately convinced that she had made a big mistake in allowing the engagement. Why, she asked everybody, could we not at least wait decently to September? "It's the biological oidge," said her husband, sensibly enough. She decided that she had always thought I had shifty eyes and wrote me a crushing letter. "A young man with no money and no position," she pointed out (this cut, because I thought I was doing pretty well), cannot possibly marry a girl like Jean just like that.

In both these blows, which hit hard in my highly emotional state, Jack played to perfection the part of a sober, understanding older friend. When I came out of Dean Ferguson's office, pale with anger at what seemed to me bureaucratic rigidity but still more at the dean's dismissive manner, Jack—who must have expected this result—was waiting to take me home for a stiff drink. When I told him about Mrs. Bower's letter he advised me with Bismarckian realism and restraint. Of course Jean was on my side, but I must remember that her grandmother had known her longer and would always be important in her life. I must answer politely so that she could eventually find a way to back down. With some difficulty, I did as he said. He lent us the key to his apartment, and we took to spending evenings there while he was at meetings. He and his friends, returning, would stumble and cough loudly on the stairs.

At this point Jean's mother in Toronto intervened with real heroism, defying her own mother for the first time in her life. She invited us to make a short visit to Toronto. I would go back to Cambridge, leaving Jean alone a few weeks, and then we could be married in Toronto in June.

We accepted gratefully. In Toronto I got my first glimpse of a country at war. Roosevelt and Churchill glared down from the billboards; Canadian and Scandinavian air force cadets swarmed the streets. When we went to get our marriage license the office was jammed with teenage soldiers and their girls.

263

Back in Cambridge alone I wound up the term's work and, with the help of several friends, found a small house on my favorite bicycling road in Lincoln, which we could have for the summer for thirty dollars a month. That seemed a lot, but again Jack, from the sober experience of several years' marriage assured me and also (by letter) Jean that it would really work out all right.

We were married on June 18 in the Terraces' garden, in the presence mainly of family friends even Jean hardly knew. Money and my mother's health prevented my family from making the long train trip. Until the last minute Jean's grandmother bombarded her daughter with letters expressing her agonized unhappiness and foreboding.

Duly married despite the opposition, we took the train to Boston and Lincoln, where we spent the whole summer in a small isolated house overlooking a lake. Every day we rode our bicycles along the network of country roads that existed even that close to Cambridge. We developed a taste for colonial graveyards. There were plenty of blueberries and blackberries. Mackerel was six cents a pound. Our Cambridge friends visited us and I tried my hand at cooking. Mr. Merk invited us to dinner in Belmont. When we left he insisted on holding our bicycles for us to mount, as politely as if he had been helping us into a Packard. Eventually Jean's grandparents relented and came to see us. Mrs. Bower decided that the trouble had never been my fault, but rather "dear Jeanie's impetuousness." With the formula established, she and I became good friends and allies in many family crises.

Gradually the outer world reasserted itself. I began working on my thesis, and we started looking at want ads for secretaries in the New York papers. My political commitments had fallen apart with Hitler's June attack on the Soviet Union. The Cambridge antiwar group disintegrated. Some of its members immediately became partisans of a transforming, united war against Fascism. Others hung back, trying hard to explain to themselves and others how, if one really understood history, it was clear that they had been right earlier in opposing the war and now in supporting it. Some were still appalled by the thought of war and its human costs. I switched more quickly than many, arguing that now it was possible to defeat Hitler, while before it hadn't been. A number of surprising people suddenly became Russophiles. My mother reported that she was much impressed by the Dean of Canterbury's book on the Soviet Union, an extraordinarily rose-colored view. What I really thought about most was when I would have to leave Jean and enter the army. Married men were not immediately subject to the draft, but it surely couldn't be long. I began to get letters from friends in basic training or navy boot camps.

One day I got a call from Professor Merk, who told me that there was a job available at Lawrence College, a liberal arts institution in Appleton, Wisconsin. Candidates were being interviewed by Henry Wriston, former president of Lawrence, now president of Brown. I went down to Providence on the train and Wriston grilled me. When it came to religion, he said, "I suppose you are one of these modern agnostics." "Yes, sir," I answered. Apparently this was all right. He telephoned the president of Lawrence, recommending that I be hired at a salary of two thousand dollars. Hanging up, he gave me a tough look and said, "Young man, I want you to remember that I could have got you for eighteen hundred." This was quite true, and I was to remember it acutely when I found that some of my young colleagues at Lawrence were jealous.

The beginning of the term was only a few weeks away. We spent the rest of our time in Lincoln in a flurry of packing as I tried to pull together something to say in two brand-new courses of lectures. The countryside around Lincoln had reached its best season—serene and lovely full summer with a hint of fall in the air—when we got on the train for the unknown Middle West.

Of course nobody quite lives happily ever after. Nonetheless, I had made very great gains in my second two years in Cambridge. No other part of my life has been so crowded with inner experience. These two years were quite different from the other happy period I had spent at college in Berkeley. When I think of Berkeley in the 1930s I think of sitting on a hillside in the sunshine in Marin County, passing a bottle of wine and talking with my friends. When I think of Cambridge at the beginning of the 1940s I think of walking fast through the crisp snow of the Yard, perhaps on the way to a political meeting, my mind bursting with exultation, ambition, frustration, and sheer uncontrolled emotion.

I left Harvard not only with a wonderfully happy marriage but also with an important lesson deeply learned. This was that the best decisions are not those one thinks through but those one can't help making. This was to be very helpful in the future, though of course the inward, gloomy, fearful part of my nature did not disappear. Both this tendency, derived from my father and remotely from Attleborough, and also a newly discovered potential for happy, cheerful decision and action were quite real. By the fall of 1941 I probably had most of the intellectual and emotional equipment, good and bad, that I was ever to have.

This was, however, 1941, and everything I had learned was to be tested in the next few years of upheaval. My wartime experience was neither heroic nor terrible nor even boring. It was, for me as for others my age, a test I had to pass before I could get on with my life.

14

The Last
Good War

Faculty life at small colleges, before the war and for a few years after—before the academic boom of the fifties—had a good deal of archaic charm. Young professors were so poor that we almost had to be honest and disinterested. Most of us tried very hard to do a good job with our heavy teaching schedules, hoping somehow, some day to find time for the book that would eventually take us to Yale. The poverty was shared; when people had babies or serious illnesses the hat was sometimes passed. Our way of life contrasted sharply with that of our students, mostly children of the rich who lived in expensive dorms or fraternities. The merchants of the college town knew our incomes precisely and also our politics, of which they disapproved. Since college government was autocratic, we were likely to be fraternally united in opposition to the college president.

I was a green newcomer, and all this dawned gradually. We were met at the Appleton station by the president of Lawrence College. He took us to our small upstairs apartment on East Franklin Street and explained that he had persuaded the landlord to let us spend a hundred dollars of his money on badly needed additional furniture. Everything available turned out to be overstuffed and came from Grand Rapids. Nonetheless, I thought this a very kind gesture on the part of the president. It was some time before I realized (Jean caught on sooner) that this president did nothing without careful thought. His paternalism disguised a natural propensity to tyranny. Like most tyrants, he had his loyal spies and informers. The college, in many ways a pleasant place, was for this reason poisoned by petty intrigue. Gradually finding this out was, for a foolishly idealistic young man, distinctly instructive.

While we were struggling to make our apartment livable and I was desperately trying to write my first lectures, the faculty made formal calls, leaving cards and sometimes asking us to dinner. There were several kinds of faculty. The college was in the process of changing from a school for training Methodist ministers to a select and expensive academy designed to attract parents who feared the godless and radical University of Wisconsin. Many of the older faculty came from the earlier phase and were simple, kindly, unambitious people who knew their subjects well, exactly as they had learned them long years ago. There were a few excellent middle-aged scholars, who had made themselves a good life in Appleton and settled into their work. And there were young men like me—as yet very few young women—just out of Harvard or Yale or Wisconsin and glad to have a job at all. In Appleton Jean and I soon found a group of close and trusted friends, bound together by left-wing political views of exactly the same kind I was used to at Harvard and by shared hostility to the president. (This was cordially returned as the dissident element was identified for the president by his cronies.) Our group of friends included one middle-aged couple, Howard Troyer and his wife Doris. Howard had been at Lawrence long enough to have some standing and even some clout with the administration, and he spent a great deal of effort and energy trying to protect his young friends. Don't leave, he used to beg us; stay here and make a better Lawrence. Cultivated, humorous, savvy without being cynical, with little personal ambition, Howard was a splendid man. I was to find a few like him in each of the three small colleges I taught in; in major universities his kind hardly exist.

During the first term I struggled desperately to have six lectures ready every week. At four in the morning Jean would hear my typewriter rattling. In the middle of the year the president called me in and told me that since one of the political science professors had become dean, I was to add three more lectures a week in international relations. I can't say that my lectures were good, but they were conscientiously prepared and always ready on time, whether I got any sleep or not. One morning, lecturing at eight o'clock in Wisconsin winter, with the windows tightly closed and the heat on full, I found my eyes closing and my knees starting to buckle from sheer exhaustion. This was the only time my own voice ever put me to sleep.

For Lawrence, I was a severe grader and a little proud of myself for flunking two members of the football team in elementary American history. They were genial fellows and did not hold it against me. It was a little different with Miss Karen Schmidt, who was both May queen and prom queen. The dean called me and asked if it was true that I was about to give Miss Schmidt an F. Stiffening, I said it was. "I suppose," he said with a resigned sigh, "that you couldn't make it a D?" I refused—Miss Schmidt knew nothing whatever about the term's work. "Well," said the dean, "she's giving a solo concert next Friday—could you please hold the grade till after that?" This seemed reasonable enough. Nothing at Harvard or Berkeley had helped prepare me to make such delicate moral decisions.

By tradition and because many of the wealthy papermill owners who were trustees were Methodists, the college was dry. If a student encountered a faculty member in one of the bars that lined Main Street, they were both quite safe; each knew the other was at risk. When we invited friends in we served them Blatz beer at fifteen cents a quart bottle. Everybody knew that if there was a knock at the door we had to grab the bottles and glasses and put them out of the way until we saw who it was. On the days of faculty meetings, when we were likely to be treated to an antidrink or antisubversion harangue by the president, a small procession of the younger faculty wives made their way to a drugstore, where each could buy a quarter-pint of whiskey and bring it home in her purse to her bored and irritated husband.

One December afternoon when we were planning to go to a concert in the college chapel, we turned on the radio and got the news of Pearl Harbor. There were reports of the imminent bombing of San Francisco, and we telegraphed my mother inviting her to come to Appleton. For a while people talked about how long the war would take to win, whether the college would close, how soon we would all be in uniform. But in Appleton the war seemed a long way away, and gradually most conversation went back to college affairs.

Living in our upstairs apartment, eating meat loaf when alone and meat loaf with mushrooms when we had guests, we were able to save enough from my two thousand dollars to get our teeth fixed (badly as it turned out) and to plan on going to California for the summer. But the long hard winter and the long hard days and nights took a heavy toll. Despite the happiness of being married, some of the grim compulsiveness of the Perkins Hall days inevitably returned. At one point in December I found myself so tense that for a couple of weeks, for the first and only time, I found myself unable to communicate with Jean. This frightened us both, but we were able to talk it out, and I resolved to put first things first, lectures or no lectures, from then on.

When spring came, even though the hard work continued, life got better. Lilacs came out all over town, and I wrote Jean a poem apologizing for my winter crankiness. We were invited to a party by three refugee scholars, one Italian, one German, and one Yugoslav. The only other guest was the attractive young women's gym teacher. Once everybody had drunk enough red wine, beer, and slivovitz, the three foreign visitors, all mild academics, started exchanging insults. Some of these dealt with the history and fighting ability of their respective countries. We all had a good time and the party went on until three o'clock. As we were leaving, Giorgio Tesoro of the University of Bari kept repeating incredulously, "Three o'clock in zee morning in Appletone, Weesconsin," and looking around the deserted streets. He was sure his landlady wouldn't let him in, so we invited him to spend the night on our couch.

At the end of the year some of the faculty men gave a quite different kind of party the night of commencement. Everybody got drunk, and a great deal of the latent ugliness in the Lawrence situation emerged. A dean who had given a particularly pious talk at the morning ceremonies passed out cold. As he lay back, somebody inserted a candle in his fly, sticking up like an erect penis. Somebody else lighted the wick, and another person took a flashlight photograph. This was not a mere prank in bad taste; the picture was intended for use as blackmail if it ever became necessary. A senior colleague to whom I had talked much too freely all year told me, in his cups, that my future at Appleton would look much brighter if he and I had been better friends. Naif as I

was, I knew a warning when I heard one, and took full note
of this one.

\#

That June we got on the train, first to Chicago and then to
Berkeley. At the end of the long ride in the chair car Jean got
up early and put on her best clothes. My mother, my sister,
my brother and *his* new wife, and Mungie were all at the
station. For me, two worlds seemed to be coming together,
happily and without strain. Self-centered in my happiness, I
failed to understand that my sister, still unmarried, felt lonely
and neglected in the presence of two euphoric, recently married brothers. She and I had been close as children; from this
point on our relations were to be chancy.

In Berkeley and especially in San Francisco the war was
much closer. The harbor was full of ships, the streets full of
sailors—U.S., British, Chinese, occasionally Free French.
Classics professors were working part-time in the Richmond
shipyards, along with black and white newcomers from the
South and Southwest, many of whom were sleeping in their
cars for lack of housing.

By this time I was getting letters from friends in training
camps all over the country. Many of them had learned a new
vocabulary, with words like *orders, report, duty, unit*. Nobody
I knew questioned the need to win the war. I was feeling more
than a little defensive, and finally decided I did not want to go
back to Appleton, start a new term, and get drafted in the
middle of it. Jean agreed. I told my mother that I had decided
I'd better get into the army or navy. I thought she would be
upset. Instead, she answered, "Well, I wondered when one of
you boys would say something like that." When I called my

boss, the president of Lawrence, my resignation was cordially accepted. "Good luck, May," he said, "we'll all be thinking of you."

We moved to San Francisco and found an apartment on Filbert Street, half-way up Russian Hill from the splendid Italian grocery stores and cheap restaurants of North Beach. The place had only oil stoves for heat and the landlady was a wino, but there was a magnificent view of the Bay.

When I set about trying to get in the armed forces I found that this was by no means easy. I applied for everything in sight, including a commission in the armed guard, the navy unit that was assigned to the defense of merchant ships. "Do you think you could command a tough gun crew?" asked the recruiting officer. "I'd try, sir," I dutifully replied. My blood pressure knew better and its wild gyrations caused my application to be refused. In desperation, I even wrote to my Cambridge draft board, saying that I was ready to be drafted. I was led to this extreme step by a curious set of emotions, made up somehow of fear, anxiety, and a wish to get it over.

Meantime I had to make a living. In wartime San Francisco this wasn't hard; all sorts of labor jobs were going begging. The one I held longest was in a small sandblasting shop, where my duties were to sweep up the sand, and when the truck drivers brought in large metal objects like torpedo tubes to attach these to a hoist and haul them up. All there was to learn was not to attach the tubes in such a way that they would swing around and kill somebody. I had a very proud moment when one of the truck drivers said casually, "You guys sure know how to handle that stuff." I learned other things also. One was that in this kind of job when you had nothing to do, you did not ask the foreman what to do next. You shoveled sand from one side of the shed to the other until he *told* you. When you went with a buddy to the garbage dump with a load of refuse, the two of you sat in the sun for an hour before driving back. It was all very different from academic life and in some ways I liked it a lot. When I got home in the evening, dark gray with sand and dust, I took a luxurious bath, realizing that I could do whatever I wanted till the next day. For instance, I could read without taking notes. Weekends we went to the park or the museum, and since Jean had found a secretarial job we could easily afford Italian or Chinese dinners. It was not at all a bad kind of limbo. Later, in a letter from a ship in the Pacific, I was to tell Jean that I would rather work for the sandblasting plant than repeat the year at Lawrence.

One day in December 1942 I read in the paper that Professor Hindmarsh of Harvard was in town recruiting former graduate students and others to study the Japanese language in a navy school at Boulder, Colorado. In our interview he started telling me almost immediately that I would like the climate and scenery at Boulder just fine. "Sir," I said, "can you tell me what are my chances of getting in?" He looked at me with surprise. "Oh, you're in all right," he said. And that, for the next fourteen months, was that.

In Berkeley and San Francisco, in intervals, I had managed to write several chapters of my thesis and before leaving for Boulder I sent them off to Mr. Schlesinger. I was proud of myself for having written anything at all under the circumstances and perhaps expected a little special consideration as a potential war hero. I should have known Mr. Schlesinger better.

His return letter, which I got in Boulder, was, of course, written after a careful reading of my text. Early in the letter, he said that my research was excellent. "At this stage, however," the letter went on, "my job is to criticize rather than to praise." The rest of the letter was all about minor lapses in form and organization. The last paragraph began, in what sounded like an exasperated tone, "As for your mechanics of citation, I didn't think anyone could make so many mistakes."

Mr. Schlesinger certainly wished me well, and he was doing his job as he saw it. Yet when I got this letter in Boulder, so far from Widener Library, it made me angry. Together with some mixed memories of graduate school and still more of my stint at Lawrence, it made me feel that I probably did not want to go back to teaching American history after the war. Maybe I would be a Far Eastern expert, I thought, and I began to read a lot of second-rate and a few good books about Japan and China. This future turned out to be illusory, but for the rest of the war I felt oddly liberated, ready to consider all sorts of new choices. This was good for me, and made my wartime experiences a little more than an interruption.

We arrived in Boulder on New Year's Eve. In the Navy Language School unmarried students lived under strict discipline in one of the college dorms, but married students lived with their wives wherever they could find housing in the crowded town. During the first half of our fourteen months there we shared a basement with some very smelly chickens; then we inherited from a graduating friend one of the best student apartments in town. On one side of Boulder were the steep red Flatirons, especially magnificent when I saw them while I was walking to class at six o'clock on winter mornings, with the sunrise hitting the powdered snow. On the other side of town the plains stretched away toward the Midwest. We did a lot of hiking, and were taken to visit ghost towns by Miss Muriel Sibell, who had come from Brooklyn to the Boulder art department and fallen in love with the region. Every day the language students had classes all morning. In the afternoon there was an hour of exercise, first calisthenics, then games. In that wonderful climate we were quite comfortable with the winter sun on our bare backs and a dusting of snow on the ground. Evenings, we memorized Chinese characters. On Saturday night, after the morning's examination, we gathered at somebody's house to drink, dance to records, and talk about our civilian lives.

The politics of the students were generally leftish, which meant that nobody questioned the need to win the war, though many were suspicious of the people in power. In general we were too busy for politics. Occasionally somebody was discharged as the result of a security check, but apparently nobody knew or nobody cared about all the meetings and signed protests in my own record. Halfway through the course we were all suddenly transformed from yeomen second class to ensigns, which meant that many of us had more money than we were used to having. Jean and I could afford to have a fine dinner in Denver once in a while, and once we took the train to Berkeley for a week's leave.

The Japanese language, I slowly learned, was a strange mixture of native Japanese sounds with several layers of Chinese characters, imported at different times over the centuries. Only a handful of Americans had been fluent in Japanese at the outbreak of the war. We heard a lot about the school's great breakthrough in teaching methods. There was indeed a breakthrough. The successful formula was to select people who had proved they were good at academic memory-work, keep them at memorizing characters fulltime under navy discipline, and send the few who couldn't make it back to the draft. The system worked, and we learned a good deal of Japanese. Mostly former graduate students, the language men worked even harder than they had to. Some eyed the posted results of the weekly tests as though their lives depended on the difference between a 4 and 4.5. On Monday morning there were lines of students outside the head teacher's office, waiting to complain about grades. Perhaps because I was a little older than most of the students, I did not get involved in this kind of extreme competition. The work was demanding, but essentially simple, and nobody really cared whether one did brilliantly or just satisfactorily. The symptoms of strain that I had known in Perkins Hall and Appleton did not return.

All this time the Denver papers were complaining about how the "Japs" (mostly American citizens) were being coddled in the camps to which they had been sent. Boulder, however, had been convinced by the navy that the Japanese-American instructors were essential to the war effort and must be treated well. As for the students, when we saw a Japanese it was our instinct to bow politely and address him in honorifics. Dogs, cats, and a few babies were given Japanese names, and some of the wives studied flower arrangement. In some of our textbooks we read about the blood heroically poured out on the plains of Manchuria for the Greater East Asia Co-Prosperity Sphere. It was a strange place and a strange year, remote from the war, in fact extraordinarily peaceful, except for the haunting realization that the end of the course would probably mean assignment overseas and painful separation.

Finally we graduated, with the best student making a carefully rehearsed speech in polite and reasonably fluent Japanese, and all of us singing our Japanese school song. My class was sent to something with the unfortunate acronym of ANIS, the Advanced Naval Intelligence School, in the Henry Hudson Hotel in New York City. There we were to study Navy intelligence (photo reading, plane and ship recognition, and so on) with lectures in navy tradition and even a bare smattering of navigation. (Apparently reports had come back that some of the Boulder eager beavers did not fit in easily aboard ship.) The first day an officer told us that after all, we had been working hard and here we were in New York City. Most of us caught his meaning, left homework alone, and spent our evenings going to shows. The only thing wrong with this picture was that we knew it would end very quickly. I cannot now hear tunes from the shows Jean and I saw— among them *Oklahoma!*—without a return of a peculiar combination of dismay and excitement. One morning our next assignments to duty were posted on the bulletin board. With most of my classmates I was to go to Pearl Harbor. Some were ordered to Brisbane, Australia, and a few lucky ones to Washington, D.C.

For a few days' leave, Jean and I simply moved upstairs to another room in the same hotel, leaving the room number with the school authorities in case they wanted to get in touch. Finally the morning came that we had been dreading for years. The hardest thing I have ever done was to say goodbye, take the elevator to the street, and call a taxi to go to the train for San Francisco. On the train one of my classmates, surprised, asked me what I was doing there. "Don't you know your orders were changed and you're supposed to go to Washington?" he asked me. When the train stopped at some station I got off and phoned the school's executive officer. "Why yes, May," he said, "we did have you changed to Washington, but since we couldn't find you we put you back on the Hawaii list. Good luck, May." If they had telephoned upstairs, Jean and I would have spent the rest of the war together. I did not tell her about this episode till well after the war was over.

Miserably unhappy, I was also determined to put a good face on things. When the train stopped in Chicago I forced myself to go to the Field Museum and write Jean a letter about it. We had agreed to write every day. I was to know lots of men who spent all their spare time writing home. Pictures of wives and children looked up from nearly every desk in offices and on ships.

When I got to San Francisco I learned that I might have to wait weeks for a ship. Of course I stayed with my mother, who seemed to be in splendid shape, younger and less formal or timid in dealing with people outside the family. For the first time in her life, she was working and liked it. She had been offered a job selling real estate and had taken and passed the state licensing test. After so many years of worry about money, she was now making enough to live on, in a little house on Pine Avenue with a cherry tree in the garden. She had bought a car. She had some younger friends, who brought her their babies to hold and invited her to new kinds of informal parties.

We talked freely about many subjects, including how much I missed Jean. One day she took me to lunch at a good restaurant in San Francisco and said she had something to tell me. This was that the doctor said her cancer might be recurring. She was not yet sure, had needed to tell somebody, but made me promise not to tell my brother, who was already in Pearl Harbor as a communications officer.

It was a relief when, in June 1944, the ship finally sailed out the Golden Gate, carrying about fifty junior officers to Honolulu. From the deck I could see Russian Hill, where our apartment had been. As we emerged into the ocean, guards were posted and the blackout enforced, though by that time the eastern part of the Pacific was nearly as safe as the Great Lakes. In the ship's newspaper we read of the Normandy invasion and the beginning of the Marianas operation. There was no doubt that we were going to win, but Japan still controlled thousands of miles of ocean, and nobody knew how many years of war still lay ahead.

The trouble with life in wartime Oahu was that it was too nearly normal. At Waikiki one even saw families who were still together. I swam a lot, hitchhiked around the island, and practiced Japanese at small restaurants. My brother and I, both lonely, became good friends for the first time. My Harvard friend Leo Marx turned up as skipper of a sub chaser. When he was in port we spent all the time together we could, swimming, drinking, and especially talking—about the civilian world, about politics, Harvard, our careers, and our wives.

Most of the language men worked in a translation section, a large room in Admiral Nimitz's Joint Intelligence Center on Makalapa Hill. Three shifts a day, we translated Japanese documents, including the diaries that Japanese enlisted men obligingly carried. Occasionally something really valuable would turn up, for instance a map of an island, including gun emplacements. The atmosphere of the translation center had all the bad characteristics of a college faculty, with few of the good ones. Petty jealousies were rife; people with a half-stripe seniority bore their authority heavily. All this occurred only when a lot of language officers were grouped together. When one of them was sent to a ship or a forward area, I later learned, he usually behaved excellently. There were even a few authentic heroes, like the man who swam alone to a small unoccupied island off Okinawa and persuaded the Japanese garrison to surrender.

I was very glad when I was requested as the language man

on a small weekly intelligence bulletin run by a former newspaper man and a bright graduate student pretending to be a
newspaper man. But I soon became disillusioned and bored.
There was very little need for a translator, and it didn't seem
to occur to my new colleagues that a pedant like me could
actually write. Finally, after too much stewing, I went to my
immediate superior and said that if I did not get some writing
assignments I would like to be sent back to the translation
section. He said that I should have made this clear much
earlier and immediately gave me some trial assignments. Nobody, he said, would speak for me unless I spoke for myself.
This was one valuable lesson, and as I wrote more articles for
the bulletin I learned another, still more valuable. What I had
to do was to forget my graduate student meticulousness, to
get the words out and let them go. If I was assigned an article
on Japanese radar and didn't really know what radar was, it
was my job to interview somebody who did know. The idea
was that it was better for the fleet in forward areas to learn
what we could tell them quickly than to wait for complete
research. I also learned the self-protective military jargon: "It
is believed by Allied sources that . . ." I turned out a few
special pamphlets—on Japanese merchant ships, on shipyards,
on naval ground troops—that I was told were useful. Instead
of checking in for eight hours daily, I could more or less make
my own hours, sometimes arriving late mornings and staying
in the office late at night.

My work life had become satisfactory, but the rest of my
life was not. Evenings at the bars or movies or the officers'
clubs were dreary. Swimming at Waikiki or Kailua and ex-
ploring the island were a little better, especially when I could
find some company. But it was an empty time, and despite all
my efforts there were hours of longing and brooding. It was
also, however, a lazier and more relaxed time than I had ever
spent. I seldom thought about my work after leaving the

office. Between bouts of acute loneliness I was sometimes able to accept the lazy life of sun, sea, and drink with a sort of half-awake semicontentment.

My lifeline was the daily letter from Jean, telling me her thoughts and commenting on mine, connecting me with the real world, giving me a past and future beyond the peculiar present. My own daily letters to her constitute the only diary I have ever kept. Since I could say nothing about my work and was not supposed to refer to any particular place, they were necessarily subjective. Many, of course, expressed mainly love and longing. Large sections make pretty terrible reading, and I have been told by officers who spent a lot of time on censorship that this is true of most wartime letters home. Yet I was also doing some occasional hard thinking: after all, I had plenty of time.

None of the really hard thinking was about politics, which occupied many pages. Usually I repeated the left-wing platitudes I had to believe, about the increasingly progressive effects of the war and how the Soviet ally, if not perfect, was obviously growing more democratic all the time. More surprisingly, an occasional letter hints at some faint stirrings of religious belief, a tendency I was not to admit fully, either to myself or to others, until long after the war. I was much impressed with my roommate Tom Murfin, who was like nobody I had known before. Tom was a person of no special intellectual pretension and a simple, unquestioned Christian faith. When I asked if he had a Bible with him, he produced it as casually as though I had asked him for a match. He made no attempt to argue with me. He admitted, I reported to Jean with surprise, that he could not answer all my questions about his beliefs. "This attitude," I commented, "seems to me immensely sensible. . . . I decide more and more definitely that it doesn't make sense not to admit that one is something of a mystic." This was much too exalted a word for what I meant;

282

at most I was beginning to admit that I too, like Murfin, believed some things that I could not explain.

I was trying, in this period of tropical indolence and boredom, to improve my character. No doubt my Attleborough ancestors would have approved of this, but they would hardly have approved the particular directions in which I was trying to move. I knew that I was too much of a worrier and too inclined in every new situation to adopt all sorts of theories about it that later turned out to be wrong. Some of my new acquaintances, I told Jean, seemed to do very well with the maxim "When in doubt, take it easy." This advice seemed to me quite new and strange, probably impossible for me to accept fully, but well worth thinking about.

Much that I am saying implies that the war was good for me, as in some ways it was. I realize how callous and shocking such a statement sounds. No doubt it is blasphemous to suggest that such an immense avalanche of blood and sorrow could have any good consequences, and it would certainly be crazy to suggest that effects on the character of an individual—even of many individuals—can be weighed against the great balance of horror. It remains true that I know many people who learned a good deal from their military experience, and that I was one of them. It is important to remember two things. First, nearly all Americans believed that this war was necessary and had to be won. Second, in this war—in sharp contrast to the later war in Vietnam—the armed forces were a cross-section of the male population. Thus we all had to get along, sometimes in close quarters, with people quite different from ourselves. Sometimes I disliked my associates and had to toughen my hide. Other times I learned something from people I never would have known in civilian life. In itself this was valuable, for me and for many.

There was certainly a lot I did not like about the atmosphere of the desk navy on Oahu. I was bored with the cliques and the rumors, and detested the bloodthirstiness of some of these civilians in uniform. "Will it kill Japs?" was supposed to be the question asked about every enterprise, and once the bombing of the home islands had begun this did not mean just Japanese soldiers. I enjoyed my writing job well enough but was becoming curious about life in the forward areas. I wanted to see what war was really like and, probably still more, what I would be like in a war. I wrote Jean asking if she would mind if I tried to get an assignment farther forward, and she understandingly consented. Next I spoke to Captain Holmes, the all-wise and all-powerful intelligence officer who supervised our bulletin. Not without misgivings, I asked him whether he would be willing to recommend me for a forward-area job.

I was duly requested by Amphibious Group 12, whose intelligence section proved to be a wonderfully congenial group, mostly of New Englanders, who had been together in the Normandy landings. Now the group was to take part in the attack on Okinawa, a good deal closer to the main Japanese islands than any island previously invaded. Planning was already under way, and I started learning all I could about this island, long barred to foreign visitors. Just before leaving Pearl Harbor, the Phib Group had a cheerful drunken luau, and the intelligence section a dinner at a Japanese restaurant, where I interpreted. Coming back to Pearl Harbor, singing heartily in our truck, I could not get over feeling that I had somehow been cast in a movie about World War I. Finally our command ship put out to sea, together with a long string of transports and protective destroyers.

Aboard ship I learned several things. The first was that navy language, rules, and etiquette make some sense when a lot of men are crowded together for a long voyage. The second was that in circumstances of mild hardship (close quarters, lack of occupation, increasing heat) most people behave better rather than worse, and that in circumstances of gradually increasing danger many become better still. Much the same cross-section of American young men who in the comparative luxury of Pearl Harbor were often competitive, discontented, and bored tended aboard ship to be polite, uncomplaining, and mutually supportive. A still more unexpected lesson was the laziness—except in time of action, of life aboard a navy ship. One comparatively experienced navy man suggested to me that the reason old-time navy officers didn't live long was not combat, but the toll taken by heavy food and lack of exercise.

Most of our long trip seemed safe and mildly pleasant. I had few duties except to read the daily dispatches from all over the world and from them to update the big chart in the intelligence office. On this I plotted our course, enemy sub and ship sightings, and, since there was plenty of time, actions all over the world, including the advance, by now rapid, of the Russians into Germany. The rest of my time was spent playing chess or poker and reading through the selection of books in the chaplain's office. (The chaplain, an earnest but unvisited Methodist, put out a bulletin on Reading, Recreation, and Religion—in that order.)

It got hotter and hotter. The air conditioning often didn't work, and the small cabin I shared with three other junior officers became stifling. I learned, like many, that it was better to sleep on deck on a couple of blankets. The metal deck was hard, it sometimes rained, and one had to clear off at five-thirty. On the other hand, cool winds came up, and there was something pleasant about looking at the bright stars and watching the deck heave up and down. The idea of insomnia did not occur to me.

Letters came in random batches when we met another ship or touched at an island. I still wrote Jean almost every day. My letters sound far more contented than those from Pearl

Harbor. Thinking over the past and future, I was more doubtful than ever that I wanted to go back to my thesis about late
nineteenth-century Protestantism and more certain that I
never wanted another year like that at Appleton. But instead,
what? I could not get beyond vague ideas about freelance
writing or possibly some undefined government position as a
Far Eastern expert. In some ways I had liked the job on the
bulletin at Pearl Harbor. I decided I much preferred getting
assignments to the long grind of planning a book or preparing
a course. Perhaps, I even thought, I would like a life with
more outer, less inner activity.

Going ashore at our first tropical islands had been a holiday, with beer, shell collecting, and swimming. The islands
of Leyte and Samar in the Philippines were grimmer. Towns
were collections of shacks; people were barefoot and some of
them dressed in gunnysacks. As we headed north toward our
target, the air grew colder, the wind stronger, the sea rougher
(we were dodging a typhoon). When we got close the admiral
announced to our command ship by loudspeaker just where
we were (only the intelligence section had officially known)
and urged us to do our best in the coming action. I suggested
to my immediate superior that perhaps the intelligence section
might prepare a brief analysis of the military importance of
Okinawa for the ship's company. I was thinking, for instance,
that a steward's mate whose main job was to wait on table and
make officers' beds might like, in a time of danger, to have
some idea why he was where he was. This suggestion got
nowhere. Of course, I did not even suggest saying anything
about the Four Freedoms or the purposes of the war. Such
matters were almost never mentioned. What people were
fighting for was to get it over and get home, or sometimes to
show that their own unit was better than another. Morale in
this army and navy of civilians was generally good, but ideol-
ogy had nothing to do with it. Once while we were off the

Philippines an army entertainment group came aboard. Everybody clustered on deck to enjoy the band, the stand-up comics, the raw jokes. At the end a wimpy looking comic character said *he* didn't want to go home, he wanted to stay out here and serve his country. Immediately two men in white coats hauled him off to ringing applause.

On Easter Sunday, 1945, I came on deck to hear continuously rolling gunfire and see thousands of boats filled with troops heading for the nearby shore. The beaches turned out to be undefended, but a few days later the troops ran into heavily fortified lines. The fleet of about a thousand vessels, stuck offshore to support the action with supplies and naval gunfire, was attacked about twice a day by kamikaze planes that took a heavy toll, especially of small picket ships. A few times the intruders came very close to our command ship. Usually, however, a heavy screen of smoke was put up in time. Like everybody else, I came to take the morning and evening air raids for granted. Aboard ship, we were comfortable, eating and sleeping as well as ever. Only occasionally I thought what it would be like if, for instance, the way out of our cabin were suddenly blocked by fire or collapsing bulkheads. Once, when I was standing on deck after dinner watching the nightly fireworks—the guns of the fleet bombarding the island—I told a friend, a very likable Dartmouth man from the intelligence section, that I hated to think of the people getting killed ashore. Obviously most were women, children, and old people, since the young men had been conscripted. Worse, I went on to say that I sometimes felt the same way reading the daily dispatches about the bombing of Japanese cities. My friend was shocked, and told me I really couldn't afford to think that way; these were the enemy. It was not that he hated them particularly. The only time I heard hatred expressed on the ship was when a kamikaze plane, lost in the fog, fell on a hospital ship. Some people then said that every Jap—man, woman, and child—should be wiped out. But these statements really sounded perfunctory and the mood didn't last. We all returned to the daily routine of war.

Soon some of Okinawa was secured, and I could go ashore. As Commodore Perry said when he stopped there on his way to Japan in 1853, it was a very beautiful island looking a little like England, except for some of its semitropical plants. Small villages fitted the green landscape as if they had always been there. Now, however, the ones I saw were deserted. An occasional swollen cow or sheep sprawled in a village street, its feet sticking out in all directions. Large areas were being bulldozed for roads and landing fields. The Okinawans, mostly a rather primitive people, smaller and darker than other Japanese, were roaming about dazed until they were herded into camps and guarded villages. They had undergone heavy bombing, then shelling by naval guns, and the Japanese soldiers had kept the shelters strictly for themselves. On the whole the Americans treated Okinawan civilians fairly well, and the language men tried hard to argue that these were not really Japs or enemies. One typically small dark man got the idea. "Me gook," he explained earnestly.

Part of my work became very interesting. Every now and then an unsuccessful suicide pilot was fished out of the sea, and I was sent to interview him on the ship that had him. To the navy, a kamikaze man was an important source of intelligence about a new and highly dangerous weapon. To me, the prisoner usually looked like a scared and disoriented kid. Our conversations followed a polite formula: "Would you please have me killed right away?" "No, I'm sorry, that's against our rules." "Oh. Then could I have a cigarette?" "Sure." "What will happen to me now?" "You will be sent back to Pearl Harbor, and then at the end of the war returned to Japan." "Oh no, that is absolutely impossible."

Since the Japanese code of honor left no place for capture,

nearly all prisoners decided that they were morally dead and might as well throw in their lot with the Americans. Quite willingly, most of them told me what airfield they had flown from. When I got back to the command ship this information was immediately reported to Pearl Harbor and the airfield was bombed. I learned something of the strange preparations for suicide flights. Many of the pilots had just graduated from training school. Often they were sent to resorts with their families for ceremonial farewells. Some carried in their pockets cherry blossoms, the symbol of a warrior's brief life, wrapped in patriotic poems written by high school girls. They were given enough fuel for a one-way trip and were supposed to crash into the first American ship they saw. Quite a few connected with an unlucky escort vessel. As we learned to put up heavy smoke over the fleet, the young pilots' task became harder. Those I talked to had tried and missed, they insisted, and woke from unconsciousness aboard an American ship as prisoners.

My only real terrors during these months came from going up and down jacob's ladders swung over the sides of ships. For a young man with a deep fear of all heights, it was not easy to stand up in a tossing boat, grab the bottom of a ladder when the boat rose, and struggle up a few rungs before the boat rose again and smashed my feet. The side of a ship seems very high, and at the top you have to swing your leg over the rail, pull yourself together, and salute the quarterdeck. None of this is made easier by grinning seamen watching the alien staff officer with a good deal of critical enjoyment. Several times I had to board a ship actually under way in rough weather. Once I failed utterly in a mission. On a rough and rainy night I set off in a boat with an enlisted man to steer. In the crowded anchorage we were supposed to locate a ship that had a prisoner aboard. Some of the ships' sentries, alert for Japanese suicide boats, fired warning shots. After going round and round for a couple of hours, lost and drenched, I gave up and told my steersman to head back to the command ship. When I reported to my immediate commanding officer, the head of the intelligence section, he told me to come to his cabin. I thought I was going to get a reprimand. Instead, he gave me a stiff whiskey he had procured from his friend the doctor and told me to try again in the morning.

When there were no prisoners to talk to I joined the nightly poker game, carried on behind the locked double doors that separated off the intelligence section. Here officers from ensign to commander were equal. Since there was nothing for us to spend our money on, we played for what seemed to me high stakes. On May 7 the ship got a dispatch saying that General Jodl, the German chief of staff, had surrendered to Eisenhower and the Russians. That night nearly every senior officer in the intelligence poker club produced an illegal bottle from his cabin. We all felt that we would soon be going home.

It became clear, however, that the Pacific war would drag on a while. When the Okinawa operation was over, I said a reluctant good-bye to my friends of Phib Group 12 and was transferred to another staff, slated for another operation still closer to Japan. Fortunately for me this mission was canceled, and I was sent back to Pearl Harbor to await the final assault on the home islands of Japan. I got my old job back, and the routine seemed drearier than ever, the swimming, drinking, and movies even less satisfying, the time of waiting longer and more meaningless. Endless rumors about the end of the war increased the tension.

Suddenly we got the unintelligible news of Hiroshima, and a few weeks later, the surrender. All the antiaircraft guns in the harbor started firing, and a group of us spent the night singing all the songs we knew. The bulletin ceased to publish, and I was sent back to the language section, where some of

my Boulder acquaintances had long resented my relative freedom. A lieutenant, who was really a graduate student in English, kept me standing in front of his desk while he debated
with himself whether to send me to Korea or possibly Tai-
wan. Finally he decided that I was to be flown to Manila to
wait for a transport squadron bound for Japan.

Manila was hot, smashed, and stinking, a once-handsome
city blown up by the defeated Japanese army. I was quartered
in a ship in the great harbor, now dotted with the superstruc-
tures of sunken warships. Finally I joined the ship to which I
was assigned, the command ship of a transport squadron
bound for Wakayama, Japan. For a long time we waited in the
tiny hot harbor of Subic Bay. There was nothing for me to
do, ashore or afloat. I learned which officers played chess and
when each was off watch. I rationed the detective stories in
the ship's library. Sometimes I spent long periods simply lean-
ing over the side, watching the toilet paper floating slowly
away in the warm green water. A metal ship lying still in a
hot harbor can be a good deal like a prison.

The staff to which I was assigned were again a likable
group, though I never felt as close to them as I had to Phib
Group 12. Most of them spent a lot of time studying the point
system, the rules issued daily that established individual priori-
ties for discharge from the service. Points were given for total
service, service overseas, time in war zones, and so on. I
would have come out fairly well except for one sentence saying that all language officers were for the present outside the
system. Every week or so there was a shipside farewell ceremony for a boatload of men leaving for transport home. A
three-piece band would play "Sentimental Journey" and "It's
Been a Long, Long Time," and jokes would be made about
the sexual prodigies expected of discharged veterans. Sometimes a well-intentioned lieutenant commander would comfort an ensign, depressed because of his lack of points: "I

know how you feel, Joe, but just think of Henry here—excuse me, Henry—who will probably be patrolling the streets of Tokyo for ten years."

After once more dodging a couple of typhoons, we finally got under way. Immediately things got better. Every day it got cooler, and since the war was over, we could keep the lights on and the portholes open. One September morning we found ourselves passing brown hills that looked a lot like Marin County. We were entering Wakayama Harbor.

The next day some of us went ashore, in a light October rain, at the little resort town of Waka-no-ura. It was a heartwarming experience. The Japanese townspeople were bowing and smiling, trying a few words of English. "Why these are *nice* people," a lot of sailors said. "This is a *good* island, not like those others. I thought I might see one woman with a baby on her back, but there are *lots*. Let me get a picture." Because of my language training, I was much in demand to buy souvenirs or ask questions. Soon half a dozen small children were hanging onto my uniform asking, "What's that ship?" "Who's he?" "How long will you stay?" Later, of course, corruption and boredom set in and relations deteriorated. Yet during the six and a half years of the occupation—on the whole, I think, the most successful military occupation in history—neither side was to lose completely the memory of those first encounters, when each side learned that the other was not a horde of monsters and sadists. (This feeling of delighted surprise was confirmed to me much later by Japanese acquaintances.)

Being in Japan early in the occupation was so fascinating that for a while I almost forgot to be homesick. From our ship at Waka-no-ura I was sent with three officers in a jeep through as-yet-unoccupied territory, to the city of Nagoya, to make contact with an advance army staff. Our squadron was to bring the occupying troops to that city. As we drove through the country we found nearly all towns, large and small, had been burned flat by our firebombs. People were digging in the rubble and working on improvised shelters. The same people smiled, waved, and cheerfully gave us directions. We felt foolish at wearing sidearms, as ordered. The countryside, unmarred by the billboards and freeways of twenty years later, was the most beautiful I had ever seen. Everywhere villages of thatched cottages were grouped around the gates and stone stairs of Shinto shrines, backed by dark trees. In Nagoya the castle and much of the town were destroyed, but a six-block section labeled Bright Pleasure Garden was being prepared for the entertainment of the American troops. The Japanese seemed entirely unembarrassed about this. On the way back to Waka-no-ura we stopped at Kyoto, beautiful and unbombed. Unfortunately, I had to spend most of my short time there buying cultured pearls for a superior officer.

Back in Waka-no-ura I continued to go ashore every day and got to know a young man about my age who was a student of economics at Tokyo Imperial University. "Fraternization" was as yet discouraged, but I went anyway to his house, where his mother, bowing low, served us tea and tangerines, about all she had.

When the squadron took off for Nagoya I had one really important professional duty. As the squadron sailed into the seaway leading to Nagoya I was on the bridge of the command ship, standing between the ship's captain and a wizened Japanese harbor pilot, once an NYK liner captain. "Migi" or "hidari" he would say, and I would silently translate this to *right* or *left* and then tell the captain "starboard" or "port," a command he would immediately relay to the ship and the squadron. I realized that if I got mixed up in my double translation the whole procession of ships might plow into a breakwater.

After being moved around Japan a certain amount, I landed

with most of the language men on a ship in Tokyo Harbor, which was even fuller of sunken warships than Manila Bay. By this time the charm of strangeness had worn off, and the language officers were bitter about being kept in service longer than anybody else. Finally a rumor started flying around, with more and more plausible confirmation. It seemed that General MacArthur did not want naval language officers in the occupation; he preferred his nisei sergeants. Before this decision was put into effect, however, I returned one day from a trip to the Hakone Mountains to find my immediate superior waiting for me with a special dispatch. I knew what it would be. My mother's letters since I had left had been cheerful and sustaining, but I had not forgotten what she had told me in San Francisco. The message was from my brother, saying, "Come home, Mother's trouble spreading." Within a couple of days I had my emergency leave papers, with orders to report for discharge when the leave expired. I was flown from Yokosuka to Kwajalein to Guam to Johnston Island to Pearl Harbor. There I learned, with considerable pleasure, that I had been given a commendation ribbon for my work in Pearl Harbor and Okinawa.

The next day I got another plane for Oakland. From the airport I took a taxi to my mother's house. Jean met me in the street in front. It had been about a year and a half. After a few minutes we went in, to find my mother sitting in a chair doing her best to look well and happy. This curious chapter, this strange interruption in my life, was suddenly over. Now when I read through my last letters from Japan, written after censorship had been relaxed and I felt free to say what I pleased, I seem to encounter a person somewhat different from my prewar self—a little tougher, more adaptable, more confident. Perhaps some of these gains were permanent; certainly some were not. A great many Americans somehow put on a different personality in wartime and then took it off with their uniforms.

15

Endings and Beginnings

My mother faced her decline and impending death with exemplary courage. At Christmas she rallied enough to sing carols and exchange presents. With many ups and downs, but with increasing pain and exhaustion, she hung on until November 1946. My sister, who as an unmarried woman was seen by the code of those days as more expendable, quit a USO job to live at home and take care of our mother. My aunt Nina came from England to be with her. John and I, living in San Francisco with our wives, came to Berkeley every few days to see her. When Jean and I spent time with her, she was often capable of unforced gaiety. She loved to hear about our life, dinners out, friends, explorations of the city. She hoped, as we did, that before she died we might have a child under way—in this we were disappointed. When death was very near my mother called each of us in separately—Mungie, Nina, my brother, my sister, and me—for a special and appropriate word of farewell. When she died she had just turned sixty.

Sad as I was when I thought over my mother's often unhappy life and early death, both at the time and later I was conscious of large elements of triumph in her story. The timid

English girl in Denver, who hated the social game she had to play and took refuge in sick headaches, had ended as a serene, apparently happy woman. Twelve years before she had reacted to her illness with panic; this time she met it with superb control. I knew I had a lot of thinking to do about the various kinds of courage and their sources.

My mother's death was a major event for me. In some ways it was the end of this story of growing up and coming to terms with ancestors, parents, and childhood. Both my parents were now gone; I was on my own. Yet my thinking about them had hardly seriously begun, and my growing up was certainly not finished. The next few years were to end at least a stage of this process and bring me to a position in which I was forced to make full use of whatever I had learned so far. A brief account of these postwar years will round out the story.

Despite the continuing sadness of my mother's illness, in many ways the first few months after my return from the Pacific were a time of happiness, excitement, and it seemed, wide-open choices. Sometimes I wondered whether it was wrong to be having a good time while my mother was dying, a question that would never have occurred to her. There were many reasons for feeling good. First, Jean and I were back together and found little difficulty in getting used to this fact. The world we read about in the newspapers seemed frightening but also full of hope. Despite my radical opinions, as yet stronger than ever, I could not avoid the euphoria that had pervaded San Francisco since the founding, right there, of the United Nations. The misery of Europe and Asia were a long way off. Perhaps the Soviet Union and the United States would manage to get along together and the world would really, finally, get better—I wanted very much to think so.

Letters from my friends all over the country were full of this sort of political optimism and of excitement about possible new career decisions. Was it a retreat to go back into the academy? Should one find some way of life that would be more of a contribution to peace and progress—braver, more active, more exciting? Only one of my close friends was entirely outside this cheerful excitement. I was distressed to learn that the marriage of Jack and Mary Rackliffe—to me an admired model of modern marriage—had broken up. Jack, after briefly holding several good jobs in publishing, was unemployed. This sounded very bad. I was still too uncritical a disciple of Jack's to understand much about his tragic combination of great talent and crippling disabilities.

With great good luck, Jean and I found a small apartment with a great view on Macondray Lane, a charming wooded alley in our favorite part of San Francisco, halfway up Russian Hill from North Beach. Mysterious checks from the navy—demobilization pay, per diem for time spent in forward areas—seemed to arrive regularly at short intervals. For a while we had plenty of money to buy cheese, sausage, panettone, and wine in North Beach, and even to go downtown for fine dinners. We saw a lot of my brother and his lively young wife, and played poker with Mark and Charlotte Hawkins in the kitchen of their apartment on Telegraph Hill.

Still hankering after the life of a freelance writer, I immediately wrote an article trying to convey the feel of Japan at the beginning of the American occupation. I was, after all, one of the first Japanese-speaking Americans to get discharged. The article took only a few days to write. It was promptly accepted by *Harper's,* which paid me $250, and then picked up by *The Reader's Digest* for $1,000. I thought I had it made in a new career and promptly wrote another article on the Okinawans and the problems of the new American Pacific empire. This went back and forth to various magazines—with no takers.

I was still not eager to return to my old field and my boxes full of cold thesis notes, but events seemed to push me that

297

way. First I got a generous demobilization fellowship from the Social Science Research Council. Then I met Professor John D. Hicks of the Berkeley history department at the house of one of my mother's friends. We talked a bit, and he offered to recommend me for a one-semester position at the University as a lecturer in American history. I decided to give this a try, got the job, and dusted off my Lawrence lecture notes and my none-too-assured lecturing technique.

Finally and with much reluctance I decided to get back to the thesis. I resolved that this time I would write it exactly as I chose, with no regard for Mr. Schlesinger's opinions except in such matters as putting commas inside or outside quotation marks. A wise letter from Henry Smith helped; he told me that it was possible to say something interesting and important about almost any topic—including the social opinions of nineteenth-century ministers.

Every weekday morning through most of 1946 and into 1947, Jean and I settled down after breakfast to two typewriters. I turned out new copy while Jean retyped my work of the day before. When I got up from my desk, staggering from sheer concentration, we went for a walk on Russian Hill. It was a strange way of life, equally detached from Harvard and from San Francisco. I once heard an American Veterans Committee acquaintance explaining with baffled incredulity what I did: "All he does is sit there and read all day."

In March 1947 I was approached for a job by Scripps College in Claremont, California. I did not altogether like the idea of an expensive women's college in southern California. We visited Scripps, and I was not reassured when I saw the tanned young men in white tuxedos dancing with the pretty young women on the flagstones of the campus under the orange trees. However Frederick Hard, the college president, a rather elegant Louisianan, seemed to be also a decent and honest man— unlike my prewar boss. (This impression turned out to be

298

correct.) Also, I had come to accept the fact that I needed a job and did not really know how to get any other kind.

In April we took the train for Boston so that I could turn in my thesis and take the final examination for the doctorate. We left San Francisco in eighty-degree heat and arrived on a day of cold wind and sleet. I was surprised to find how happy I was to see the red bricks and barely budding trees. Jack met us, apparently unchanged, with a bunch of flowers for Jean. We stayed in the apartment of Jane and Leo Marx, on the "wrong" side of Beacon Hill, halfway between the staid handsomeness of Pinckney Street and the raucous slum of Scollay Square. At Widener Library the guard at the stack entrance greeted me pleasantly enough. I had the strong impression that he and others had not really noticed that I had been away.

On a Sunday, exactly according to pattern, we called on the Schlesingers at Gray Gardens East. They were cordial as we sipped our tea, but nothing was said about the thesis I had mailed him. I had come prepared to fight against any serious changes. Finally, when we were ready to leave, I asked if he had received it. "Why, Henry," said Mr. Schlesinger, beaming, "didn't you get my note? It's just fine." After spending some weeks frantically trying to review all I knew about American history, I took the final examination in the Schlesingers' garden. I passed without much distinction, doing best, I thought, on questions from Perry Miller.

For a week of recovery we went to Matthiessen's house at Kittery, Maine, then occupied by the Marxes. We dug clams, fished in the bay for flounder, ate lobster occasionally, and spent a lot of time singing, discussing politics, and strolling on the beach. Finally, Jean and I boarded a train in Boston, stopped for a few days to see Santa Fe, New Mexico, and arrived in Claremont very early one morning. We got some coffee at a rather sleazy cafe near the tracks. I innocently asked where I could get a bottle of whiskey. "Not in Claremont,

you can't," was the obviously hostile answer, "but those professors up at the colleges sure do put away a lot." This was the
unpromising beginning of five good years.

Good years indeed, placid and on the surface unexciting,
but in many ways deeply fulfilling. I was back in the world of
the small college—a world of frugality, friendship, and an
odd kind of security. Security in a small college does not
depend mainly on formal rules of tenure but on a tight social
nexus. Each individual is so well known that it would shock
the whole community if he were fired. Therefore a lot is
tolerated, except in specially bad circumstances, like those at
Lawrence when I was there. I was still a radical and soon
everybody knew that. Doubtless I was disapproved of in
some quarters, but I was never threatened, even though right-
wing organizations kept close watch on the colleges, mutter-
ing darkly from time to time.

Major universities tend to be somewhat alike; small colleges, despite some traits in common, are highly individual.
Scripps had been founded in the 1920s with a strong commitment to the humanities, rather narrowly defined. I remember a
faculty meeting in which the question discussed was whether a
girl could get credit for an economics course taken at one of the
other Claremont colleges. She could if the course was theoretical, but not if it had any practical business use, a decision that
would have delighted Thorstein Veblen. Rather uneasily
mixed with the commitment to the humanities was a peculiar,
old-fashioned kind of feminism. It was the special job of
women to "civilize" society. The girls were nearly all attractive
and well dressed, and most came from wealthy western families. Some were bright, and much of the teaching—especially
in the arts—was excellent. The best thing about the job for me,
at this stage in my career, was that there was nobody else at
Scripps in American studies except one retired college president in his eighties, who did a little desultory teaching in the

humanities program. I was free to develop my own subject matter and teaching style, without the pressure from peers that I would have felt in a larger place.

The president, in his gentlemanly manner, had warned us that the college house he had found us was "unpretentious." This was no exaggeration. It was a four-room frame shack, with vines pushing through the thin walls and no heat except unvented space heaters. Winters are cold in Claremont, and much of the time we had headaches from the gas heaters. Occasionally we were asked by the college administration to invite some of the girls to tea. They had impeccable clothes and manners, and we learned that they found our way of life "brave" and "picturesque." We were indignant: it was our first house and we were proud of it. In a couple of years we were able to move to a much more attractive college house as a vacancy occurred.

We developed close friendships. Fred Bracher taught English at Pomona and was a gifted and wise man, ten years older, from whom I learned a lot. His wife Agnes was a poet and a brilliant woman, troubled with mental illness. Bob and Betty Palmer, he a classicist, were young and juicy companions. Golo Mann was unlike anybody I had ever met. He was, of course, the son of Thomas Mann, who was then living in a brilliant circle of European expatriates in Pacific Palisades. Golo taught history at the new, conservatively oriented Claremont Men's College. Deeply loyal to his father, he also wanted to be independent of his towering image and somewhat disapproved of his recent turn toward the political left. Golo was the product of a first-rate European classical education. He had a profoundly gloomy temperament, which had been deepened by his experience of the German disaster. He presented me, in short, with my first experience of a real European conservative. On most current political questions he was liberal to radical by Claremont standards. The conservatism was fundamental: Golo had little belief in the goodness of human nature and the possibility of progress. Unlike anybody I had known, he did not even pretend to entertain these beliefs.

When Golo drove to Los Angeles he was made physically sick by the ugliness of the urban sprawl. Very often on weekends he and Bob Palmer and I hiked into the San Gabriel Mountains, where one could start, after a half-hour drive, among massive cedars and pines, and see the desert six thousand feet below. Once after a hike Golo, the Palmers, Jean, and I were sitting in front of our fire drinking wine. "Some day," Golo said suddenly, "we will remember the Claremont time as a good time."

Letters from my Harvard friends were full of books and babies. My thesis was accepted for publication by the religion department of Harper's, and I spent a summer revising it—trying to make it read a little less like a thesis. It was very well received and I promised myself I would never write such a conventional book again.

In 1948 we decided to adopt a child, and while proceedings were under way Jean found herself pregnant. We were overjoyed, and in a couple of years decided that our daughter needed a sibling. Again we started adoption proceedings, and the same thing happened—to our delighted amazement, we had two daughters, Hildy and Ann. Before long, it seemed as though we had always been a family of four. When your own children are young, just as when you are yourself a child, it seems as though the life of the family is fundamental and essentially unchanging.

In these years families were very much in fashion. In our circles it was taken for granted that fathers must help with shopping, housework, and child care. It was also taken for granted, however, that in most families the husband and father had a job and the wife and mother stayed home. A good

Endings and Beginnings

deal of semipopular, semi-Freudian psychology emphasized the importance of accepting traditional sex roles. A remark made to Jean by a Claremont faculty wife—not one of our favorites—says a lot about several attitudes common among academic liberals in this period. "For a few years," she said, "you must try to be just like a black mammy." Rejecting the implications of this advice, we made our own compromises, like everybody else, between beliefs, customs, and the needs of the situation.

I was promoted to associate professor and my salary was raised from $3,800 to $4,000. In Claremont this was almost enough to get by on. We had no car, partly because I had never learned to drive—a reminder of my timid adolescence. A taxi would take us anywhere in town for thirty-five cents. We were surprisingly contented, though from time to time I began to want a bit more scope.

Slowly and painfully, my political ideas were changing. No doubt some would say that this was the result of a comparatively secure and stable life, and they would probably be partly right. Any number of intellectual autobiographies of this period explain their authors' movement away from sympathy with the Soviet Union in terms of public events from the takeover of Eastern Europe through the Berlin blockade, and they are right too. I moved slower than most. The ideas I had absorbed at Harvard were part of my identity; loyalty to them was loyalty to my closest friends. On the other hand, none of my new friends at Claremont was particularly radical, and Golo was a strong influence in favor of a fresh look at the world.

In 1948, when Henry Wallace argued that the developing Cold War was largely the fault of the United States, I tried hard to believe in his cause and gave talks, in Claremont, on behalf of his presidential candidacy. Before the campaign was over I found it increasingly impossible to deny that the Wal-

303

lace movement in California was dominated and manipulated by the Communist party. Two years later I could not go along with the view of Paul Sweezy's *Monthly Review*, justifying the North Korean attack on South Korea. Paul had been a much-admired mentor at Harvard, and I wrote him a long polite letter of dissent. In these years I was always writing letters to politicians and periodicals. Occasionally I wrote a political essay, and a few of these were published. As I read over these letters and essays, I find that I am really arguing with myself. My position in the Cold War years was full of uneasiness. Increasingly hostile to the Soviet Union, I also continued to be critical of American foreign policy. I spoke and wrote against McCarthyism; I did not even consider breaking with friends who remained on the left, though in some cases communication was gradually to become more difficult. I was—and to some extent still am—nostalgic for the times when I had been able to be at least a fellow traveler in a movement that seemed to promise a better world.

Just before and just after leaving Claremont I began seriously reading and teaching Reinhold Niebuhr. Like many others, I found that his message fit my needs. A long-time radical, who had been something of a Marxist, he still insisted that one must give one's best efforts to making society more just. While doing this, however, one must realize that the result will always be partial failure. To expect utopia in the world will always lead not only to illusion but to dangerous cruelty. So far his message seemed to me to fit the facts of contemporary history. But there was more to it than that. If, as this implied, politics cannot be the focus of one's ultimate trust and loyalty, what can? For Niebuhr, of course, the answer to this question lay in the essential teachings of Christianity. I had to believe in something and slowly began to consider this alternative. The stories and metaphors of Christianity had always attracted me, and Niebuhr, Paul Tillich, and others seemed to be suggesting that one could believe in their meaning without quite believing in the New Testament as historical fact. We moved in this direction very slowly, but we did sympathize with a young minister who was dismissed from the staff of the Claremont community church. Fresh from Union Seminary and Niebuhr, he was too radical in politics and—even worse—too conservative or at least neo-orthodox in theology for his congregation. The solid citizens of Claremont wanted comfort and reassurance in church, not callow, complicated, and disturbing talk about sin, suffering, and contrition.

In 1950 I got a letter from the chairman of the history department at Berkeley, offering me an associate professorship. Nothing could have delighted me more, except for one thing. The University was embroiled in a fierce controversy over a loyalty oath, imposed by a narrow majority of the regents in a hysterical effort to root out alleged Communists on the faculty. Twenty-two professors—some of whom I knew—had left the University rather than sign, and the national academic profession had called for a boycott against the University. Obviously, I could not accept this tempting invitation and keep either my self-respect or the confidence of my friends. I wrote a careful answer, trying hard to leave the door open for later. The next year the faculty loyalty oath was abolished and the exiled nonsigners returned. When the invitation was repeated I accepted enthusiastically. I did not quite realize—I probably did not *want* to realize—that instead of the special faculty oath, a new oath, at least as offensive, had now been imposed by the legislature on *all* employees of the state of California. In this curious Pyrrhic victory, new faculty members had to promise in writing that they did not want to overthrow the state or national government by force or violence. I had no such intentions, but did not like to be forced to sign the oath.

Since we knew that life in Berkeley would not be as simple as life in Claremont, we decided that we would have to have a car. I hired a Claremont graduate student to give us both driving lessons. Passing the driving test exorcised, for me, a number of fears, though I was never to become a really skillful and confident driver. We bought a big second-hand Hudson and with our two daughters and a lot of luggage left for the far north. Sticking to back roads, we made it to Berkeley in four days. I have always been rather proud of this; I know plenty of people who have made this trip in six hours, but none who has taken four days. When we got to Berkeley and I reported to the department office, the secretary said, "Welcome home, Mr. May." Few things have ever pleased me more.

\#

The rest of my life and career have taken place in Berkeley. The next thirty years were a crowded period, in which writing, teaching, and campus affairs left hardly enough time for family and friends, let alone reflections about youth and origins. It was not until the children had grown up and I had retired that I was able to get started on that demanding task.

I have written about my time in Berkeley elsewhere, and that period is beyond the scope of the present book. By way of summary, however, it seems worth explaining that my Berkeley experience was sharply divided into two parts. During the first stage, from my arrival to 1964, the Berkeley campus was rapidly changing from the relaxed provincial university I remembered into a far more ambitious, larger, more cosmopolitan institution, vigorously contending for national and international standing. In all this I took a full and enthusiastic part. For me this was a period of almost complete involvement in the affairs of the University and the national historical profession. I say *almost* because in my historical writing I tried hard to remain independent of current professional trends and vogues.

In this effort at independence I was not altogether successful. I taught, wrote, and believed in American intellectual history. In my writing and teaching I tried very hard, always fascinated and at times obsessed, to understand the ideas, beliefs, and also the emotions that had shaped a complex, vital, and baffling national culture. When I came to Berkeley intellectual history was a satisfyingly radical cause. The wise old men of the historical profession, at Berkeley and elsewhere, tended to dismiss it as impossibly vague and subjective. During the fifties, however, the vogue changed, and my kind of history became, for a short and heady few years, the rising fashion. To my surprise and slight discomfort, during my first decade at Berkeley I found myself, in writing, teaching, and university affairs, increasingly a part of the winning side.

My second period at Berkeley began in 1964 with the Free Speech Movement, the Concord and Lexington of the American student revolt. During the sixties it seemed increasingly as if not only public order but—still more important—the loyalties and goals by which I had lived in the fifties were in a state of upheaval and threatened collapse. Scholarly detachment, intellectual discipline, sometimes even learning or scholarship themselves became bad words; spontaneity, participation, and feeling were to be admired instead. Intellectual history was especially suspect—it was associated, perhaps correctly, with elitism.

Deeply involved in campus controversy, I found myself in the most uncomfortable position—the middle. I tried repeatedly to formulate compromises between the side of order and the side of rebellion. Of course, these efforts succeeded only in drawing fire from both sides. For me the time of maximum upheaval, from 1964 to 1969, was a period of extreme tension, of making speeches and attending caucuses, of frequent frustration and defeat. It was also a time of learning and self-searching, and thus in the long run part of the background of this book.

There were obvious immediate reasons for the ambivalence I felt during the controversies of the sixties. Despite my ardent participation in the academic ethos of the previous period, with its strong emphasis on performance and competition, I had never felt entirely at home in that world. For instance, it had not been my experience that real excellence was always associated with intense competition or maximum production. I could not deny all sympathy with the dreams or even the illusions of those who said, in the lingo of the day, that they wanted to make the University a loving community. I was often pretty sure that if I had been young in this period I would have found a place somewhere among the rebels. On the other hand, I was repelled by the frequent mindlessness and anti-intellectualism of the early period of the revolt, and still more by its later hardening into New Left rigidities. Trying hard to discriminate between what was and was not valid in the various proposals for transforming the University and the community, I began to realize that my habit of ambivalence arose partly from the situation but also partly from my character.

I have seldom for long been able fully to accept group programs and loyalties. Realizing that any political effectiveness requires such acceptance, I have tried hard to swallow my doubts from time to time, never quite successfully. I am a born fellow traveler, for instance with Marxism in my youth and with Christianity later. With regard to the latter, it is its paradoxes and not its credos that have seemed to me profound. Creeds and ideologies have never seemed to encompass much of reality.

I also find in my own makeup another major trait, related and also opposite, and harder to describe or explain. This might be called ultimate intuitionism, or perhaps in religious terms fideism, or even, I am afraid, romanticism—the worst possible trait to accuse anybody of in the hard-boiled thirties or the social scientific fifties. I have been a strong partisan of careful research, of disciplined and systematic inquiry, of an effort at impartial understanding of issues. But I know that I have not myself made important life decisions on this basis, nor have I found that many other people seem to take this course. In the real crises one does what one has to do; the decisions make themselves. For me, allegiances to causes have usually been a matter of allegiances to people. I am not happy to admit this. Recent history and personal experience have combined to make me aware of the dangers involved in trusting the emotions. I have every respect for the generations of brilliant scholars and writers who have tried to analyze the workings of the human mind and emotions in order to improve human behavior. At the moment, however, this brave effort does not seem very close to success. I find it necessary to admit that I have to live by certain values whose basis I cannot really explain. Once my friend Henry Smith, probably in a discussion of religion, told me that he felt uncomfortable with anything he could not understand. I answered that I felt uncomfortable with anything I thought I *could* understand fully—this was sure to be illusion.

This combination of incessant ambivalence and rock-bottom intuitionism is not an easy one to live with. It often makes life difficult for me, decreases my effectiveness, and irritates my friends. I am, however, stuck with it.

For the writing of history, as opposed to the handling of

present problems, this combination of tendencies has some advantages. I do not find much merit in historical polemic. In dealing with present crises or decisions one has to take sides, whether this is congenial or not. In dealing with the past, however, it is useful to have some sympathy for many sides and individuals—never, of course, for all. And in the process of writing itself I find a large place for the workings of the subconscious. If you are dealing with any large part of human experience, you are never going to be able to understand it fully. At some point, after all the research is done, you have to put away your notes and ask yourself what you think really happened, and even why. The result will of course be no more than a tentative and partial glimpse of the truth, but there is some chance that it will be interesting.

I undertook this study in large part because I thought I might better understand my own character and its contradictions by looking back at my youth and especially at the lives and characters of my parents. I think that I have learned something about what I got from each of them. From my father and from his ancestors in "Attleborough and after," I think I have inherited a lot, including a strong compulsion to moral and intellectual rigor and an even stronger tendency to self-doubt. I could not possibly cheat on a tax form, and I am never really comfortable without a demanding project under way.

Yet I have never been a card-carrying Calvinist, and I have many reservations about the powerful set of post-Calvinist values my father lived by. He sometimes thought and said that everything important—improvement, education, achievement—came by forcing oneself to do unpleasant things. For me this has not been true. The least pleasant parts of my early life—junior high school, Perkins Hall, Pearl Harbor—were not the most productive or educational. Nor were the most placid periods—Berkeley in the thirties, Claremont. Rather the formative and valuable episodes have been times of stimulation, enjoyment, and also challenge, emotional as well as intellectual—Dunster House, Phib Group 12, and Berkeley in the sixties.

From my mother, whose personality I have found it harder to describe convincingly, I drew a different kind of lesson. Though she never went in for precepts or formulas, her real practice was—increasingly as she developed increasing self-confidence—to trust and live by the affections. This is what sustained her through the many difficulties of her life and strengthened her at its end.

As I have thought more about the lives of both my parents, I have realized that it is always a mistake to treat people too simply, in terms only of their most obvious characteristics. I have begun to see the more subtle obverse qualities of each parent. Perhaps the most admirable quality in my father was *his* capacity for affection, which despite his Puritan quirkiness led always to strong friendships and eventually to an essentially happy marriage. And perhaps what I finally admire most in my mother is *her* kind of strength and discipline, in the long run stronger and less brittle than her husband's. I am grateful to both of them, and would like to think that in my best moments I have managed to draw some strength and insight from each.

Sources and Acknowledgments

In the sections of this book that deal with my ancestors and parents, my principal sources have been family papers in my possession. I have supplemented these by considerable research in libraries, archives, periodicals, and books. I will be glad to furnish my particular source for any fact or impression to any interested reader. In quoting from manuscripts, I have made minor changes in spelling and punctuation for purposes of clarity.

I want to thank the following people for their help: the manuscript has been read by my wife, who shares the memories covered by the last two chapters, and my brother, John R. May, who remembers our childhood and our parents. My sister, Elizabeth M. Slater, helped me with her memories of the Denver period and with material about certain ancestors that she found on a trip to Winthrop, Maine. For my mother's family the recollection of her half-sister Nina Rickard were invaluable, and I was also assisted by my cousin Leontine Rickard Watt. I had one interesting encounter with my uncle by marriage, Sir Alfred Chester Beatty. Mrs. Margaret Worcester Briggs, the daughter of my father's college friend Will Worcester and the niece of Margaret Worcester, was generous with her memories and impressions of my father's youth. Professor J. Leonard Bates of the University of Illinois, the author of an excellent monograph, *The Origins of Teapot*

Dome, cheerfully gave me copies of all his notes dealing with my father's work on the oil cases for the U.S. Department of Justice. My colleague Gunther Barth shared with me his knowledge of Denver history. The manuscript has been critically and most helpfully read by my friends David Bailey, William J. and Beverly Bouwsma, Frederick Bracher, Robert and Hope Davis, Peter Frederick, and Kenneth Stampp. Several versions have been patiently and intelligently typed by Dorothy Shannon. I am grateful to the staff of the University of California Press, especially Barbara Metcalf, for understanding and support.

Index

315

Index

Index

Designer: Sandy Drooker
Compositor: Huron Valley Graphics, Inc.
Text: 10/13 Bembo
Display: Bembo
Printer: The Murray Printing Co., Inc.
Binder: The Murray Printing Co., Inc.